THE RENAISSANCE GARDEN IN ENGLAND

ROY STRONG

THE RENAISSANCE GARDEN
IN ENGLAND

144 illustrations

THAMES AND HUDSON

Filmset and printed in Great Britain
by BAS Printers Limited, Over Wallop, Hampshire

CONTENTS

PREFACE 7

I THE RENAISSANCE GARDEN 9

II THE HERALDIC GARDEN 23
Hampton Court, Whitehall and Nonsuch

III THE EMBLEMATIC GARDEN 45
Kenilworth, Theobalds, Wollaton, Wimbledon and Nonsuch

IV THE MANNERIST GARDEN I 73
Salomon de Caus

V THE MANNERIST GARDEN II 113
Francis Bacon and others

VI THE ECLECTIC GARDEN I 138
Isaac de Caus

VII THE ECLECTIC GARDEN II 167
Inigo Jones, Sir Jones Danvers and André Mollet

VIII CONCLUSION 199
Renaissance into Baroque and magic into science

NOTES 224

LIST OF ILLUSTRATIONS 233

INDEX 237

IN MEMORY OF ALL THOSE
GARDENS DESTROYED
BY CAPABILITY BROWN
AND HIS SUCCESSORS

PREFACE

It was the reality of planning and actually planting a large garden which led me to the subject of their history. I began, quite naturally, by looking for an authoritative account of the period that has preoccupied me most in my writing, that of the England of the Tudors and Stuarts. One did not exist. There were admittedly chapters on what was categorized as the formal garden in general histories, but I soon discovered that no detailed attempt to reconstruct from the sources, both visual and archival, how England responded to the new art form of the Renaissance garden had ever been made. This book simply sets out to remedy that defect.

As an area of academic study, garden history is a relatively new one. I therefore freely acknowledge my debt to the pioneers in the field of Italian Renaissance garden studies, in particular the exemplary work by David Coffin and Eugenio Battisti. In respect of England I am grateful for the researches of literary historians, who more than any others, have begun to open up the subject for serious consideration. I have attempted to relate their findings to the reality of the actual gardens as far as we are able to reconstruct them.

This book is not concerned with the horticultural aspect of gardening but takes as its theme the garden of the palace and the great house from its inception in the reign of Henry VIII until the outbreak of the Civil War. As a country we are so obsessed with our contribution to the world in the form of le jardin anglais *that we have forgotten that England once had some of the greatest garden complexes of the Renaissance. By resurrecting these I have attempted to restore a balance in the history of English gardening, in which our attitude to the formal garden has been essentially one of condescension and, in the case of Tudor gardening, one of downright naïvety.*

The writing of this book owes much as usual to many friends and colleagues. In particular I would like to express my thanks to the following: Robin Harcourt Williams for access to the archive at Hatfield House; Christopher Gilbert for information about Temple Newsam; Professor A. G. H. Bachrach for transcribing and translating Huygens's description of Wilton; Professor David McKeen for information on the gardening activities of William Brooke, Lord Cobham; Peter Thornton and Maurice Tomlin for information on Ham House; Michael Archer for the reference to Francis Bacon's 'plot' for a water garden; John Nevinson for help over the manuscripts of Thomas Trevelyon; Sir John Summerson for information concerning the Works Accounts; G. C. G. Thomas of the National Library of Wales for help over the Wynnstay manuscripts; Stephen Calloway for material from the Department of Prints and Drawings of the Victoria and Albert Museum; Miss Pamela Sigl for translating the descriptions by Neumayr; and the staffs of the Witt Library of the Courtauld Institute, the London Library, the

Warburg Institute and, by no means the least, that of the Victoria and Albert Museum.

More particularly I have benefited from many enlightening discussions with John Harris and Stephen Orgel. Garth Hall has loyally fed me with hundreds of books and articles. Above all I owe a debt to Dr Sylvia England, without whose unstinted labours in the British Library and the Public Record Office this book would be noticeably poorer. And, of course, once again it is a pleasure to thank one's publisher and those in particular who nursed first the author in the writing and then the book through the press.

Roy Strong
Victoria and Albert Museum
September 1978

CHAPTER I

THE RENAISSANCE GARDEN

In 1604, one year after his accession to the English throne, James I and his queen, Anne of Denmark, went a-maying to Sir William Cornwallis's house at Highgate.[1] At the gates the household gods dutifully hailed him as 'monarch of this isle' and paid tribute to his 'admired queen', leading them through the house out into the garden. Here they were met by Mercury, who presided as master of ceremonies in a typical witty, elegant, yet courtly entertainment by Ben Jonson. While they were being escorted through the garden, Mercury told them that Highgate, which looked downwards towards the spires of London – 'those statelier edifices, and towers' as he called them – was the Arcadian hill, Cyellene, on which he had been born, and pointed towards a flowery bower where his mother, Maia, the month of May, sat accompanied by Flora, the goddess of flowers, Zephyrus, the wind god and Aurora, goddess of the dawn. The theme of the entertainment then unfolded itself in a song inextricably interweaving the advent of the royal couple and of spring with its warm winds and flowers:

> *Raise Larke thy note, and wing,*
> *All birds their musique bring,*
> *Sweet* Robin, *Linet,* Thrush,
> *Record, from euery bush,*
> *The welcome of the King;*
> *And* Queene:
> *Whose like was neuer seene,*
> *For good, for faire.*
> *Nor can be; though fresh* May,
> *Should euery day*
> *Inuite a seuerall paire,*
> *No, though shee should inuite a seuerall paire.*[2]

In the afternoon, after dinner, James and Anne returned into the garden. This time Mercury presented Pan and a group of wild satyrs dancing around a fountain made to run with wine, an opportunity for sport with both courtiers and ladies. In this way the visit came to its end.

When this alfresco entertainment took place, the country had been at peace for nearly half a century and was still basking in the aftermath of golden Gloriana's reign. Part of that new civilization, created by internal economic and political stability, was the setting for this fête: the garden. Jonson mirrors this in a series of images in which the house, the garden, the beneficence of the seasons with their fruits and flowers and the reign of the deities of the ruling house are interconnected. In this entertainment, therefore, we are able to catch one of the central threads of this book in microcosm, that is the link between the advent of the Renaissance garden in England and what might be described as the Tudor and Stuart 'idea' of monarchy.

For those interested in the history of garden design this 'idea' may indeed seem a strange point of departure for a book on the formal gardens of Tudor and early Stuart England. And yet, as I shall demonstrate, it can be taken as perhaps the most significant motivating force. The palace or great garden begins with Henry VIII's Hampton Court, Whitehall and Nonsuch, in which the garden is made a symbol of the new monarchy's power and prestige. It becomes the setting for a deliberate display of heraldry celebrating the descent of the royal house. The beauties of nature tamed, the ingredients inherited from the medieval garden, the walks, mounts, roses, fountains, grassy banks and arbours, are architecturally held together by the marshalling of heraldic beasts and coats of arms proclaiming the Tudor pax. Under Henry's daughter, Elizabeth, gardening moves out from the royal palaces to become a feature of the great houses that were a product of the long Elizabethan peace. Heraldry was gradually overlaid and eventually replaced by allegory. Gardens came to symbolize the Queen's peace and part of the cult of the Virgin Queen found its expression purely in horticultural terms. Each flower within a great garden was seen to mirror one of her regal virtues while its overall composition could proclaim Elizabeth in her varying roles as Spenser's 'most royall queen or empresse' or 'most vertuous and beautifull ladie'. The garden in short became Gloriana's glass.

The Jacobean age inherited this royalist garden and, although its style and mythological vocabulary changed, its meaning as a symbol of the King's peace remained constant. James I's reign witnessed a revolution in gardening styles. Until then gardening fashions had arrived in the main from Italy by means of France, but increasingly they began directly to reflect experiences of Renaissance Italy. Not only did design change; but also elaborate fountains, grottos and automata were introduced. Succeeding the Henrician heraldic garden and the Elizabethan emblematic one came the era of the Mannerist garden. Its guiding force was from abroad in the person of a forgotten but vastly important figure, Salomon de Caus, a French hydraulic engineer who supervised and transformed the royal gardens of Anne of Denmark and Henry, Prince of Wales, at Somerset House, Greenwich and Richmond Palace. The impact of his visit was enormous and the opening decade of the new reign saw an unprecedented creation of new gardens making use of esoteric symbolic designs and complex water effects. It was during this period that Hatfield, Ham House, Twickenham Park, Worcester Lodge, Chastleton, Ware Park and the earlier Wilton were planted.

After 1615 Inigo Jones enters our story. His return from Italy coincides with the introduction of the garden as a setting for the display of antique sculpture. Arundel House, Somerset House and St James's Palace reflected this development. At the same time Englishmen learned that fundamental tenet of Renaissance garden design, the relationship of house and garden in architectural terms as a single unit. This began with Sir John Danvers's Chelsea House in the 1620s and spread across England in the thirties in gardens such as Little Hadham, Temple Newsam and Rycote. Salomon de Caus's brother, Isaac, was active from the 1620s onwards, continuing to create gardens, grottos and waterworks in the Mannerist style, often working directly in conjunction with Inigo Jones. Isaac de Caus was responsible for the two most famous gardens of the age: Moor Park for Lucy Harington, Countess of Bedford, and Wilton for Philip Herbert, Earl of Pembroke. The latter enjoyed a fame European in its extent. Both were to embody the eclecticism of the civilization of the Caroline court.

By 1642, when civil war broke out, new forces were at work. André Mollet, a member of the great gardening dynasty at the French court which preceded the genius Le Nôtre (creator of the gardens of Versailles), laid out St James's Palace and Wimbledon House for Charles I and Henrietta Maria. His work heralds the broad monumental planning of the Baroque. In 1660 he was to work for Charles II to restore the garden tradition which had been swept away in the war.

All this is by no means an isolated story, but one deeply related to the other arts of the Renaissance in England. The garden was a setting for masques and alfresco entertainments, for philosophical contemplation and melancholy meditation. It was a symbol of pride and an expression of royal and aristocratic magnificence; man conquered the earth, tilled and planted it, subjecting it to his will. By means of the garden we can follow the change in attitudes to the natural world as the viewer studied its contents firstly as a series of emblems telling of virtues and vices and then gradually as a series of botanical specimens. The magical world of the late Renaissance, with its preoccupation with occult forces and influences, gives way to the age of experiment and of the Royal Society. Gardens also speak of the change in optical principles which overtook early Stuart England, the arrival of what John White has categorized as 'the invention of pictorial space'. The garden evolves from a series of separate, enclosed, emblematic tableaux to a sequence of interconnecting spaces whose vital link is the vista and *point de vue*.

Where, in fact, can we today go and see these gardens? The answer unfortunately is nowhere. The formal gardens of sixteenth- and seventeenth-century England are a totally lost art form. This is owing to a number of factors. In the first place gardening is a strangely ephemeral art. The palace or great house is less quickly altered than the garden surrounding it, which could so much more speedily and inexpensively be updated in fashion. When houses were given a face-lift the garden was done before anything else. Gardens inevitably grow and in the end invariably outgrow themselves, changing the whole visual intent of the planter. They are, moreover, the setting for transitory modes of architecture in the form of pleaching and *treillage* or pavilions and gazebos made of painted wood, which easily rot and decay. None of these foes, however, was to be as devastating in its effect as the advent of the one style for which England was famous, *le jardin anglais*. Bridgeman, Capability Brown and Repton and their imitators from 1720 onwards were responsible for the mass destruction, on a scale unmatched in any other European country, of the old formal gardens in the Renaissance, Mannerist, Baroque and Rococo styles. There is no English equivalent to the Villa d'Este at Tivoli or to the palace at Heilbronn outside Salzburg. The loss was total.

There is, in fact, no garden surviving from before the Civil War and only fragmentary examples, such as Levens, Melbourne or Westbury, from the period up to the introduction of the landscape style. What a tragic loss! A whole phase of visual creativity within the arts in this country has vanished beyond recall – so much so that it is hardly ever discussed or even referred to by students of Tudor and Stuart culture. Architectural historians mostly ignore gardens, although during the seventeenth century in particular they were integral parts of the overall *mise-en-scène*. What is worse, those who do write about the formal garden lump together what was an incredibly complex phenomenon stretching over two hundred years, failing to distinguish between a number of quite separate and distinct phases not only of design but also of ideas. Of all these phases, that before 1642 is to me the most tantalizing. What was Burghley's Theobalds really like? How did something like the grotto room at Woburn arrive in England? Who was responsible for the great garden at Wilton in the 1630s, how was it laid out and what did it mean? All these gardens were celebrated in their time, connected with famous people – with Elizabeth I, Charles I, Lucy Harington, Francis Bacon, Henry, Prince of Wales, the Pembroke brothers, that 'incomparable pair of brethren' to whom Shakespeare's editors dedicated the First Folio. In studying the gardens of Tudor and early Stuart England we are comprehending not only a lost art form and aesthetic but something more: an attitude to nature as it was conquered and tamed by the arts of man under the impact of the culture of the Renaissance.

We are so removed from all this because our existing views of Tudor and Stuart gardening hardly rise above vague visions of clipped topiary yews and knot gardens, mazes and arbours, quaint fountains and obelisks. And this has been entirely formed in our minds by visiting Elizabethan and Jacobean houses which are now surrounded by what are believed to be re-creations of their long-vanished formal gardens. Nothing could be more misleading; let us dwell on this for a moment. Montacute is the ideal house by which to make the point. Inigo H. Triggs in his *Formal Gardens in England and Scotland* (1902) writes of the 'practically unaltered state' of both house and garden.[3] So, too, does Avray Tipping in his *Gardens Old and New* (*c.* 1909?) who praises it as 'marking an historic moment in [the] English mode and manner of living' and 'as an example of gardening both interesting and elaborate, and certainly one of our best illustrations of the period to which it belongs'.[4] Alas for Triggs and Tipping the famous north garden which we see today was laid out in the 1840s; the pond in the centre was added in the nineties. Conceivably the banking and terracing might have been Elizabethan but what may have been a mount in the middle was demolished for the fountain. The forecourt, too, centres on a late nineteenth-century fountain surrounded by flower-beds in the Jekyll vein that can give no notion of the real appearance of a forecourt of an Elizabethan great house.[5] Chastleton, Oxfordshire, and Hatfield, Hertfordshire, are two other gardens which are of the same type, replantings under the impact of Romanticism but which are often cited and seen as authentic specimens of Jacobean garden design. In none of these so-called early gardens are we looking at anything which Francis Bacon, to judge from his essay *Of Gardens*, would have found remotely recognizable. Instead we are nostalgically evoking a vision of Merry England of the type enshrined in that best seller Nash's *Mansions of England in the Olden Time*. The reality of a Tudor or early Stuart garden, let alone the ideas which motivated its planning and creation, would come as something of a shock.

12

1 The medieval garden was one of a series of enclosures containing simple plantings of fruit trees, roses and herbs. Turfed banks against walls or, as here, beneath trees were made to be sat upon. Often the focal point was a simple fountain. The miniature from the *Roman de la rose* also captures its role as a setting for amorous dalliance.

Nonetheless, such Romantic re-creations were necessary for the rediscovery and serious study of these early gardens. This began in earnest at the close of the last century with Reginald Blomfield's and F. Inigo Thomas's *The Formal Garden in England* (1892), which was designed primarily as a polemic against the landscape style of William Robinson. Blomfield defends the role of architecture: 'We protest entirely against the view that there is one art of the house and another of the garden. . . . They rest on the same principles and aim at a common end'.[6] As a result of this battle Blomfield produced the first seriously researched account of early gardening, although there is no attempt to differentiate its evolution, and illustrations of the *hortus conclusus* of the *Roman de la rose* appear cheek by jowl with the Baroque splendour of Badminton. Half a century later Ralph Dutton in *The English Garden* (1937) advances no further and still amalgamates the years between 1500 and 1720 as 'The Age of Symmetry',[7] an attitude which if applied to architecture during the same period would assume that Wolsey's Hampton Court and Vanbrugh's Blenheim were motivated by the same guiding stylistic principles. What could be more absurd?

From this we can get an idea of the rudimentary state of garden studies. In this book I am only going to take one period and one thread. The period stretches from the accession of Henry VIII (1509) to the outbreak of the Civil War in 1642 and the thread is the evolution, design and meaning of the palace and the great garden. This is immensely complicated as it is, for England responded to all that had happened in garden design in the Italy of the Renaissance. Both the forms and the phases which we shall be studying had their roots there so that it is at that point that we must get out initial bearings.

The history of garden design during the Italian Renaissance is an enormously complex subject that has only in the last decade or so become the province of serious art historical inquiry, and as that develops in respect of France as well as Italy it may well be necessary to modify our conclusions concerning England.[8] The broad history of the Italian Renaissance revival of the classical garden, however, is clear and it will be an essential point of reference throughout this book. Knowledge of Italian gardens in England in any profound detail was to ebb and flow. Sometimes it was transmitted direct by means of travellers such as Fynes Moryson or John Evelyn, more often through books such as the *Hypnerotomachia Poliphili*, but mostly it arrived second-hand by way of France or the Low Countries. Although it is an over-simplification, for convenience the garden development from *c.* 1450 to *c.* 1600 can be categorized as successively Humanist, high Renaissance and Mannerist.

(1) *The Humanist garden: Pliny, Alberti and the 'Hypnerotomachia Poliphili'*
In its most basic form the Italian Renaissance garden was a revival of the gardens of classical antiquity under the aegis of Humanism. This movement overlaid and transmuted a rich medieval gardening tradition, one which reached its apogee in thirteenth- and fourteenth-century France and which, in its use of water and fountains, owed much to Arabic influences. Whereas the monastic garden was strictly practical, even the symbolic flowers being grown to decorate the church, these new secular gardens were planted purely for pleasure. They were walled or hedged enclosures in proximity to the castle or palace with an idealized, controlled representation of nature. Their ingredients were mounts, walks, grass, roses, banks for sitting upon, alleys, wooden arbours and pavilions and simple fountains. All these constituent parts of the medieval garden, which are caught in several late medieval manuscript illuminations, were destined to linger on, relabelled or transmuted, as part of the Renaissance garden. Their arrangement was also basically geometrical thus anticipating the revolutionary Renaissance concept, that the garden was to be the domain of the architect.

The most potent influence that re-shaped the medieval into the Renaissance garden in fifteenth-century Italy was the re-creation of the villa ideal as described in the letters of Pliny the Elder. Here is how he describes his house and garden:

> The greater part of the house has a southern aspect and enjoys the afternoon sun in summer and gets it rather later in the winter. It is fronted by a broad and proportionately long colonnade in front of which is a terrace edged with box and shrubs cut into different shapes. From the terrace you descend by an easy slope to a lawn and on each side of the descent are figures of animals in box facing each other. You then come to a pleasance formed of soft acanthus. Here also there is a walk bordered by topiary work and further on there is an oval space set about with box hedges and dwarf trees.[9]

He goes on to describe the hippodrome, an open lawn shaped into a half-circle at one end and surrounded by a ring of plane trees covered in ivy. Behind this there was a wall of trees, cypresses and a curving walk.

> In one place there is a little meadow; in another the box is displayed in groups and cut into a thousand different forms; sometimes into letters spelling the name of the

master or the signature of the topiarist; whilst here and there arise little obelisks intermixed alternately with apple trees.[10]

In the midst of these formal geometrical gardens there is a wild one, full of 'the careless beauties of nature'. There are also marble benches shaded by vines, marble fountains for coolness and places to eat in.

Pliny more than any other source gives seemingly the most complete account of the classical garden. The villa was to be set on a hill for a southern view. The garden was to be linked to the house by means of loggias and terraces; its planning was to be geometrical with walks, avenues and open spaces; its architectural quality was to be enhanced by the art of the topiarist, who subjected box to the shears to form innumerable different shapes. There were to be seats, fountains and banqueting houses. Not all the garden was to be formal, for parts were deliberately to be naturalistic as a foil. As no gardens survived from antiquity the importance of Pliny's descriptions for the Humanist re-creation of the villa garden can hardly be overestimated. In one sense it was specific; in another it left enormous latitude for the re-creator.

Alberti's *De re aedificatoria* (1452) brought together not only Pliny's references but all the others from classical texts known to mid-fifteenth-century Humanists in an attempt to restore to reality the villa and garden of antiquity.[11] He begins by discussing the site, advocating a hillside for the view. The garden is seen in architectural terms as an extension of the house, both being conceived in terms of Renaissance harmony and proportion expressed by means of geometry. The planting was to be symmetrical, with trees and shrubs arranged in stately avenues, circles and semi-circles. There were to be pergolas, labyrinths and groves; loggias, cast as the vital intermediary between house and garden, were to be built to provide both summer shade and winter sun and everywhere there were to be fountains and pots or amphorae filled with flowers. Sculpture is regarded as befitting a garden and there is a long description of a grotto. Following Pliny, he describes topiary work in box cut into extraordinary shapes and patterns. The influence of Alberti on the development of the garden of the Renaissance villa was, of course, immense. In concrete terms the result, in late fifteenth-century Italy, might be said to be a multiplication of the single medieval garden into many gardens. These retained their arbours, mounts and roses but were rearranged to reflect the new ideals. The most important single concept propagated by Alberti, however, was that the garden was the province of the architect. It was not until the 1620s that this idea was to reach England.

These new Humanist ideals found expression in the second half of the fifteenth century, especially in Florence, where the garden became a second courtyard aligned axially with the palace. Into this topiary work was introduced on a large scale. The Rucellai garden, for instance, which was possibly created with advice from Alberti, contained 'spheres, porticoes, temples, vases, urns, apes, donkeys, oxen, a bear, giants, men, women, warriors, a harpy, philosophers, Popes, Cardinals'.[12] The Medici garden had 'elephants, a wild boar, a ship with sails, a ram, a hare with its ears up, a wolf fleeing from dogs, an antlered deer'.[13] These not only prove that the antique *ars topiaria* was revived but presuppose a symbolic function. The garden becomes a fantasy world of escape where box sculpture fulfils the metamorphoses of Ovid.

From the point of view of northern Europe, however, this vision of the garden as a place for fantasy about the classical world found a much more imaginative and evocative form in Francesco Colonna's *Hypnerotomachia Poliphili*, published in Venice in 1499.[14] There were several Italian editions, a number of French ones from 1546 onwards and an English translation by Robert Dallington in 1592. Most important of all it was illustrated with a large number of pictures of gardens which incorporated into a basically medieval format an overlay of classical allusion. This book was to have a powerful influence north of the Alps, not least because it showed how antique detail could easily be superimposed and introduced into an existing garden tradition. Its translation into English prefaces the expansion in size and change in character of gardens during the late Elizabethan and early Jacobean periods.

The book describes the dream of Polyphilo and his search for Polia, a journey which takes him through a Humanist dreamland filled with pyramids and hieroglyphics, classical ruins and inscriptions, antique trophies and statues. In particular there are pages of detailed descriptions of topiary work in box in the form of circles, of mushrooms, one in the shape of the figure of a man, with his feet resting upon two vases, his hands supporting an ornament composed of two towers, and another clipped into three peacocks growing out of

2 The Humanist garden was the medieval garden with a classical overlay. This is epitomized in the illustrations to Francesco Colonna's *Hypnerotomachia Poliphili* (1499). Here the enclosed *jardin d'amour* is articulated by a fountain and by architectural forms and motifs which are classical in inspiration.

3, 4 The clipped trees in geometric or figurative shapes illustrated in the *Hypnerotomachia Poliphili* were a revival of the antique *ars topiaria*. They represented a major step towards the recognition of the garden as a medium for allegory.

5 The *Hypnerotomachia Poliphili* contains the earliest plans for knot gardens, often highly complex in pattern, planting and symbolic content.

a vase which is placed upon an altar. The island of Cythera is presented as one huge circular garden arranged as a geometrical progression to the circumference through flower-beds laid out in patterns, a river, garden ornaments in the antique style, and waterworks, the whole encompassed by a wood of myrtle, the tree sacred to Venus. The plan is richly suggestive of the possibilities of symbolic gardening. Each individual ornament and flower-bed is described in minute detail, including not only its pattern but also its planting, the colours of the flowers and the construction of the antique monuments that made up the focal points. For a society such as the Elizabethan and Jacobean court, whose code of behaviour emanated from the etiquette of a revived medieval chivalry, both in its hierarchical and its romantic forms, and whose assimilation of the antique style was only surface, the *Hypnerotomachia Poliphili* was perfect in its happy alliance of antiquity with romance.

(2) *The high Renaissance garden*

Alberti's assumption that the garden was the province of the architect took a further definitive step forward in 1503 with Bramante's celebrated series of terraces and flights of steps whereby he linked the Vatican and the Villa Belvedere for Pope Julius II.[15] Here, as James Ackermann has written, 'a form of architecture which had been extinct since imperial times was suddenly brought to life'. Here also the tentative efforts to re-create the classical garden had culminated in the re-invention of the architectural garden, which takes its form from the contour of the site, and re-forms the whole environment. Contemporaries must have been stupefied at the architect's control of this vast unmanageable area. Bramante's solution stemmed from a study not only of Pliny and of the accounts of Nero's fabled Domus Aurea, which embraced a complete valley and whose parts were linked by a mile-long colonnade, but also of the archaeological evidence. Throughout the first half of the sixteenth century Bramante's project was seen as he conceived it, a re-creation of the Roman villa or palace garden. It fulfilled everything that the Pope demanded:

6 The high Renaissance garden is epitomized by Bramante's landscaping of the area between the Vatican Palace and the Belvedere. In its control of the terrain by means of terraces and flights of steps and in its use of antique statuary it had a revolutionary influence on garden planning.

it provided the link between the Vatican and the Villa, it made a setting suitable for the display of the papal collection of antique sculpture and it contained a garden and a courtyard which could be used to obtain quiet and repose or, at times, become the setting for spectacular court festivals. More even than this, it looked out to the landscape beyond and related to it. From this famous arrangement stems the whole history of the Renaissance garden in Europe up to the time when it was banished by the English landscape style in the eighteenth century. This reshaping of the terrain by means of retaining walls, flights of steps and balustrading was to reach England a century later in the gardens of Robert Cecil's Hatfield and Lucy Harington's Moor Park.

As a setting for the display of the papal sculptures the Belvedere was likewise of supreme importance. Such pieces had already found a place in the Humanist gardens of the fifteenth century but the garden museum of the Belvedere took this a stage further. The figures, instead of being isolated items of display, were integrated into the new architecture by being set into niches or turned into fountains. This basic idea, born of many years' study of antiquity, married water and sculpture again in a way as revolutionary in its consequences as the steps and terraces. Instead of the usual cup-shaped fountains of the previous century standing in the middle of the garden, the ancient river gods, Nilus and Tiber, were arranged as sources of water and the Apollo and the Laocoön stood in alcoves decorated with painted trellis, climbing plants and birds. The Tigris and Cleopatra were transformed into fountains within grottos made of rustic stone and water plants. All this, too, was to arrive in early Stuart England,

18

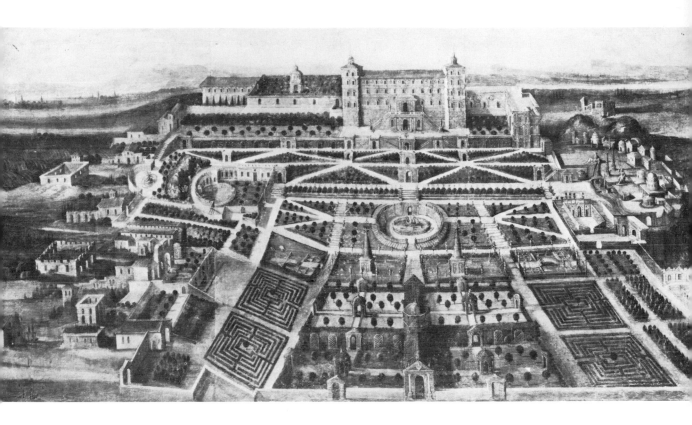

7 The Mannerist garden was not only larger in scale than its forbears but it developed the garden as a vehicle for princely magnificence and regal apotheosis. Nature tamed by art in the form of spectacular hydraulic engineering created a symbolic *mise-en-scène*, of which the Villa d'Este is perhaps the most famous exemplar.

mainly by way of the French hydraulic engineer Salomon de Caus, but the antique statuary appeared even later. It was from Rome in 1615 that Thomas Howard, Earl of Arundel, accompanied by Inigo Jones, returned to England with his earliest purchases of antique statuary. With it he created the first museum garden in England at Arundel House on the Thames. A decade later Charles I was to send the sculptor Hubert le Sueur to Rome to obtain moulds of some of the most celebrated of the statues to adorn the relaid out gardens of St James's Palace.

Following from this, during the opening decades of the sixteenth century there was an enormous expansion in garden making within Italy under the aegis and using the refound repertory of the architect. The Humanist garden room gave way to the Roman conception of moulding the terrain to an architectural form axially related to the building of which it was an adjunct. The theme was taken up, for instance, by Raphael, San Gallo and Giulio Romano at the Villa Madama and the Palazzo del Tè. And gardens of this kind implied something else, an acceptance and use of the new rules of scientific perspective. Design increasingly relied on a series of spatial relationships dependent on vista and avenue created either by means of foliage or stone.

(3) *The Mannerist garden: the Villa d'Este*
By the 1540s the garden repertory had established itself in Italy. What was to typify the Mannerist phase that followed was the application to the garden of allegorical programmes such as had already been applied to the interior of the

palace or the villa. Up until about 1540 the aristocratic and middle classes had decorated their garden with antique statuary as a means of exhibiting their humanistic learning and of raising the prestige of their family. Now new statuary, commissioned in relation to definite symbolic programmes, began to be made for gardens. One of the earliest instances of this is described in Vasari's account of the plans of Tribolo and Benedetto Varchi for the gardens of the Medici villa at Castello in the 1540s.[16] This was to be an allegory of the city of Florence and its surroundings. At the top of the garden there were to be statues personifying the mountains and rivers, from which streams flowed down to a labyrinth, in the midst of which stood a fountain topped by a statue of the nymph Florence wringing water from her hair. Varchi's scheme consisted of statues of the seasons, into which he worked allegories glorifying the Medici. In this way the Medici were among the first to use the garden as a means of intertwining the natural world with a dynastic apotheosis. As a result of this gardens began to assume an increasingly symbolic function.

By the middle of the sixteenth century the development of the garden was being influenced by some of the central ideals of the Renaissance. It still carried with it the medieval tradition of the garden as the earthly paradise and as a setting for courtly dalliance, but it had become much more. Under the impact of the classical revival it became the location for solitary meditation and for philosophical discussion. It was the setting for feasts and entertainments. It could be an open-air museum of antique sculpture, a horticultural encyclopaedia, a centre for botanical and medical research, a source of moral instruction and a means of demonstrating man's ability to harness the magical forces of nature. It drew to itself visions of the idyllic whether expressed in terms of poetic yearnings for the Golden Age or of the ideals of the pastoral life of Vergil's *Eclogues*. Although conceived initially, and still looked upon by visitors from the north, as a re-creation of antique gardens, it had taken on an existence of its own. And that existence became increasingly governed by late Renaissance literary *topoi* and symbolism. The garden evolved into a series of separate yet interconnected intellectual and physical experiences which required the mental and physical co-operation of the visitor as he moved through them. Strange though it may seem to us, plants become almost incidental, apart from their contribution towards achieving a symbolic effect.

To amplify this, and to demonstrate the rapidity with which the symbolic garden developed in mid- and late-sixteenth-century Italy, let us take a single example. The Villa d'Este at Tivoli is not only a garden whose fame and influence was European but one that has also been the subject of a major modern scholarly study by David Coffin.[17] It was designed by Pirro Ligorio, Humanist and antiquarian, for Ippolito d'Este, Cardinal of Ferrara. Following the precedent of the Belvedere, it is set on a hillside falling away from the villa in a system of terraces and balustraded staircases which lead the visitor from the house into the gardens. The initial impact looking down on it must have been one of staggering size, a *coup d'œil* aimed at establishing immediately in the mind man's total control over the forces of nature. Its plan, a central vista interrupted by cross axes, is one which preserves symmetry. This geometrical framework is enlivened by the most complex use of water, moulded like sculpture to form jets, veils, heavy cascades, vaults and emblematic shapes. Originally the water also assailed the ears, as it boomed out like artillery from the Fountain of the Dragon or set in motion the music of the water organ.

The features of the Villa d'Este garden are statuary, fountains, staircases, terraces, *treillage*, plantings of groves of trees and evergreens, and formal patterned flower-beds. Ligorio retained the classical contrast between the more formal, cultivated parts of the garden and the wilder, informal parts. The whole area is divided by avenues and vistas focusing on statuary and fountains, but between the avenues are dense plantings of trees and evergreens. This principle, seen in action at the Villa d'Este, was to be taken up and extended on an even larger scale later in the century in the two Medici gardens of Boboli and Pratolino.

The whole point of the garden, however, was Ligorio's symbolic programme. This stemmed from a celebration of the two Greek heroes, Hercules, patron of the Este family and tutelary deity of Tivoli, and the Cardinal's namesake, Hippolytus. The Cardinal's personal device or *impresa* was the white eagle of the Este family clutching a wreath adorned with three golden apples, the apples of the Hesperides, symbolic of the virtues. The garden as a whole is seen in allegorical terms as the Garden of the Hesperides, into which was set a series of tableaux extolling the hero Hercules as an emblem of heroic virtue. Together with Achilles he stands close to the villa: Hercules attained immortality, something which Achilles failed to do because of the vulnerability of his heel. The garden develops its theme in subtle ways with the many levels of interpretation typical of late Renaissance allegory, whether encountered in a picture or a court festival. A grotto of Venus, symbol of voluptuous pleasure, for instance, is placed in juxtaposition to one of Diana, symbol of virtuous pleasure and chastity. Groupings of opposites such as these made the visitor himself experience the choice of Hercules. Certain statues stood outside the main programme: a fountain of Mother Nature in the form of Diana of Ephesus and two small fountains to the horticultural deities, Pomona and Flora.

The influence of the Villa d'Este was considerable. By the seventies its fame had spread through northern Europe. In 1573 a French engraving of it appeared. It was visited by Montaigne in 1581 and by Pighius, whose description of it in *Hercules Prodicius* (1587) was, in turn, copied by François Schott for his guidebook to Italy (1600). The latter went through several editions and was used by John Evelyn when he visited the garden. Even more relevant from the English point of view, it was known and studied by the man who was to bring grottos and mechanical hydraulic effects into the Stuart royal gardens, Salomon de Caus. Its fame was to continue unabated until the 1670s.

I have dwelt on the Villa d'Este in some detail because it encapsulates so very well the essence of the Mannerist phase. Other gardens on greater and smaller scales were created during the same period throughout Italy. The most celebrated that survives today is Bomarzo, with its incredible sculpted monsters arising out of an enchanted wood. The greatly admired Villa Lante at Bagnaia with its water parterre was laid out in the 1550s. Pratolino, which was to have an even greater influence north of the Alps but which has long since vanished, was begun in 1568 for the Grand Duke Francesco de Medici. Like other aspects of Renaissance culture all this travelled slowly, its progress constantly interrupted by political events. In the case of England, a time lag of at least half a century is the norm from the inception of a new style in Italy to its arrival in any comprehensive form in England. The explosion in garden making in the Jacobean and Caroline periods, in fact, is this Italian Mannerist phase arriving in England fifty years on.

To sum up: the Italian garden through the fifteenth century and into the late sixteenth goes through a Humanist, a high Renaissance and a Mannerist phase. In simplified terms Alberti and the *Hypnerotomachia Poliphili* may be said to epitomize the first, Bramante's Belvedere the second and the Villa d'Este the third. All three were sooner or later to have an effect on the development of garden planning in England and be the ultimate *fons et origo* of the Tudor and Stuart formal gardens. But that is to anticipate. By the close of the 1570s Italy had gone through its greatest spate of creativity, whereas England's was only about to begin. A comparison between the two countries at the end of the fifteenth century would show them to be even more distant from one another: England, a cold and remote island on the fringes of northern Europe, was then very far away from the enchantments of the Renaissance garden basking in the warmth of a Mediterranean sun. While the Medici were enjoying the delights of villa life with its splashing fountains, ordered walks, vine-covered pergolas and clipped topiary box trees, England was a land of the castle and moat still just emerging from the Wars of the Roses. Civil strife is not conducive to the arts of either building or gardening and it is only with the establishment of the Tudor pax after the Battle of Bosworth in 1485 that these arts begin again.

CHAPTER II

THE HERALDIC GARDEN
Hampton Court, Whitehall and Nonsuch

Gardening goes hand in hand with architecture and both are the products of peace and prosperity. The Tudor pax, ushered in by the accession of Henry VII in 1485, was slow to mature. Instead of indulging in profligate spending, the new king consolidated his dynasty by financial parsimony, so that the first twenty-five years of Tudor rule witness no great Renaissance in the arts. Until 1509 the efforts of the Crown centred on creating an efficient government machine, on subduing the remnants of the Yorkist party and on establishing the House of Tudor internationally, by means of dynastic alliances with the great ruling houses of Europe.

Richmond Palace on the banks of the Thames alone arose as a symbol of the power and prestige of the new ruling house, a palace–castle, still in the Gothic style, arranged around a series of courtyards: its most striking feature must have been the forest of pinnacles bearing heraldic beasts and banners that made up the skyline. No detailed reference is made to its gardens until 1501. In that year the guests at the marriage of Prince Arthur, Henry's eldest son, to Katharine of Aragon (which was the apogee of Henry's dynastic policy), were led 'through his goodly gardeyns, lately rehersid, unto his galery upon the walles'. This slight reference would indicate that Richmond had elaborate galleried gardens in imitation of those of the courts of Burgundy and France. Anthonis van Wyngaerde's view made half a century later shows these galleries surrounding pleasure gardens. Although we know so little, Richmond was to be the seed from which was to grow later Thornbury Castle and Hampton Court.[1]

With the accession of the eighteen-year-old Henry VIII the pattern suddenly changes to one of outright ostentation. For the first twenty years of the new reign the King presented himself as the focal point and hero of the ephemera of courtly pageantry. Borrowing from the traditions of fifteenth-century Burgundy, the court embarked on an endless series of fêtes, tilts, tourneys, masquerades and mummings, the most famous of which were those staged at the Field of Cloth of Gold in 1520 in which Henry set out to dazzle Europe and eclipse in splendour his rival, Francis I. Patronage of the arts by the Crown during this period found no expression in the permanent forms of building, gardening, sculpture or painting. These were to find fulfilment in the King's chief minister, Cardinal Wolsey. Largely in emulation of Georges, Cardinal d'Amboise, he embarked on an extensive programme of building and, by implication, of gardening also.

Wolsey's palaces of York Place (the later Whitehall) and Hampton Court together form a prelude to what was to come. York Place, which included gardens, was the official residence of the archbishops of York and Wolsey extended and developed these buildings by the Thames. At Hampton Court, which went up from 1515 onwards, there were also gardens.[2] George Cavendish, in the memoirs he wrote of his great master, tells us all that we know about them in the following lines:

My gardens sweet, enclosed with walles strong,
Enbanked with benches to sytt and take my rest
The Knotts so enknotted, it cannot be exprest,
With arbors and alys so plesaunt and so dulce,
The pestylent ayers with flauors to repulse.[3]

There is nothing in these verses to suggest anything more than what we know made up the late medieval *hortus conclusus*. The garden was enclosed within a wall against which banks were thrown up covered with turfs to sit upon. Within, it was set out in knots, again a late medieval feature shortly to be highly developed – raised square beds divided into quarters, each planted in geometrical patterns. There were arbours, either of foliage or of painted wood, and there were walks. In short it is the type of garden which we see illustrated in any of a number of late fifteenth- and early sixteenth-century manuscripts. In his gardens, as in his architecture, Wolsey was no major innovator.

During the period when Henry, under the direction of Wolsey, was playing the role of the warrior prince in a renewal of the Hundred Years War, one subject did create a garden which anticipates all that was to happen after 1530. Edward Stafford, 3rd Duke of Buckingham, was executed on a trumped up charge of treason in 1521. At Thornbury Castle in Gloucestershire (now Avon) he had built a residence of all but royal pretensions; it followed the courtyard plan of Richmond and also had an extremely elaborate garden.[4] It is conceivable that it was in imitation and emulation of Richmond from which the architectural formula was derived. Buckingham was evidently interested in gardens because even before he began Thornbury he employed a gardener 'diligent in making knots'. Thornbury was begun in 1515 and was still unfinished when the Duke fell from power. There were two gardens and an orchard. The smaller garden is described as follows:

On the South Side of the ynner warde is a proper garden, and about the same a goodly Galery conveying above and beneath from the principall lodgings booth to the Chapell and Parishe Churche, the utter part of the said gallery being of stoon imbattled and the ynner parte of tymbre couered with slate.[5]

Beyond lay 'a goodly gardeyn to walk ynn closed with high walles imbattled' and a 'large and goodly orcharde full of younge grafftes well loden with frute, many rooses and other pleasures; and in the same orcharde are many goodly alies to walke ynn oppenly; and rounde aboute the same orcharde is conveyed on a good height other goodly alies with roosting places coverde throughly with whitethorn and hasill'.[6]

Thornbury was far in advance of Wolsey's gardens. The first garden, the Privy Garden, was seen as an open-air room within the castle related to the privy apartments solely for the use of the Duke. The other gardens were designed as a series of enclosures connected by passages and galleries at both an upper and a lower level, again reinforcing the feeling of rooms. Here the visitor was protected against the weather and could look down from the upper storey onto the patterns of the knots beneath. Only Richmond Palace was comparable, and Thornbury; both, in scale and arrangement, anticipate in considerable detail the first great royal garden at Hampton Court.

Hampton Court   Wolsey's and Buckingham's gardens were but minor rehearsals for the major royal gardens to be planted during the 1530s. As the chivalrous warrior prince gave way to the politician and man of affairs, an obsession with building set in. In 1525 Wolsey attempted to mollify the King by handing over Hampton Court. This marked the beginning of twenty years of royal building on a scale never to be repeated in the history of the Crown. It was precipitated not only by rivalry with Francis I, who was simultaneously engaged in building a series of great châteaux but also by the events of the Reformation. Those events meant that there was unprecedented finance for major projects, especially after the Dissolution of the Monasteries in 1536, and that the King of England, as he defied the rest of Christendom and proclaimed himself the image of God on earth, needed a setting worthy of the extreme powers which were now attributed to him. During the 1530s there begins the cult of the royal palace and the development of the whole apparatus of court ceremonial and etiquette deliberately designed to exalt the monarchy. And this demanded settings, both interior and exterior, to celebrate, in the words of the chronicler Edward Hall, the 'triumphant reigne' of Henry VIII.

Hampton Court was the King's first garden. During the decade following 1525 he carried through large extensions to the palace, including the building of a great hall and a series of state apartments around what is today Wren's Fountain Court. The gardens, however, were to be the palace's most startling innovation.[7] Nothing quite like them had ever been seen before and their design and layout are of major significance for the whole development of garden design in England down to the accession of James I.

The earliest alterations to the grounds were those to what was referred to as the Privy Orchard. Seven sun-dials were purchased and in January 1531 there occurred the following payment:

> The Kinges bestes made to be sett vp in the privie orchard. Dieu to John Rypley of London Joyner for making vij of the Kinges Bestes. That is to say ij dragons, ij greyhoundes, i lyon, i horse & i Antylope at xviij^s the pece.[8]

This entry introduces us to what was to become the most distinctive feature of early Tudor garden display, dynastic heraldry. Each beast, picked out in bright colours with an abundance of gilding, surmounted a post painted either white or white and green, the Tudor colours, and clutched a small vane or flag with either the royal arms or a Tudor rose. Later this scheme was elaborated by the addition of three antelopes, three dragons, three lions, two harts, two greyhounds and three hinds.

In this way what was to become a leitmotif of Tudor gardens began. What was its source? Early Tudor royal panoply expressed itself primarily by means of heraldry. All these beasts and coats of arms celebrated the legitimacy of the House of Tudor and its right to rule. Badges and beasts became fashionable first at the court of Edward III and, from the fourteenth century to the sixteenth, badges are found more frequently than the royal arms in decoration. The period of their greatest popularity was during the Wars of the Roses when

8 Panorama of Hampton Court and its gardens from the Thames, *c.* 1555. From left to right we can see the Pond Garden, the Privy Garden and, in the foreground, the Mount Garden leading right to the Great Arbour, whose onion-shaped dome is partly obscured by the Water Gate.

their use on standards and on liveries was a mark of allegiance.[9] Beasts, in particular, were widely used in an architectural context decorating gables and gateposts and supporting banners or vanes along the roof-line of buildings. This was a common feature of the Tudor palace style and the skylines of both Hampton Court and Whitehall were dotted with them. They also adorned the roofs of the temporary pavilions which formed such a striking feature of early Tudor court festivals. In the painting of the Field of Cloth of Gold at Hampton Court, the temporary palace erected at Guisnes has these beasts holding vanes at its corners.[10] If we want an even more precise impression of what they looked like in their pristine glory there exists a design for a pavilion of crimson and gold among the Cotton manuscripts, possibly in connection with the Field of Cloth of Gold, the tent poles of which are surmounted by eighteen royal beasts derived from badges and supporters of Henry VIII and his ancestors: four lions, three dragons, six greyhounds, two harts and three antelopes. Each beast supports a banner adorned with either the royal arms or appropriate badges.[11] All we need to do is to imagine these transported into the orchard.

26

The Privy Orchard seems to have been a preliminary canter for what was to follow, for it is not referred to again in the accounts. Then in 1532 work begins on the series of three gardens which ran by the south side of the palace down to the riverside, the Privy Garden, the Mount Garden and the Pond Garden. Our only source for what this looked like is a series of topographical drawings by Anthonis van Wyngaerde made during a visit to England about 1555. Wyngaerde left a series of views of the palace from every side and the drawings constitute the most comprehensive visual account of any sixteenth-century palace garden.

The importance of these gardens cannot be over-estimated. The first two ran from north to south parallel with one another, the Privy Garden immediately below the suite of rooms which constituted the King's side of the Cloister Green Court and the small, triangular Mount Garden south of that. Together, the two gardens, according to the Parliamentary Survey of 1653, occupied three acres and one rod.

The drawing shows the Privy Garden as consisting of two groups of square beds divided quarterly, the whole encompassed by walks with a central broad walk dividing them running from north to south. There is no indication in the drawing of walks running between the quarters. The whole was encompassed on the south by a wall, on the north by the façade of the palace, on the west by a gallery running by way of a turreted banqueting house towards the Thames and on the east by the Water Gallery, which ran by way of the Great Round Arbour on to a landing place. In the Privy Garden the initial theme explored in the Privy Orchard seems to have been taken up and developed. Early in the winter of 1534 comes the following payment:

> For making bestes in tymber for the kynges new garden. Also payd to the said Edd. More for Cuttyng, makyng and karvyng of vij^{xx} xixth [i.e. 159] of the Kynges and the quenys beestes stondyng in the Kynges new garden at xx^s the pece.[12]

This is followed by something new, payments for painting hundreds of yards of wooden railing in the Tudor colours of white and green.[13] If we turn to the drawing we can see the beasts dotted about the garden at strategic points and the rails which connected them running horizontally around the beds.

The garden contained another feature, twenty sun-dials purchased at 4s 4d each from Brise Augustyn of Westminster in June 1534.[14] These, like the heraldic beasts, were scattered about the garden. Here we are at the fount of what continues to be a standard garden feature. It extended, in simplified form, the theme of the famous Astronomical Clock made by Nicholas Ourlian for the King in 1540. In embryo we have already the idea that the garden is an area for a demonstration of the sciences.

The Mount Garden, which was also referred to as the Little Garden, was a triangle as recorded in Wyngaerde's view. It is difficult to see how it was laid out and there is only one beast on a pole visible above the shrubbery. In 1533 sixty-seven apple trees were purchased for it.[15] Its most spectacular feature, however, was at the south-east end, the mount from which the garden took its name, thrown up against the wall on the east. This went up in 1533–4. On top of the mount was the South or Great Round Arbour, three storeys in height, almost all of glass, with a leaden cupola surmounted by the inevitable king's beasts and a great gilded crown. The ascent to the mount, which was thick planted with quickset, was by means of paths flanked by the king's beasts carved in stone: two dragons, two greyhounds, a luzern and a griffin.[16] The Great Round Arbour can be seen in Wyngaerde's view and also in another by Danckaerts made in the reign of Charles II but from the east side of the palace.[17]

The Mount Garden was little more than an enclosure containing the mount and arbour and allowing views down onto the Privy Garden from the south and, in the other direction, to traffic on the Thames. To the west of the Privy Garden lay the Pond Garden. We can see in Wyngaerde's drawing three rectangular fish-ponds running from east to west. These, likewise, were bordered by the king's beasts: four dragons, six tigers, five greyhounds and five harts.[18] This arrangement also was richly suggestive for the future. What had begun as the medieval fish-pond, necessary for food, and the moat, a feature of defence, is already in the 1530s beginning to develop into an attribute of the pleasure garden, water cast in a role beyond that of the purely utilitarian. Finally, to the north of the palace, was an enormous orchard in which there was a very large and several-storeyed arbour that can be seen in Wyngaerde's view.

Hampton Court is thus a development of Richmond and Thornbury but on a vast scale. The gardens are connected by galleries running around them, the Privy Garden is not sited far away from the palace or castle but in close proximity to it for ease of access, and the placing of galleries or arbours on more than one floor makes it simpler to look down onto the pattern of the garden. There were, however, features going beyond those listed at Thornbury. One was the mount, the first of any size in England. Mounts had been included in medieval gardens, designed to give views over the castle walls to the countryside around and John Leland in his *Itinerary* records a number at Wresehall in Yorkshire.[19] But the one at Hampton Court was quite spectacular in its size. This, together with the hundreds of royal beasts which were to be found everywhere, gave the garden a character far different from that of Richmond and Thornbury and made it emphatically regal.

Where can we in fact place the gardens at Hampton Court in garden history? One prime source must be France, which forty years earlier had first begun to respond to the new impulses of gardening in Renaissance Italy.[20] The French Renaissance garden is usually reckoned as beginning with Charles VIII's expedition to Italy in 1494–5 when, overcome by the beauty in particular of Neapolitan gardens, he had brought back two Italians, Pacello de Mercogliano and Gerolamo da Napoli, who introduced the Renaissance style. This is an over-simplification; up until the close of the sixteenth century only certain elements of Italian Renaissance garden planning had been introduced into France. The central principles – that the garden is the domain of the architect, that the terrain could be reshaped by means of architecture and that the garden related axially to the house – were slow to come. During the reigns of Louis XII and Francis I, Italianate features – pavilions, galleries and fountains – are introduced into what are basically still medieval gardens.

Blois, which Mercogliano laid out for Louis XII between 1500 and 1510, is the first great garden complex of the French Renaissance. There were three sections to this garden. The first, the lower part, was a revamping of an older garden. This was divided into four sections with a fountain *à l'italienne* at the centre and two *treillage* rooms placed at the corners. It was enclosed by walls and galleries, one of which had an upper storey with windows for looking down. The galleries led on to the second, more important garden, a large rectangular area laid out in squares or *carreaux*, all different, each one surrounded by wooden balustrading or fencing with walks in between; the whole was encompassed by an open arcaded gallery hung with hunting trophies. The garden had a chapel, a pavilion for the view and, at the centre intersection of the walks, an octagonal wooden pavilion with St Michael on the top and a marble fountain within it. Beyond lay a third, less elaborate, garden.

The second great early French Renaissance garden, built and planted simultaneously with this, was Gaillon, the famous château of Georges, Cardinal d'Amboise. As in the case of Blois the gardens are away from the house and repeat the same layout on a more splendid scale. It, too, is a large rectangular area enclosed by a wall with an entrance pavilion on one side and on the other three galleries. Within, there are parquets as there were at Blois, two being in the form of a labyrinth (or daedalus, as it was then known), one rectangular and one circular, with a central pavilion of carpentry with a white marble fountain beneath. The engraving of Gaillon in Du Cerceau shows what

French sources
of early
Tudor gardens

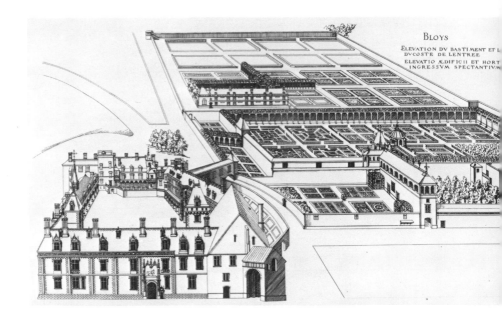

9 Blois was the earliest
French Renaissance
garden complex. The
gardens are laid out in
squares planted with
geometric knots and
enclosed by covered
galleries. This
arrangement also
characterized Richmond,
Hampton Court and
Whitehall.

10 Gaillon repeats the
design of Blois on a more
elaborate scale. Its
fountains are likely to
have influenced Whitehall
and the rectangular and
circular mazes could have
inspired Nonsuch.

11 Francis I's
Fontainebleau places the
garden beneath the state
apartments of the palace,
an arrangement duplicated
in all Henry VIII's
palaces.

facing page:
12 Burgundian gardens
were a source for both
France and England.
There, the medieval
garden was highly
developed as an open-air
room. Duke Charles the
Bold is presented with a
book in a walled garden
with a summer house,
raised flower-beds and a
topiary shrub in a pot.

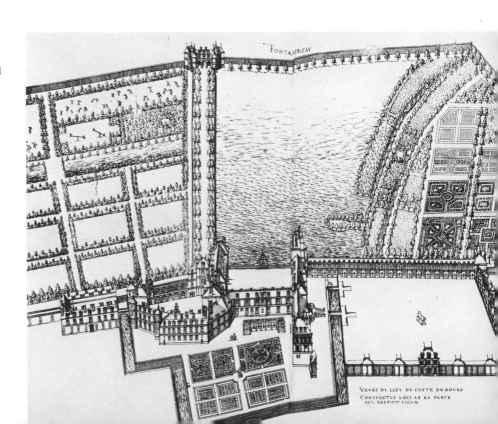

is missing from the ones of Blois – that the squares are laid out as knots, that is geometric patterns made up of plants, grass and coloured materials such as sand or coal-dust.

These two epitomized French gardening during the first half of the century. Henry VIII, however, was influenced more than anything by what his rival, Francis I, was building. The French king was not particularly interested in gardens. Chambord (begun 1519) had none, Madrid (1528) and St Germain-en-Laye (1539) had only simple parquets with no fountains. At Fontainebleau alone were the gardens developed to any degree.[21] This happened from 1528 onwards, a date which coincides exactly with Henry VIII's own introduction of gardens into his palace schemes. Du Cerceau's view of Fontainebleau shows the great avenue of trees which was planted down to the Porte Dorée. To the left, there were orchards and meadow land. To the right, there was the great pond and beyond, the Jardin des Pins laid out in the usual parquets. But the most important garden lay to the north within the canal encircling the palace. It was situated directly beneath the palace windows and consisted of four squares with, as its focal point, the statue of Diana of Versailles.

How does all this compare with Hampton Court? Henry's interest in fountains seems to follow that of Francis, and to date from the 1540s. Neither Fontainebleau nor Hampton Court had them in the thirties. Subsequently they became prominent features of Whitehall and Nonsuch. The placing of the Privy Garden below the windows of the King's apartments at Hampton Court suggests the influence of Fontainebleau but, on the whole, the arrangement at Hampton Court is much more elaborate in its articulation. The use of galleries and arbours by which to link the gardens looks surely to Blois and Gaillon. The wooden fencing surrounding the beds was typically medieval but its development in England into a vehicle for dynastic heraldic display was novel. Perhaps this feature owed something to Gaillon, which also had wooden carved animals. The concept of the use of the garden as a vehicle for heraldic celebration seems specifically English; the Privy Garden itself, however, was directly French. Its layout as a large rectangular area divided into squares is straight from Blois and Gaillon.

Both traditions, however, may go back to another source. The court which above every other set the style in northern Europe during the fifteenth century and well on into the sixteenth was that of the dukes of Burgundy.[22] There, the garden was cultivated as a part of the life and symbolic pageantry of the late medieval palace–castle and as a symbol of political power. There, too, the medieval *hortus conclusus*, the enclosed garden of the Virgin's chastity, was developed as a potent symbol of the reality of happiness. Philip the Good's wife, Isabella of Portugal, took the enclosed garden as her symbol, expressive not only of chastity but also of the theme of courtly dalliance, *le jardin d'amour*. The gardens of the Burgundian dukes at the castles of Hesdin and Germolles opened outwards as planned extensions of the building, as if they were open-air rooms within the castle. Flemish miniatures which record the ceremonial life of the Burgundian court give us a record of this interplay of castle and garden. Guillebert de Lannoy presents to Duke Charles the Bold his *L'Instruction d'un jeune prince* in a formal garden divided up into square raised beds of grass and flowers; in the background there is a large summer house or arbour. The early Henrician court strove to emulate this Burgundian model in its endless round of tilts, tourneys and chivalrous displays, at least for the first two decades of the reign, one dazzling spectacle succeeding another in an effort to establish the new king as the perfect warrior prince. Gardens were part of that Burgundian magnificence of courtly life which had to be assimilated.

Until now I have dealt solely with the evidence from the accounts and from the drawings by Wyngaerde. But the gardens of Hampton Court were also seen, admired and described by foreign visitors. The first of these was a Spaniard, the Duke de Najera, in 1544. He visited a royal palace called Hampton Court, which lay a league from London, within which he saw 'a garden which is extremely handsome, with high corridors and passages everywhere and in them there are various busts of men and women'. He goes on to refer to the 'monsters' or beasts which decorated it.[23] The description so very soon after its creation reinforces the impression that it was like Blois with its interconnecting galleries running from one garden to the next. More tantalizing is the allusion to the busts in the passages. Were these, perhaps, roundels like the terracotta heads of Roman emperors by Giovanni da Maiano, executed for Wolsey in the present Base and Clock Courts?

The next, very much more detailed, description is late Elizabethan. Thomas Platter, a German, was conducted around the Privy Garden in 1599 by the gardener. He begins by describing its layout:

By the entrance I noticed numerous patches where square cavities had been scooped out, as for paving stones; some of these were filled with red brick-dust, some with white sand, and some with green lawn, very much resembling a chess-board.[24]

In other words Platter is saying that the squares which we see in the Wyngaerde drawings were laid out in patterns as knots in which grass, brick-dust and sand had been used as materials to delineate a design that could best be read from the upper windows of the royal apartments. Knots were a feature of gardens in fifteenth-century England, the patterns in them evolving and changing through the century. They must have been there already in the thirties.

He goes on to refer to the shrubbery surrounding the garden:

The hedges and surrounds were of hawthorn, bush firs, ivy, roses, juniper, holly, English or common elm, box and other shrubs, very gay and attractive.[25]

All this would square with the purchase of plants in the accounts. He then proceeds to describe a more surprising feature:

There were all manner of shapes, men and women, half men and half horse [i.e. centaurs], sirens, serving-maids with baskets, French lilies and delicate crenellations all round made from dry twigs bound together and the aforesaid ever green quick-set shrubs, or entirely of rosemary, all true to the life, and so cleverly and amusingly interwoven, mingled and grown together, trimmed and arranged picture-wise that their equal would be difficult to find.[26]

This was the Privy Garden four years before the death of Elizabeth, but had these astounding topiary figures been a feature of her father's garden? I think it highly likely, as the accounts are full of purchases of quicksets and of willow branches or osiers with which to bind and set them.[27] Topiary had been a medieval as well as a Renaissance tradition; in the same miniature of Guillebert de Lannoy presenting his book to Duke Charles the Bold there is a sculpted shrub in a pot placed in the centre of the garden. But the scale of the Hampton Court topiary is such that it must reflect directly an Italianate influence. The account by Platter recalls the descriptions of the human figures, animals and monsters that made up the mass displays of the revived antique *ars topiaria* in the Rucellai and Medici gardens at the end of the previous century. And such a display, like the heraldic beasts, presumably had a symbolic function.

Hampton Court is the most fully documented of all sixteenth-century English gardens. It is a typical product of early Tudor civilization, in which the channels of stylistic communication were in the main through France. Above all it makes abundantly clear that the great garden has arrived as an essential attribute of the palace–castle of the reigning dynasty. Pleasure gardens are seen to pertain to the king and to the court as outward signs of regal magnificence. The English Renaissance garden from the start is strongly cast as a vehicle for symbolic display. In early Tudor terms this meant the introduction into it of heraldry. As the century progressed, and particularly after 1560, the whole range of Renaissance symbolism was taken up in England through the importation of books of emblems and *imprese*, as well as the great mythological manuals, so that the older heraldic vocabulary developed into the much richer language of allegory.

Whitehall and Nonsuch

Whitehall, like Hampton Court, was a remodelling and extension of one of Cardinal Wolsey's houses.[28] It had begun life in the thirteenth century as York Place, the London residence of the archbishops of York. Thomas Wolsey, as soon as he became archbishop, had begun to build and expand beyond the original site and to purchase neighbouring land. The splendour of York Place under his aegis is memorably described in the memoirs of his servant, George Cavendish. On Wolsey's praemunire in October 1529 it passed to the Crown and three months later the King announced his intention of elevating it to the status of a royal palace.

The conversion of York Place into the Palace of Whitehall, as it soon became known, was carried through at breakneck speed. It was complete enough by the autumn of 1533 to receive Anne Boleyn as queen. Whitehall was a much more rambling and piecemeal affair than Hampton Court. Wolsey had begun extending and remodelling the group of buildings next to the Thames. The King followed suit by purchasing large tracts of land, chiefly to the west, but in spite of the demolition of hundreds of houses even he was unable to deny the ancient public rights of way either south to the river or east to west by way of King Street. The result was that the palace was divided into two distinct parts, with the famous King Street and so-called Holbein gateways linking them. To the north there was the cockpit, the tennis court and the tilt gallery leading onto parkland and St James's Palace. To the south lay the main part of the palace and the state apartments divided as usual into a King's and a Queen's side, the whole being articulated by means of galleries.

We know that there were gardens under Wolsey; a document of 1530 refers to two, but there is no evidence for their location.[29] One, it would be reasonable to argue, must have been what became the Privy Garden, occupying an area later to become famous as the Sermon or Pebble Court. This first Privy Garden is something of an enigma. Much of it must have gone by the time it was taken over as a court for open-air sermons in the reign of Edward VI and only remnants of its role as a garden existed by 1584 when a German visitor, Lupold von Wedel, described it as 'a grass plot surrounded by broad walks'.[30]

Fortunately such an elusive quality does not pervade the Great Garden created in the 1540s to the west of the palace, where there had formerly been an orchard.[31] This was a large rectangular area bounded by brick walls on the north and west and by the palace itself on the south and east. To the south there was the Low or Orchard Gallery which had been part of Wolsey's palace but which was now altered and adorned with a series of wall-paintings depicting Henry VIII's coronation and the Field of Cloth of Gold. Part of this at least took the form of an open loggia comensurate with its southern aspect. Above ran the Stone Gallery; to the west at an upper level there was the Privy Gallery, which was a re-erection of Wolsey's gallery at Esher, linking the Privy Lodgings.

The Great Garden was in existence by 1545 but the earliest description comes forty years later:

Hence we went into the queen's garden, in which there are thirty-four high columns, carved with various fine paintings: also different animals carved in wood, with their horns gilt, are set on the top of the columns, together with flags bearing the Queen's arms. In the middle of the garden is a nice fountain with a remarkable sundial, showing the time in thirty different ways. Between the spices that are planted in the garden there are fine walks grown in grass, and the spices are planted very artistically, surrounded by plants in the shape of seats.[32]

In the Jacobean period the escort of the young Duke of Saxony gives a similar description:

Then Your Grace went down into the garden. It lies immediately next to the royal palace, so that one can see into it from the main apartments. It is quadrangular, not especially big, divided into several garden plots. At the corners of the same stand wooden columns, on them all kinds of animals. They had flags in front of themselves, carved from wood and gilded all over.

In the middle of the garden is a great quadrangular stone, hollow in the middle and round like a baptismal fount. One walks up four steps. On this stone are over 117 sun-circles, on which you can see the hours. It is a beautiful work of art. This Herologia was designed in the first place in Henry VIII's time by Joan Pieneto Episcopo Wintoniensi but was later restored by the present King [James I], as the inscription records.[33]

Shortly after the garden was completed two views of it were included in a group portrait of Henry VIII and his family.[34] Through archways to the left and right of the picture we peer out at a rare topographical record, the King's new Privy Garden. The raised beds are contained with low brick walls above which run rails painted the Tudor colours of green and white. Exactly as in the written descriptions, the beds are punctuated by marbled wooden columns topped by heraldic beasts: Edward III's griffin, the Beaufort yale, the Richmond white greyhound and possibly the white hind. Within there is a low planting of herbs and flowers. We seem to be looking out on the garden from the southern Orchard Gallery and in the distance there are the red brick boundary walls and beyond, the roofs of the tennis court and cockpit. There is also what might be the banqueting house which was put up in the orchard in 1541. It is a building whose walls are covered with grotesque work in the antique style on the lines of that we know was used at Nonsuch.

The second view is by Anthonis Wyngaerde and, in contrast to his drawings of Hampton Court, little more than impressionistic. From it we can gather the regularity of the layout in straight walks with a great central fountain. This, indeed, is our only source for the appearance of the fountain, which was very large and a major innovation. As far as we know there were none in the earlier Hampton Court gardens. Its introduction as the focal point articulating Whitehall is the first sign so far of the role of the fountain in the Renaissance pleasure garden. In northern Europe during the early sixteenth century the fountain as a garden motif in the medieval romance tradition is fused with the fountain as part of the revived antique garden as conceived by the Humanists. A small sketch of the fountain in the view of Whitehall indicates that it was of the candelabrum variety, a series of bowls descending downwards with a figure at the top. As a type its origin is Italian but this design probably came via France. Even that perfunctory sketch recalls the famous fountains at Gaillon erected during the first decade of the century.[35] Cardinal Georges d'Amboise, prime minister and adviser to Louis XII, had two elaborate fountains at

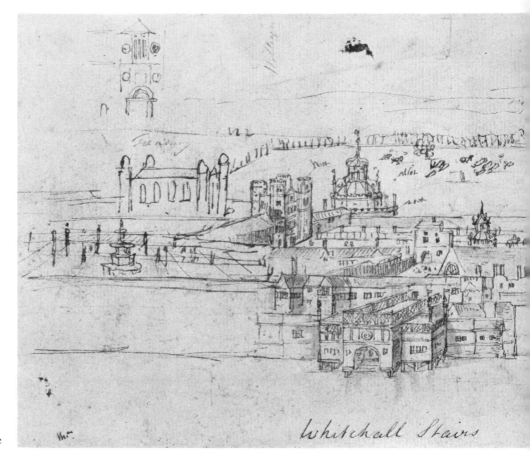

Whitehall Stairs

The Great Garden of Whitehall

facing page:

13 Two views, *c.* 1545, of the Great Garden, from a gallery within the palace. The raised flower-beds are surrounded with rails painted in the Tudor colours of green and white. The heraldic animals surmount marbled wooden columns.

14 Aerial view from the Thames, *c.* 1555, showing the garden centring on a large fountain; it is laid out in knots decorated with heraldic beasts on posts and is surrounded on two sides by galleries.

15 The royal beasts were the most ubiquitous form of early Tudor dynastic decoration. They were used not only on buildings but on temporary pavilions. Their introduction into the garden was a major innovation.

Gaillon. One, imported from Genoa, was in the *cour d'honneur*. The second, less magnificent than the first but of the same type, was inside a pavilion in the centre of the garden. Both were surmounted by figures, both had a series of bowls from which classical features such as lions' or cherubim's heads spouted water downwards and both were approached by flights of steps. On the inadequate evidence they would seem to square with what we know of the Whitehall fountain.

More topical, however, would have been the work going on at Fontaine-bleau. In 1541 Primaticcio finished the fountain in the Cour de la Fontaine, which was surmounted by Hercules, and from 1543 onwards Cellini was working on a monumental Fountain of Mars, surmounted by a gargantuan figure of the god fifty-four feet high.[36] By the 1540s Henry VIII would also have been thinking of fountains as new expressions of monarchical power and glory. The most direct link with Fontainebleau would have been the Italian Nicholas Modena who had worked there and who entered the English King's service in 1538.[37] He was principally to design and supervise the carved decoration at Nonsuch but he worked extensively on the interior of Whitehall in the forties. Unfortunately practically no accounts for Whitehall survive so that his connection with the fountain must remain pure conjecture.

Foreign visitors to Whitehall, however, were less struck by the fountain than by the sun-dial in close proximity to it. We know very little about this. In 1621–2 Nicholas Stone was paid to take it down and re-erect it, while Edward Gunter, Professor of Astronomy in Gresham College, reworked the scientific part, publishing a description at the behest of the future Charles I.[38] The attribution of the dial by the Saxon duke's escort to 'Joan Pieneto Episcopo Wintoniensi' makes no sense at all. The Bishop of Winchester at that date was Stephen Gardiner. If the dial was by anyone it must surely have been by Nicholas Kratzer, a native of Munich and the King's Astronomer, one of whose two surviving manuscripts is entitled *De compositione horologiorum*.[39]

Whitehall is basically the Privy Garden of Hampton Court transported to London. Apart from the fountain and the sun-dial there are no major innovations. The source again is French and in 1544 many French gardeners crossed the Channel to England, some of whom are known to have been in Henry VIII's service.[40] Hampton Court, as far as we know, was supervised throughout by an Englishman, Edward Gryffyn. French craftsmen during this period were, however, being recruited for the King's greatest and most celebrated folly, Nonsuch Palace, which was also to have famous gardens.

Nonsuch arose at the foot of the north downs between Cheam and Ewell, the village of Cuddington being razed to the ground to make way for it.[41] It went up at an astonishing speed between 1538 and 1547 and was designed from the outset to be the King's supreme monument to princely ostentation and splendour. As in the case of his other palaces, rivalry with Francis I was the driving force and an urge to eclipse Fontainebleau in particular. By 1545, the sum spent was £23,000 but the palace was still unfinished at Henry's death. Following its predecessors it was a series of courtyards opening one into the other and its chief novelty lay in the external decoration of the inner court which was done in emulation of Fontainebleau by foreign workmen under the supervision of Nicholas Modena and consisted of sculpture and reliefs in the antique style. The private apartments were situated on the far side of the inner court and looked south over the Privy Garden. An impression of this can best be obtained from the engraving by Jodocus Hondius in Speed's *Theatre of the Empire of Great Britaine* (1611–12). The encrusted façade can be seen flanked by huge octagonal towers crowned by windowed pavilions, pointed lead roofs with pinnacles and vanes, designed probably to outshine the towers of Francis I's Château de Chambord. Basically, however, as Sir John Summerson has observed, Nonsuch was an English structure with a French overlay.

The gardens and grounds of Henry VIII's Nonsuch remain extremely problematic. Mary Tudor sold the palace to Henry FitzAlan, 12th Earl of Arundel, whose son-in-law John, Lord Lumley, carried out radical alterations to the gardens in the eighties, making them into one of the most significant Elizabethan garden ensembles. Speed shows this garden, to which we shall come shortly. Only the general disposition of Henry VIII's gardens is known.

Following Hampton Court, the Privy Garden at Nonsuch was laid out directly below the state and private apartments on the three sides of the inner court. It was bounded by a brick wall. An Elizabethan eulogy of Lord Lumley, composed by one Anthony Watson, states that the garden on the southern side stretched five hundred paces to the boundary wall. The 1650 Parliamentary Survey refers to 'quarters and rounds set about with thorn hedges', walks, arbours, covered alleys and seats painted green, blue and russet. There was a total of twelve arbours.[42] All one can suggest is that the arrangement was the usual one of walls backed by shrubbery with the main garden laid out in squares, probably surrounded with the usual wooden rails and display of the king's beasts. These would have been obvious candidates for removal when Lumley was inserting his own dynastic heraldry into the garden. The fountain which we see in the centre of Speed's engraving is also definitely his. One feature which may pre-date Lumley is the complicated topiary. Watson describes how 'deer, horses, rabbits and dogs give chase with unhindered feet and effortlessly passed over the green'.[43] Platter more directly describes 'all kinds of animals – dogs, hares, all overgrown with plants, most artfully set out, so that from a distance, one would take them for real ones'.[44] This sounds like repetition of Hampton Court, in which quickset was bound with willow and trained into topiary shapes. Whether this is Elizabethan or Henrician remains to be proved.

To the east there was another garden laid out in knots while to the west there was a labyrinth or maze. Anthony Watson states that 'you will enter a tortuous path and fall into the hazardous wiles of the labyrinth'.[45] Platter, in 1599, says that the hedges were so high that one could not see through them.[46] That would have been extremely untypical of early mazes, in which the hedges were but little above ground level, so that the whole maze could be seen at one view and the divisions stepped over. A maze of this sort could go back to Henry VIII's day and have been planted to rival those in the gardens at Gaillon. Further west there was an orchard and, at an even further remove from the palace, an elaborate two-storeyed banqueting house set on a mount. It had balconies on the first floor and a roof which was decorated with the king's beasts.[47] It must have looked something like the Great Arbour in the Mount Garden at Hampton Court. On the available evidence Nonsuch, like Whitehall, did not advance garden design beyond the initial statement of Hampton Court.

Knots and mazes

The central feature of all gardens of pleasure in the sixteenth century was the knot, which held its own until replaced by the *parterre de broderie* of box in the Jacobean period. We have seen in the engraving of Gaillon the effect of these knots, the earliest published designs for which are those in the *Hypnerotomachia Poliphili*. The square knot divided into quarters was to dominate garden design for over a century and the tradition remained vigorous in smaller manor houses and country gardens until the close of Stuart rule.[48]

It becomes possible to find out something in detail about knots only when they were already beginning to pass out of fashion in the greatest gardens. In 1613 Gervase Markham in his *The English Husbandman* opens his discussion by stating that the knot 'which is most ancient and at this day of most vse amongst the vulgar though least respected with great ones, who for the most part are wholy given over to nouelties. You shall vnderstand that Knots and Mazes were the first that were receiued into admiration.'[49] Francis Bacon, who certainly comes within Markham's definition of a great one, dismissed them in 1625 in his essay 'Of Gardens':

> As for the making of knots or figures, with divers coloured earths that they may lie under the windows of the house on that side which the garden stands, they be but toys; you may see as good sights many times in tarts.[50]

But in the 1530s when Henry VIII's gardens were being planted these elaborately patterned knots carried out on a large scale had all the excitement of an original idea. Knots were known in the fifteenth century but it is only with the expansion of gardening under the early Tudors and with the influence of France that their full potential was realised. That they were the vital element of all the royal gardens is proved by the deliberate siting of the Privy Gardens immediately below the windows of the King's apartments so that the patterns could be looked down upon.

Markham explains that knots were of two types, open and closed. Open knots had the pattern set out in lines of rosemary, thyme, hyssop or some other plant, the intervening spaces being filled with different coloured earths and the

Another Maze.

facing page:
16 Design for a knot from
Didymus Mountain's
The Gardeners Labyrinth
(1571)

right:
17 Design for a
rectangular maze from
Thomas Hill's *The
Profitable Art of
Gardening* (1568)

below:
18 Design for two knots
and a circular maze by
Thomas Trevelyon. Early
17th century

path, where it was not grass, was sanded. Closed knots had the spaces between filled with flowers of one colour. There are no surviving designs for early Tudor knots or mazes and the earliest appear in Thomas Hill's *The Profitable Art of Gardening* (1568) and Didymus Mountain's *The Gardeners Labyrinth* (1571). These are of the same type as those that appear in the Gaillon engraving and all are closely related to designs which appear on carpets and embroidery. Who in fact designed them? Only one manuscript gives an answer and that is Jacobean. Thomas Trevelyon was a writing master who worked in Blackfriars during the reign of James I. One of his profusely illustrated manuscripts incorporates a series of designs 'For Joyners, and Gardeners . . . Knotes, and Buildyngs, and Morysies, and Termes'. In other words people went to him for designs for embroidery, marquetry and also for knots for their gardens.[51]

This is a rare single instance of being able actually to pin-point the author of a garden design. The fundamental question: Who designed Henry VIII's gardens? is impossible to answer. Like architecture, the garden was officially the domain of the Office of Works. As John Summerson writes: 'The palaces were devised and built and largely adorned not by mysterious foreigners floating about Henry's Court, but by the officers whose business it was to do these things; and most of these officers were English.'[52] The precise form each garden was to take would have been worked out by the senior officials in joint consultation. The most important person in the Works during the creation of all these gardens was the Surveyor, John Nedeham, who had previously held the office of Master Carpenter. Beneath him came the artificers and craftsmen appointed under patents; these included the Master Mason, Master Carpenter, Chief Joiner, King's Glazier and Serjeant Plumber. In addition to them, and also appointed by patent but not incorporated into the Office of Works, were the Serjeant Painter, Master Plasterer and Chief Smith. It was these men who actually designed the King's buildings and their surroundings, including the gardens, who drew 'plats' for submission to the Surveyor and to the King. And it is these men who created the style and repertory of the early Tudor palace garden.

At the time they must have made a profound impact as expressions of Tudor magnificence. In the mind's eye we need to conjure them up, first from above looking down from the state apartments, opulent with tapestries and glittering with gold and silver, to see them rolled out like some gigantic multi-coloured carpet below us. Within the chequer-board of the formal walks the squares carry patterns, some in intricate interwoven knots, others in swirling arabesques, yet others arranged in the convolutions of the labyrinth. The patterns are delineated by lines of sweet-smelling herbs and the spaces between are filled with coloured sands and earths in the case of the closed knots, or with gillyflowers, primroses, violets or sweet-williams in the case of the open ones. Occasionally these knots must have performed a symbolic function and the allusion would be caught from above. Descending into the garden we need to stroll along its walks. The walls are covered with espaliered pear, apple and damson trees, the roses of York and Lancaster scent the air and everywhere we look there will be a forest of pinnacles bearing brightly coloured heraldic beasts, their gilding catching the sunlight. There will be the marvel of the sculptured figures of men, women, animals and fabulous monsters in quickset and rosemary that seem to inhabit the garden. Perhaps there will be the spiralling walks of a mount to climb or the plashing waters of a marble fountain. Stephen Hawes in his *The History of Grand Amour and la Bell Pucelle* (1509), written perhaps with the gardens of Henry VII's Richmond in mind, evokes vividly the ambience of these early Tudor royal gardens:

Than in we wente to the garden gloryous,
Lyke to a place of pleasure most solacyous.

Wyth Flora paynted and wrought curyously,
In divers knottes of marvaylous gretenes;
Rampande lyons stode up wondersly,
Made all of herbes with dulcet swetenes,
Wyth many dragons of marvaylos likenes,
Of divers floures made ful craftely,
By Flora couloured wyth colours sundry.

Amiddes the garden so moche delectable
There was an herber fayre and quadrante,
To paradyse right well comparable,
Set all about with flours fragraunt;
And in the myddle there was resplendyshaunte
A dulcet spring and marvaylous fountaine,
Of golde and asure made all certaine.

No other lines better encapsulate the role of the garden as 'a place of pleasure'.

The great garden enters sixteenth-century England as an adjunct of monarchy, as an expression of the post-Reformation assertion of royal power and omnipotence. Not until the accession of James I was royal building to be undertaken on any scale to rival that of Henry VIII. His palaces, their parks and gardens remained virtually untouched as the visual setting of monarchy right up to the Civil War. He it was who, in emulation of Burgundy and more particularly early Valois France, established the garden as a symbol of the royal will. The channels of stylistic communication which affected the garden, France or the Low Countries, were the same as those in the other arts. After the break with Rome direct contact with Italy of a kind which France continued to enjoy, in the form of the importation of sculptors, painters, architects and designers, ceased. No more appeared in England after 1540 and knowledge of Renaissance Italy becomes increasingly second-hand as the century progresses. Isolation was only to be broken after 1603 when the wars of religion, engendered by the Reformation, gradually came to their close and direct contacts with the civilization of Renaissance Italy were re-established in the figures of Thomas Howard, Earl of Arundel, and a future Surveyor of the King's Works, Inigo Jones.

19 Elizabeth I as *Rosa Electa*, flanked by the Tudor Rose and the Virgin Eglantine (*c.* 1590–1600)

CHAPTER III

THE EMBLEMATIC GARDEN
Kenilworth, Theobalds, Wollaton, Wimbledon and Nonsuch

The middle years of the sixteenth century were not at all conducive to either architecture or gardening. The only significant building to arise was Somerset House, built for Edward VI's Lord Protector between 1547 and 1552. Although it was architecturally one of the most influential of mid-Tudor buildings, we know nothing about its gardens until they were redesigned for Anne of Denmark. Until the defeat of the Northern Rebellion in 1569 the country had been passing through a severe period of political instability, violent religious change and economic crisis. It was only after 1570, and more particularly after 1580, that the long Elizabethan peace gradually became a reality and building started in earnest again, continuing in an upward curve into the new century.

The most important development was that the pleasure garden became an essential adjunct of the great house. Elizabeth I never directly patronized the arts on any scale. The palaces and gardens of her father's reign remained unchanged as the background to her court. This absence of royal initiative resulted, especially towards the close of the reign, in what was virtually antiquated isolationism, reinforced as religious divisions sharpened in Europe from the 1560s onwards. As England went Protestant in 1558 the roads to Italy were to all intents closed until the turn of the century. By the seventies the Low Countries were totally disrupted by the long struggle provoked by the Revolt of the Netherlands and by the middle of the eighties the Valois court disappeared, engulfed in the last and most savage of all the French wars of religion, those of the Catholic League. This meant that neither country was able to act as a transmitter of the latest developments in garden design from Renaissance Italy. In spite of all this, gardens remained an essential feature of the age, so potent that four centuries later we still think of the old formal gardens of England as being Elizabethan in style. We imagine that we know much more about Elizabethan gardens than in fact we do. That they have left such a vivid impression within the realm of popular mythology is a distant reflection of a reality, the deliberate presentation of the peace of the Elizabethan age and its queen in horticultural terms. And it is with this that we must begin.

Elizabeth I and the garden

In May 1591 Queen Elizabeth I was entertained by Lord Burghley at Theobalds. As usual it was the occasion for courtly compliment. She was welcomed by a hermit apologizing for the absence of the lord of the house who had retired to a cell out of grief at the loss of his wife and daughter. The most interesting speech, however, was one by a gardener; this we must imagine taking place as the Queen strolled in the Great Garden. In it he describes to her a garden that was being created four miles away at Pymms:

> . . . the youngest son of this honourable old man . . . devised a plot for a garden, as methought, and in a place unfit for pleasure . . . and besides so far from the house that, in my country capacity, a pound would have been meeter than a paradise. . . . The moles destroyed and the plot levelled, I cast it into four quarters. In the first I framed a maze, not of hyssop and thyme, but that which maketh itself wither with wondering; all the Virtues, all the Graces, all the Muses winding and wreathing about your majesty, each contending to be chief, all contented to be cherished: all this not of potherbs, but of flowers, and of flowers fairest and sweetest; for in so heavenly a maze, which astonished all earthly thought's promise, the Virtues were done in roses, flowers fit for the twelve Virtues, who have in themselves, as we gardeners have observed, above an hundred; the Graces of pansies partly-coloured, but in one stalk, never asunder, yet diversely beautified; the Muses of nine several flowers, being of sundry natures, yet all sweet, all sovereign.
>
> These mingled in a maze. . . . Then was I commanded to place an arbour all of eglantine, in which my master's conceit out-stripped my cunning: 'Eglantine', quoth he, 'I most honour, and it hath been told me that the deeper it is rooted in the ground, the sweeter it smelleth in the flower, making it ever so green that the sun of Spain at the hottest cannot parch it.'[1]

What was being described to the Queen was a garden designed by Lord Burghley's younger son, Sir Robert Cecil, which had been conceived as an emblem of herself. It was sited (unusually) away from the house, and laid out in the customary four quarters, each to be filled by a knot. Only the first of these knots is described; it was planted as a maze on the lines of those illustrated in the garden books or in the manuscripts of Thomas Trevelyon. The gardener explains that it was laid out not with the customary herbs but with symbolic flowers: the twelve Virtues in roses, the three Graces in pansies and the nine Muses in nine different types of flower. Cecil then commanded his gardener to make an arbour entirely of eglantine.

The entertainment was written by George Peele who, although a poetaster on the fringes of the court, was deeply imbued with the basic assumptions of its mythology. Peele is describing something which almost certainly existed and even if it did not, this approach to reading the contents of a garden takes us onto what is perhaps the most important path to pursue. During Elizabeth's reign early Tudor royalist heraldry is transmuted into allegory of a kind related to the complex cult of the Virgin Queen. The Queen was, of course, always the Tudor Rose, the union of the white rose of York and the red of Lancaster.[2] Through that rudimentary equation she was ever present in any garden in the kingdom. What is more significant is that that flower represented only a fraction of what came to be, as the reign progressed, an enormously diffuse horticultural image in which the Queen, the kingdom, the spring, the garden and flowers became inextricably intertwined. In Cecil's garden she is, for instance, unequivocally presented as the single five-petalled eglantine rose whose power was such that it could vanquish the might of Catholic Spain. Elizabethan literature is sprinkled with allusions to Elizabeth as the eglantine, from Sir Arthur George's poem eulogizing her as Eglantine of Meryfleur, descendant of the ancient kings of Troy, to passing exhortations of the kind George Peele wrote in celebration of the thirty-fifth anniversary of her accession to the throne:

> *. . . Wear eglantine,*
> *And wreaths of roses red and white put on*
> *In honour of that day . . .*

The eglantine can also be found in her portraits. The Phoenix Jewel in the British Museum depicts her profile encircled by a wreath of Tudor roses and eglantine in enamelled gold. William Rogers depicts her during the last decade of the reign as *Rosa Electa*, enshrined between branches of the Tudor and the eglantine rose.[3]

Perhaps the most important of these 'horticultural' visions of the Queen comes in Edmund Spenser's April Eclogue in *The Shepheards Calender* (1579), in which Elizabeth is celebrated as 'fayre Elisa, Queene of shepheardes all'. Spenser is a key figure for naturalizing the Renaissance pastoral tradition as part of the Elizabethan myth and investing its imagery with a Protestant gloss.

> *See, where she sits upon the grassie greene,*
> *   (O seemely sight!)*
> *Yclad in Scarlot, like a mayden Queene,*
> *   And ermines white.*
> *Upon her head a Cremosin coronet,*
> *With Damaske roses and Daffadillies set:*
> *   Bay leaves betweene,*
> *   And primroses greene,*
> *Embellish the sweete Violet . . .*
>
> *Bring hether the Pincke and purple Cullambine,*
> *   With Gelliflowres;*
> *Bring Coronations, and Sops in wine,*
> *   Worne of Paramoures;*
> *Strowe me the ground with Daffadowndillies,*
> *And Cowslips, and Kingcups, and loved Lillies:*
> *   The pretie Pawnce,*
> *   And the Chevisaunce,*
> *Shall match with the fayre flowre Delice.*[4]

Here in the seventies that fundamental aspect of the Elizabeth cult, her association with spring and its flowers and by implication their further association with the principles and success of her rule, is already clearly enunciated. The garden under Elizabeth, therefore, becomes drawn into the network of symbolic royalist imagery, a connection that was only to be shattered by the English revolution. It is a phenomenon deeply related to the late sixteenth-century cult of monarchy which was expressed symbolically in imagery dwelling upon the almost magical powers of the sovereign over the physical universe. This view is central to the Elizabethan image and can be most easily studied in the celebration of the Queen as Astraea, the Just Virgin of Vergil's *IVth Eclogue*, whose return from the heavens to earth brings again the Golden Age.[5] John Davies's twenty-six *Hymnes to Astraea* published in 1600 cover every aspect of this cult and they are deeply revealing when read in relation to the development of gardens during the last twenty years of the reign.

At the beginning, in the Golden Age, spring reigns eternal, in this case a spring which is equated with the rule of Elizabeth Tudor.

E arth now is greene, and heauen is blew,
L iuely Spring which makes all new,
I olly Spring, doth enter ;
S weete yong sun-beames doe subdue
A ngry, aged Winter.

B lasts are milde, and seas are calme,
E uery meadow flowes with balme,
T he Earth weares all her riches;
H armonious birdes sing such a psalme,
A s eare and heart bewitches.

R eserue (sweet Spring) this Nymph of ours,
E ternall garlands of thy flowers,
G reene garlands neuer wasting;
I n her shall last our State's faire Spring,
N ow and for euer flourishing,
A s long as Heauen is lasting.[6]

May, the month of spring, is her month; the rose is her flower, because she is also beauty's rose. But perhaps the best Hymn associating the art of the garden with the cult of the Queen is number IX:

TO FLORA

E mpresse of flowers, tell where away
L ies your sweet Court this merry May,
I n Greenewich *garden allies?*
S ince there the heauenly powers do play
A nd haunt no other vallies.

B eautie, vertue, maiestie,
E loquent Muses, three times three,
T he new fresh Houres *and Graces,*
H aue pleasure in this place to be,
A boue all other places.

R oses and lillies did them draw,
E re they diuine Astraea *saw;*
G ay flowers they sought for pleasure:
I nstead of gathering crownes of flowers,
N ow gather they Astraea's dowers,
A nd beare to heauen their treasure.[7]

The Rainbow Portrait of Elizabeth at Hatfield is a visual equivalent: it presents her as the flower-bedecked Astraea, her bodice embroidered with spring flowers – roses, lilies and pansies – while the rainbow in her hand tells of the peace she has brought her kingdom after storms.[8]

This 'royalist garden' could be multiplied in the courtly entertainments, or progresses, in which the cosmic powers of the Queen were continually celebrated. When she visited Lord Hertford in September 1591 she was met by the Graces and the Hours who walked before her sprinkling flowers in her path and singing of the springtime that she has ushered in in the midst of autumn:

Now birds record new harmonie,
And trees doe whistle melodie:
Now euerie thing that nature breeds,
Doth clad itselfe in pleasant weeds . . .[9]

On another day the Fairy Queen and her maidens danced in the garden beneath her window and presented flowers made in the form of 'an imperiall crowne'. Her departure was seen as that of the passing of summer.

When we turn to examine her portraits they too are filled with flowers. In many she clasps the olive of peace or the virgin or Tudor rose.[10] In one she holds a pansy recalling Shakespeare's tribute in *A Midsummer Night's Dream* to her as 'a fair vestal throned by the west':[11]

. . . a little western flower;
Before, milk-white; now purple, with love's wound,
And maidens call it love-in-idleness.

So insistent and pervasive is the floral theme that one might look for the submerged layer which probably accounts for its potency. One of the most familiar of all celebrations of the Virgin Mary shows her enshrined within a medieval enclosed garden. The *hortus conclusus* is a symbol of the Immaculate Conception and is borrowed from the Song of Solomon: 'A garden inclosed is my sister, my spouse; a spring shut up, a fountain sealed.' Medieval paintings and illuminations depict the Virgin and Child seated within this garden surrounded by the horticultural attributes of the Virgin: the violet, the lily, the white and red rose. Much of the imagery of the Elizabeth cult suggests the deliberate replacement in Protestant England of the worship of the Virgin Queen for that of the Queen of Heaven. It is hardly surprising, therefore, to witness the *hortus conclusus* of the Virgin Mary take on a new life as the symbolic garden of Elizabeth of England.

Five Elizabethan gardens

We have surprisingly little evidence concerning garden planning between 1550 and 1600.[12] In fact we are able to discuss in detail only five of them: Kenilworth, Theobalds, Wollaton, Wimbledon and Nonsuch. Even then our approach has to be fragmentary by means of surveys and plans together with written descriptions by foreign visitors. No topographical views exist to show us the marvels of Burghley's Theobalds or Lumley's Nonsuch. Nonetheless the five cover garden planning in some detail from the sixties through to the nineties. They illustrate the isolation of England from all that had happened and was still happening in Italy. At the same time they show the enormous growth in the actual size of gardens and their importance as an adjunct of the great house. As the houses were conceived to receive the court on progress they were either directly framed or could be adapted to meet the needs of palace planning. The Queen always had to have a sequence of guard room, presence chamber, privy chamber and bedchamber. In addition, following the development of the early Tudor palaces, there should also be a privy garden. This ensured that in garden design there was nearly always a division between the private and the public domains, the former reserved for the delectation of the owner or of the visiting monarch, the latter for public display. Gardens, therefore, share the development of rooms. The combination of a desire for privacy and the increasing formality of aristocratic life led to a multiplication of rooms and a division between the state as against the private apartments. It could also lead to a multiplication of gardens.

(1) *Robert Dudley, Earl of Leicester, and Kenilworth Castle*

The earliest and longest description of an Elizabethan pleasure garden comes in a letter by Robert Laneham narrating the entertainments given by Robert Dudley, Earl of Leicester, for Queen Elizabeth I in July 1575 at his castle at Kenilworth in Warwickshire. That the garden was exceptional must account for the extremely detailed description, so exact that we can construct a diagram of its plan and layout. This, in its turn, should be read in relation to Sir William Dugdale's plan of the castle in the *Antiquities of Warwickshire* (1656). Kenilworth is the first great garden born of the Elizabethan peace.

Leicester was granted Kenilworth Castle in 1563 and entertained the Queen there in 1565 and 1575.[13] The garden must, therefore, have been laid out during that decade. Laneham opens with a eulogy of this 'paradise' which is worth quoting as it captures the prolonged rapture with which he describes the garden as a whole. It is, he writes,

> Beautified with many delectable, fresh, and umbragioous bowerz, arberz, seatz, and walks, that with great art, cost, and diligens wear very pleasantlie appointed; which also the natural grace by the tall and fresh fragrant treez and soil did so far foorth coommend, az Diana herself myght have deyned thear well enough too raunge for her pastyme.[14]

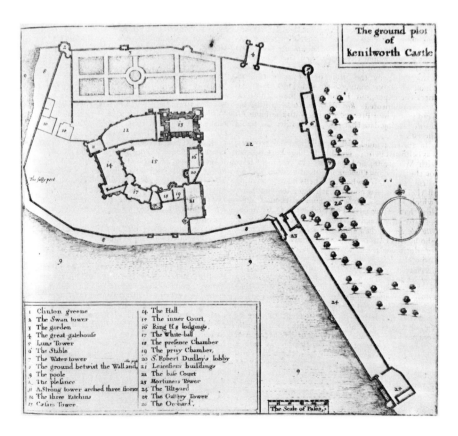

20 Kenilworth Castle. Plan of the garden as it was in 1656

Such enthusiasm reflects more than a degree of novelty in the whole idea of a garden solely for pleasure.

The garden lay to the north of the castle and occupied over an acre. It was immediately inside the castle walls and was prefaced by a walk ten feet high and twelve broad, bordered by obelisks, spheres and Leicester's personal device of the bear and ragged staff. At either end were arbours of trees and flowers. In the centre of the terrace walk on the garden level there was a large aviary on a raised bank. This must have been made of wood because it consisted of window arcading painted and gilded to represent diamonds, rubies, sapphires and emeralds. The garden itself was square and divided into quarters with the walks meeting at a fountain. This was eight feet high and of white marble. Two athletes stood back to back supporting a ball which spouted water into the basin beneath and there was the inevitable bear and ragged staff on the top of it. The garden walks were of grass edged with sand and in each of the four quarters there was an obelisk with an orb on the top of porphyry, surrounded by fragrant plants and herbs (not specified in detail) and planted with apple, pear and plum trees.

Kenilworth is the first garden that we know about in detail since the early Tudor palace gardens of the late thirties and forties. Although smaller in scale than these, it was basically the format of Whitehall and Hampton Court transferred to the nobleman's great house. Instead of the royal beasts the heraldic ornaments celebrate the owner of the house, so the garden is dotted with the bear and ragged staff. Yet in certain respects Kenilworth was different. In the first place it was a reworking of a medieval castle and for this Leicester may well have been influenced by what he had seen as a young man in 1551 at Amboise. Early French Renaissance gardens dealt with precisely the same problem of adding a garden to a fortress. Kenilworth, like Amboise and Bury, was essentially an enlargement and extension of the medieval castle garden. It was placed outside the inner defence walls but also, as at Amboise and Bury, within the main walls and moat. Two features are, however, new: the obelisks, a distant echo that the garden was the place for formal statuary; and, more significantly, the terrace. As the garden could not be placed immediately below the windows of the state apartments the patterns of the knots could not be appreciated without the introduction of a terrace from which to view them. This is the earliest instance we have of the landscaping of the terrain into a terrace descending into a garden. That it was largely dictated by necessity seems to be proved by the fact that terracing was not taken up as a general principle of garden design until the Jacobean period.

(2) *William Cecil, Lord Burghley, and Theobalds*

Sir William Cecil purchased the manor of Theobalds in 1564 with the future needs of his younger and brilliant son, Robert, in mind.[15] The house lay just off the main road from London to Ware and thence to Stamford and his first great house, Burghley. In an area of the country studded with royal residences he began first to alter, then entirely to rebuild the house. Already by 1571, when he was created Lord Burghley, it was large but it was to grow to palatial proportions in the following decade. Theobalds grew 'encrease by occasion of her Majesty's often coming' and so by 1585, when for practical purposes it was finished, it could be regarded as an auxiliary royal palace, something which became a fact in the next reign when Robert Cecil exchanged it for Hatfield.

Burghley had an intense personal interest in gardening, a weakness which he freely admitted. Amongst the manuscript collection at Hatfield there are a number of garden plans in his own hand. His London house also had elaborate gardens, about which we know little, and both these and Theobalds were superintended by the great herbalist, John Gerard. Gerard's famous *Herball* was dedicated to Burghley in 1597.[16]

Theobalds, like Hampton Court and Nonsuch, from which it descends, was a courtyard house. For the purposes of studying the garden we cannot do better than refer to Sir John Summerson's study of the building of Theobalds and his ground-plan reconstructing the house, which is based on the large amount of surviving contemporary material, in particular the plan amongst the drawings of John Thorpe who carried out a survey sometime between 1606 and 1610. The plan of the house was a series of courtyards, one in succession to another, stretching over a quarter of a mile axis. It was the final courtyard, the Inner or Fountain court, that contained the royal apartments, which directly related to the gardens. These fell into two main sections, the Privy Garden on the east side beneath the owner's personal accommodation, and the Great Garden on the north side beneath the state rooms.

The fact that the gardens were grouped around this last courtyard, for which there is a drawing dated 1572, places their design and planting during the decade 1575–85. The sources for any conjectural re-creation of the garden scheme are two: a detailed Parliamentary Survey of 1650; and the visitors' accounts from the 1590s onwards.[17]

The Privy Garden on the east side is not described by any of these travellers, whose tour took them to the Great Garden only.[18] For this, then, we have to rely on the 1650 Survey. The Privy Garden covered seventeen poles (a pole is five and a half yards) and was enclosed by a wall. Within this was a gravel walk followed by 'a hansome quicksett hedge cutt into formes' interset on the north, east and west sides with twenty-eight cherry trees. On these sides only flights of steps led down to a grass walk bounded by a second low hedge and then a third, nine feet in height, which surrounded the central square knot. Jutting T-shaped buttresses of hedge met the descending stairs on the three sides and on all four there were two entrances by which access was had to 'a square knott . . . turned into a complete fashion and shape, with 3 ascents, boarded and planted with Tulipps, Lillies, Piannies and divers other sorts of flowers'. In the corners of the great hedge were round arbours. What did this look like? The description reminds one more than anything of the type of gardens by Vredeman de Vries as presented in his *Hortorum viridariorumque formae*. De Vries's work was widely used in England as patterns by builders and although, as a studious follower of Vitruvius, he divided his gardens into the orders Doric, Ionic and Corinthian, they are all virtually of the same type. The grander gardens are surrounded by hedges and pergolas often with arbours at the corners. They are square and within turf is laid out in geometrical patterns punctuated by trees with occasionally a pavilion or fountain in the middle. Very little use is made of statuary.

The Great Garden, by contrast, was enormous – over seven acres in extent, twice the size of Henry VIII's Hampton Court garden. Like the Privy Garden it was surrounded by a wall within which it was divided into nine knots or squares. In a plan endorsed by Burghley these are seventy feet square with walks between twenty-two feet wide. Each knot had a hedge around it of whitethorn and privet 'cutt into a handsome fashion with cherry trees planted at the angles'. The central knot had a white marble fountain; a second was 'sett forth with box borders in ye likenesse of ye kinges armes verie artificiallie and exquisitely made' (this must have been immediately below the façade of the house and was later in date, although it may have continued an existing tradition of an armorial knot); a third was 'planted with choice flowers'; while the remainder were 'all grasse knotts handsomely turfed in the intervalles or little walkes'. Two of these knots had 'figures of wainscott well carved' in them; later accounts record these to have been wild men.[19]

Accounts by visitors expand our picture of this garden. The approach was through a loggia painted with genealogies and, more surprisingly, for no mention of it is made in 1650, the garden was surrounded by a canal or moat. This is how Paul Hentzner describes it in 1598:

> ... from this place one goes into the garden, encompassed with a ditch full of water, large enough for one to have the pleasure of going in a boat and rowing between the shrubs.

This arrangement could come from only one source, France, where the evolution of the moat into the decorative canal was one of the most striking features of garden design under the Valois. Lord Burghley had visited France and was no doubt also familiar with engravings of this type of garden in Du Cerceau. Hentzner goes on to refer to the layout of the Great Garden as being in 'labyrinths', presumably knots, decorated with wooden columns and obelisks, a description which yet again evokes the engravings of de Vries. In particular, he describes a summer house, which the Parliamentary Survey places on the southern side in the middle of a walk:

> ... in the lower part of which, built semicircularly, are the twelve Roman emperors in white marble and a table of touchstone; the upper part of it is set round with cisterns of lead, into which water is conveyed through pipes, so that fish may be kept in them, and in summertime they are very convenient for bathing. In another room for entertainment, very near this, and joined to it by a little bridge, was an oval table of red marble.[20]

This again reinforces the supposition that some of the areas must have been divided by canals.

Two later visitors go on to refer to another feature which is described as follows in 1613:

> There is also a little wood nearby. At the end you come to a small round hill built of earth with a labyrinth around. [It] is called the Venusberg.[21]

It is totally unclear as to whether or not this was part of the Great Garden, but the mount could have been within one of the nine enclosures. Whatever it was, the mount as a feature clearly derives from the one at Hampton Court in the 1530s. But, instead of providing the setting for a blaze of early Tudor heraldry, it has here a symbolic function, a maze leading to the goddess Venus. We do not know when this maze was planted, and whether by Lord Burghley or his son, Robert Cecil, but it is important because it implies that the garden was being thought about in allegorical terms. Renaissance symbolism is here replacing

21 A melancholy young man seeks the solace of the greenwood tree outside the walls of a garden of the de Vries type.

22 Design for a garden in the Ionic style, enclosed by a pergola, with turf laid out in patterns and with trees. From a pattern book by Vredeman de Vries, whose work in the Antwerp Mannerist vein was a powerful influence in Elizabethan England. Theobalds probably looked very similar.

facing page:
23 Conjectural plan of the gardens, showing the division into the Privy and Great Gardens. The latter was laid out in nine large enclosures or knots with a fountain in the centre.

Theobalds

Planted in the decade 1575–85, Theobalds was the most influential Elizabethan garden, although its actual appearance and detailed layout can only be a matter for speculation.

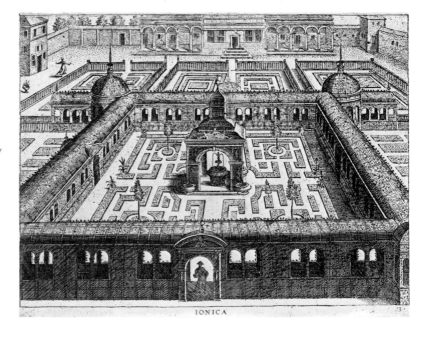

IONICA

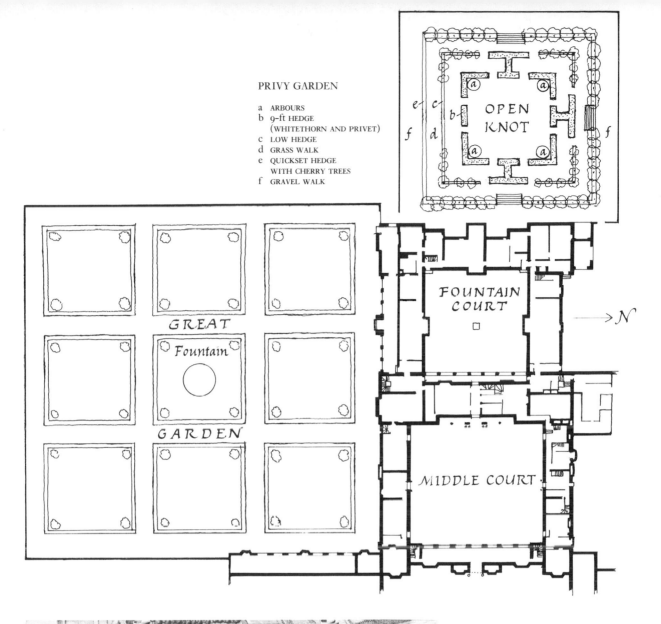

PRIVY GARDEN

a ARBOURS
b 9-ft HEDGE
  (WHITETHORN AND PRIVET)
c LOW HEDGE
d GRASS WALK
e QUICKSET HEDGE
  WITH CHERRY TREES
f GRAVEL WALK

OPEN KNOT

GREAT
Fountain
GARDEN

FOUNTAIN COURT

MIDDLE COURT

→N

Fürstlicher Lustgarten zu Hessem

Grundtriß warauff das Schloß Hessem stehet.

24 The most helpful
descriptions of English
gardens, including
Theobalds, are those by
visiting Germans, and the
old-fashioned garden of
the Duke of Brunswick in
the 1630s at Hesse reflects
much of what we know
Theobalds to have been
like.

heraldry. Was the mount a tribute to Elizabeth I as the Goddess of Love? At first glance this would seem an unusual role for her to occupy but it is not unparalleled. In some of her portraits she appears holding up a jewel bearing the image of a sea-born Venus-Virgo, a cult which stems directly from the appearance of Venus disguised as nymph of Diana in the *Aeneid*. During the last decade of the reign, the cult becomes overt with endless celebrations of Gloriana as 'Queen of Love' and 'Queen of Beauty'.[22] It would have been inconceivable for a programme for the garden of Theobalds to have been in praise of anyone other than Elizabeth.

It is not easy to get a very precise visual picture of the garden. The most important impression it made on every visitor was one of size; it was said that one could walk for two miles through its pleached arbours and covered walks. The area it occupied far exceeded that of any early Tudor palace garden and was not to be surpassed until Wilton in the 1630s. From the start it was conceived in terms of splendour, magnificence and royal compliment. Its arrangement as a series of knots, each with its own theme and focal point, develops the tradition of the early part of the century but now overlaid by Antwerp mannerism. If I had to choose a garden by which to evoke the atmosphere of Theobalds it would be a surprisingly late one, the garden of the Duke of Brunswick at Hesse laid out in the 1630s.[23] In style it was by then extremely antiquated. As in the case of Theobalds it is surrounded by canals with little wooden bridges over them. Its layout in knots is bordered by a pleached walk on three sides of the garden. Each knot has a hedge surely matching the description in the Parliamentary Survey of that in the Privy Garden 'cutt into formes', for the hedges at Hesse are trained into the figures of huntsmen and mermaids, animals, letters and numbers. Within each enclosure there is a different knot; some are armorial and some focus on an obelisk or a fountain. German Protestant visitors are our main source for descriptions of late Elizabethan and early Stuart palaces and gardens. That the garden of the Duke of Brunswick should re-echo Theobalds so very closely may not be as far-fetched as it sounds. It may indeed reflect direct influence from England.

(3) *Sir Francis Willoughby and Wollaton Hall*

Wollaton Hall in Nottinghamshire was designed by Robert Smythson for Sir Francis Willoughby, sheriff of the county.[24] He had entertained Elizabeth in his old house but, in anticipation of further royal progresses, began in 1580 to build what can only be described as a palace. Willoughby was something of an eccentric and this is reflected in the resplendent egomania of the house. His family was connected with two great aristocratic families, the Seymours and Dudleys, pillars of the new Protestant establishment, and his wealth stretched back to before the advent of the Tudors. All of this is reflected in the architecture of the house, which is described by Mark Girouard as 'original, extravagant, uncomfortable and restless, to the fringe of lunacy'.[25]

The house still stands but the gardens have long since vanished. What we know of them comes in the main from three sources: a plan among the drawings of John Thorpe in the Sir John Soane Museum;[26] a second plan, which includes the gardens, by Robert Smythson, the designer of the house, in the Royal Institute of British Architects; and a view of the house from the garden side dated 1697 by Jan Siberechts in the Mellon Collection. As is typical of all late Elizabethan and Jacobean houses, Wollaton was built on an eminence to see and be seen. What is unique for its period is its unity: the house, its outbuildings, courtyards and gardens were combined in a completely rigid four-way symmetry. Compared with any other sixteenth-century garden Wollaton Hall was an enormous advance, looking forward to the strict relationship of house and garden that was to be the guiding principle in the next century. Thorpe's plan tells us little beyond the fact that the garden was at the back of the house and that the orchard was to one side. Smythson's plan shows more, although it is not always easy to read because there is no clear way of differentiating between walls and what must have been hedges. The approach to the garden was by means of a flight of steps flanked by a terrace, both features which are clearly visible in the Siberechts painting. The centre garden was exactly the width of the façade of the house and was presumably enclosed by a wall within which there was a hedge on three sides, the furthest one concealing the laundry and dairy. Four beds surrounded a central fountain, whose successor occupied exactly the same place in 1697. On one side there is a second garden laid out in quarters, presumably in knots, on the other another consisting of a single square enclosure. From the Thorpe drawing we know that the orchard occupied the enclosure that contained the stable block. The three remaining ones must presumably also have contained kitchen and other gardens apart from those designed purely for pleasure.

Wollaton is a strange phenomenon; its garden arrangement is as peculiar as its architecture and these vividly reflect the Elizabethan preoccupation with the 'device', a novel arrangement of geometrical shapes, symbolic or otherwise, to cause delight and surprise in the eyes of the onlooker. This is how the garden would have struck the visitor, rather than as the fulfilment of a Renaissance architectural theory. Wollaton is perhaps the only known Elizabethan example of what in France had become standard practice in the second half of the sixteenth century. The earliest instance of this is Ancy-le-Franc, built in 1546, after designs by Serlio, in which the garden was axially joined to the house, the whole being encompassed by a moat. De L'Orme's Château d'Anet (1548-55) was laid out in the same manner, the garden being placed in total symmetry at the rear of the house and surrounded by a stone gallery with a terrace on the top of it. Verneuil (1565) and the projected palace of Charleval (post-1560) for Charles IX followed suit.[27] Views and plans of all these were available in Du Cerceau's *Les Plus Excellents Bastiments de France*, which was known and studied in England.[28] Du Cerceau's book, published in 1576, is exceptionally important as it was about the only architectural book to give views of gardens. It contained a virtually complete series of engravings of French royal and aristocratic gardens, which had an immense influence in England. Wollaton Hall is the most outstanding instance of this impact.

(4) *Thomas Cecil and Wimbledon House*

Wimbledon House in south London was begun the year that Wollaton was finished, 1588 (John Aubrey records that the date was inscribed over the entrance), by Lord Burghley's eldest son, Thomas, later Earl of Exeter.[29] As a young man, he had travelled not only in France but also in Germany and the Low Countries. His father had recognized that he was a man of less ability than his younger brother, Robert, and history would not have remembered him but

Wollaton

Sir Francis Willoughby's house at Wollaton, built in the 1580s, is the unique Elizabethan instance of house and garden conceived as a single architectural unit.

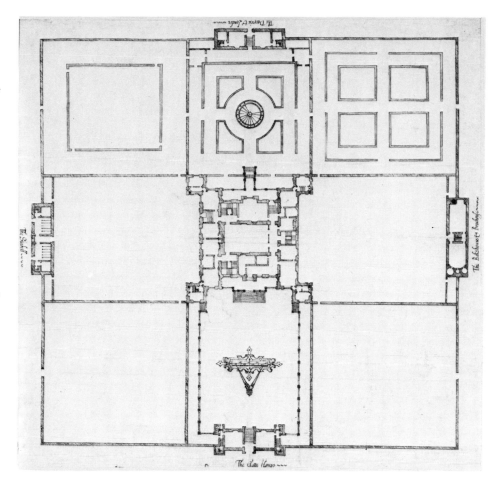

facing page:
25 Jan Siberecht's view of
Wollaton as it was in
1697. The house is the
same and, in spite of great
changes to the gardens,
the layout at the back in
three squares, with a
central one focusing on a
fountain, directly reflects
the original plan.

26 Robert Smythson's
plan shows the four-way
symmetry including the
back entrance of the house
lined up axially with a
garden walk and central
fountain.

27 Anet is one of a series
of French châteaux built
from the 1540s onwards
which carry out the
Renaissance principle of
the architectural
relationship of house and
garden. These were the
model for Wollaton.

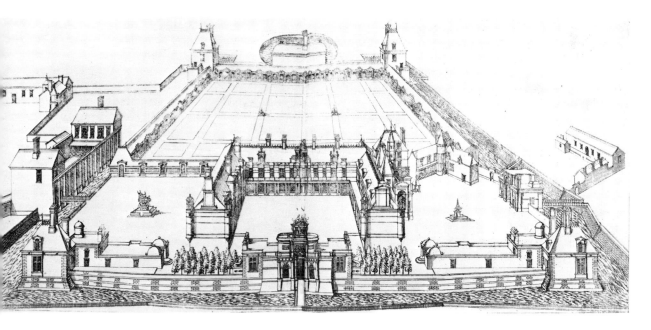

for the accident of his birth. His career during the seventies and eighties was largely either in Parliament or as Governor of Brill in the Low Countries and it was not until 1599 that he received his first major preferment as Lord President of the Council of the North.

Wimbledon was a Cecil property and it was here that Thomas was to build one of the most dramatic and picturesque of all late Elizabethan houses. It was sited, as was Wollaton, on a hill but he made skilful use of the rising site to preface the H-shaped house, whose designer is not known, by a series of courtyards with stepped terraces which Sir John Summerson believes to have been inspired by the Farnese Palace at Caprarola. What is important is that this landscaping of the approach, which is directly in the tradition of the Renaissance treatment of a garden site, was not applied to the garden itself, which stretched up the hill at the back of the house in a totally unsymmetrical way, making no use of terracing.

Our knowledge of this garden comes from Robert Smythson's plan of 1609, which is inscribed 'A great Orcharde with walkes now In Plantinge', so that it was continuing to be altered and expanded in the first decade of James I's reign.[30] Most of the planting must have been carried out during the late eighties and nineties, but Smythson's plan is the most important and complete we have from the Elizabethan period.

Contrary to Wollaton, but entirely typical of the majority of Elizabethan gardens, symmetry is of no primary concern in the planning. The garden is a series of enclosed squares and rectangles, separate visual experiences bounded by walls and hedges. Following Hampton Court and Nonsuch, the garden faced south and, like Theobalds, there was a Privy Garden as against a 'Great Garden'. What must have been the former lay to the east of the house and, like

Wimbledon

Thomas Cecil's house at Wimbledon, built from 1588 onwards, epitomizes the last phase of Elizabethan gardening.

28 Wimbledon in 1678. The Italianate terracing used in the approach to the house was not used for the gardens.

29 Robert Smythson's plan of 1609 shows the two main phases of garden development. The earlier, near the house, is a series of enclosed squares in the Theobalds manner, but irregular. The later lime walk, orchard and vineyard are on the large scale typical of the Jacobean period.

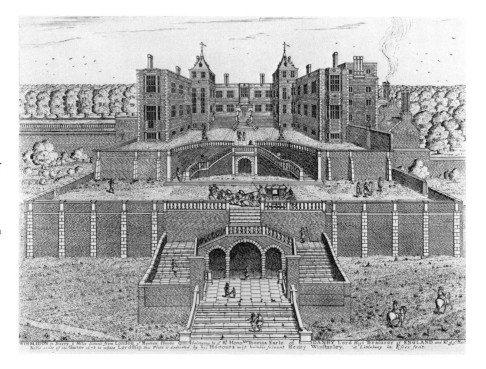

60

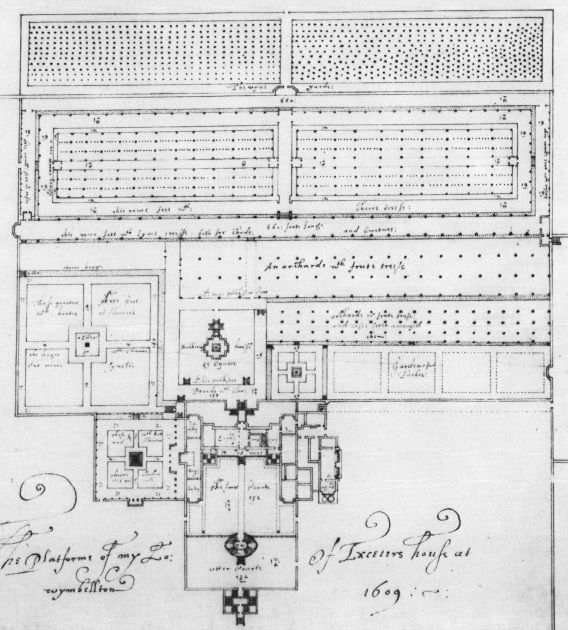

The Platforme of my Lo: of Exceters house at
wymbellton 1609

Wollaton, is an early attempt to marry house and garden. It was prefaced by an Italianate feature, an open loggia, and consisted of a walled enclosure exactly the width of the east façade of the house, with an entrance from the loggia leading to the central walk from west to east. We can see the loggia in Henry Winstanley's engraving of 1678. The cross-axis walk from north to south linked a summer house or arbour set into the north wall with a flight of steps leading up to the 'Great Garden' on the southern side. On that side it was enclosed by a hedge. Within, the garden was laid out on the lines of Kenilworth, with what was presumably a central fountain around which there were four beds edged with thorn borders 'cutt verie well' (perhaps as topiary) and set with open knots with flowers. The cross-walks were six feet wide and the walk around next to the boundary walls, which were probably planted with espaliered fruit trees, was fifteen feet.

The flight of steps along the south side led to the 'Great Garden', laid out in the same way. It was partly enclosed by hedging and partly by boundary walls; its four large beds were again arranged as open knots set with flowers. Smythson gives an interesting fact that its focal point was a 'Piller'. Elizabeth I visited Wimbledon as many as four times between 1592 and 1602 and at least one of these occasions was dramatized with customary pageantry.[31] The pillar, in particular a crowned pillar, is a device of Elizabeth I, in one sense an adaptation to Gloriana of the famous *impresa* of the Emperor Charles V – the Pillars of Hercules with the motto *Plus Ultra* expressing the expansion of the Empire into the New World. After the defeat of the Spanish Armada in 1588 the pillar device appears with great frequency in relation to Elizabeth. At the 1590 Accession Day Tilt, that flower of chivalry, Sir Henry Lee, had resigned his office as Queen's champion by laying down his arms at the foot of a crowned pillar embraced by an eglantine tree. Later, in 1592, when he received her at his house in Oxfordshire, a song took up the theme:

> *Constant Piller, constant Crowne,*
> *Is the aged Knightes renowne.*

In her allegorical portraits the Queen also appears with both double and single pillars.[32] In the atmosphere of queen-worship that pervaded the last decade of the reign surely a pillar set up in the centre of the garden of a great house built to receive her and her court on progress could only ever have had one significance, homage to the Queen?

Access from the Pillar Garden to the next enclosure could only be gained by means of one corner, which had flights of steps leading to a banqueting house set into a sunken garden immediately to one side of the south façade of the house. The banqueting house stood in the middle of an eighty-five-foot square surrounded by high hedges. To the west of this lay another smaller garden on exactly the same lines as the first, perhaps with a fountain in the centre, but Smythson does not indicate how it was planted. Further to the west lay a herb garden and south of that two oblong orchards, one with trees interset with roses, a type of planting which went back to Thornbury at the beginning of the century.

This may have been the boundary of the initial planting, which was already on a scale far beyond that of either Kenilworth or Wollaton. But in 1609 it was extended even more. These additions must have astounded Smythson that year when, having arrived in London from the Midlands, he began to study the latest fashions in house planting and garden design. There was a great lime walk 'for both shade and sweetness' which ran from east to west, a huge new orchard and beyond that a vineyard. Their flavour is quite different from the nineties' planning. They ascend the hill linked by flights of steps and a central vista which take up, alas too late for total unity, the Italianate theme of the terrace approach to the house. When André Mollet relaid out the garden for Henrietta Maria in 1642 these were the areas which he was to leave virtually untouched while the earliest gardens, cast higgledy-piggledy around the house, were to be swept away.

Wimbledon is surely a garden where heraldry has given way to allegory. In planning it preserves the arrangement of Theobalds. There is a Privy Garden, of which the component part is the square knot garden, focusing on fountain or monument, multiplied on various scales surrounding the house in a virtually random manner. There is the placing of the pleasure gardens around the central block and the west wing, where the state and the private apartments were, and of the herb garden and orchards in proximity to the kitchen wing. Understandably, as the builder was Lord Burghley's eldest son, the greatest debt is to Theobalds.

(5) *John, Lord Lumley, and Nonsuch Palace*

The gardens of Nonsuch Palace were transformed in the Elizabethan period by John, Lord Lumley. Nonsuch was sold by Mary I to Henry FitzAlan, 12th Earl of Arundel, who entertained Elizabeth there in the summer of 1559. Arundel had no male heir and after his death in 1579 the palace, together with his debts, passed to his son-in-law, Lord Lumley. And it was under his auspices that the gardens considerably changed their character.[33]

These alterations were essentially a reflection of the strange personality and preoccupations of the new owner. John, Lord Lumley, was Roman Catholic and, as a result of the Ridolfi Plot, which had centred on an attempt to assassinate Elizabeth and replace her by Mary Queen of Scots, Lumley was excluded from office and the circle of the court. Henceforward his main obsession in life became the family genealogy and, under his auspices, Lumley Castle, the family seat in the north of England, was gradually transformed into a shrine devoted to his ancestral glories. This primarily took the form of an enormous collection of portraits, by far the largest in Elizabethan England, of ancestors and contemporaries, both real and imaginary. In addition the castle and its interior were decorated with heraldic devices, sculpture and inscriptions lauding the Lumley family and its achievements over the centuries. James I, when confronted with this *mise-en-scène*, was said to have remarked: 'I did'na ken Adam's ither name was Lumley.' The garden at Nonsuch was to be the southern equivalent of his northern castle.

Lumley, furthermore, was one of those rarities, an early Elizabethan nobleman who had travelled and seen the wonders of Renaissance Italy. In 1566 he had visited Italy and in particular Florence, to deal with the Grand Duke over a matter of debt. This must have had some effect on him because he was, for the period, more than usually interested, for example, in sculpture, and the collection of portraits that he formed reflected the Medici array of worthies assembled in imitation of Paolo Giovio. During his visit Lumley must

Nonsuch

The garden of Henry VIII's palace was relaid out by Lord Lumley in the 1580s. It is the earliest instance of a garden in the Italian Mannerist manner, designed with a symbolic programme to celebrate simultaneously the Lumley family and its sovereign.

30 The marble Obelisk with the Lumley arms

31 The Privy Garden with, from extreme left to right, half the Obelisk, the first Falcon Perch, the Diana Fountain, the second Falcon Perch and the Leaping Horse

also have seen Italian gardens with their extensive use of trees and shrubs planted in clumps or *boschetti* focusing on sculptural or architectural groups, each with its symbolic or allegorical meaning. In other words he had seen and understood some of the principles of the Mannerist garden; all this combined to have a powerful effect on the replanning of Nonsuch.

The changes to the garden must have been made between 1579 and 1591, when the Palace was returned to the Crown, although Lumley still continued to live there. The engraving by Jodocus Hondius, which is indicative rather than detailed, shows us exactly what the Privy Garden on the south side looked like in the early Jacobean period. We can supplement this, as we can in the case of other sections of the garden, with descriptions by foreign visitors, and the fanciful one by Lumley's employee Anthony Watson, with the account drawn up by the Parliamentary commissioners in 1650, and with the drawings of most of the garden statuary and fountains in the famous Lumley Inventory of 1590.[34] The Inventory is a unique document not only listing the contents of his collections and containing his pedigree but also, more significantly, including watercolours of the furniture, tombs and sculpture he had commissioned.

To the early Tudor disposition of the gardens around the walls of the final courtyard he made no significant change. In all his alterations to the gardens and

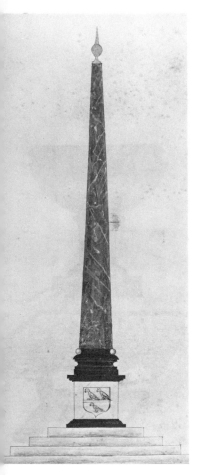

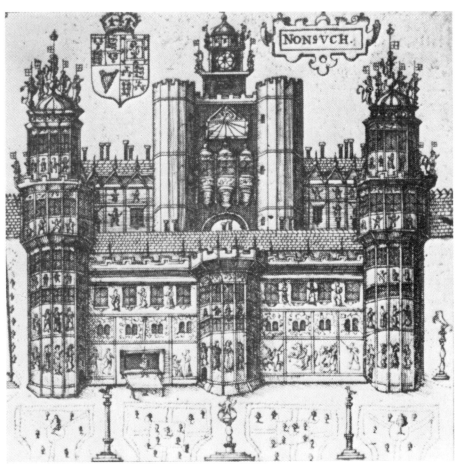

wilderness beyond, two themes predominate: his own heraldry, which presumably replaced that of Henry VIII, and, overlaying it, an allegorical programme in praise of Elizabeth. The main part of the Privy Garden was on the south front and stretched towards a wall enclosing the garden. The latter is visible in Georg Hoefnagel's famous drawing of the palace, in which Queen Elizabeth is depicted riding by in a fantastic coach.[35] For what lay beyond that wall we have only the rudimentary but precise information provided by the engraving in Speed. This shows a garden set out in knots, which is how Watson describes it: 'plants and shrubs mingled in intricate circles as by the needle of Semiramis'. Watson further describes how 'deer, horses, rabbits and dogs give chase with unhindered feet and effortlessly passed over the green',[36] a feature which the German visitor Thomas Platter also records: '. . . all kinds of animals – dogs, hares, all over grown with plants, most artfully set out, so that from a distance, one would take them for real ones'.[37] As I pointed out in the previous chapter these could have been part of the original planting under Henry VIII. On the iconographical evidence, however, they could equally, as we shall see, have been dictated by Lumley.

These knots were laid around what must have been Lumley's most striking additions, described thus by a German visitor:

In the pleasure and artificial gardens are many columns and pyramids of marble, two fountains that spout water one round the other a pyramid, upon which are perched small birds that stream water out of their bills.[38]

32 One of the Falcon Perches with the Lumley popinjay on its summit

Returning to Hondius's engraving, at the extreme left we can just see half of an obelisk, one for which there is a drawing in the Lumley Inventory. On its pedestal are the arms of Lumley, the three popinjays. The 1650 survey goes on to describe how near it there was 'one large marble wash boule or bason, over which stands a marble pellican fed with a pipe of lead to convey water into the same'.[39] This is not only illustrated in the Inventory, but still survives in the possession of Lumley's descendants, the Earls of Scarbrough. In the main garden itself, there are two marble columns flanking a central fountain; the columns were referred to, in 1650, as 'the Fawlcon perches', a misreading of the Lumley popinjays. Watson describes the main fountain as 'a shining column which carries a high statue of a snow-white nymph, perhaps Venus, from whose tender breasts flow jets of water into the ivory-coloured marble, and from there the water falls through narrow pipes into a marble basin'.[40] In other words the fountain was of the usual early Renaissance type. Watson states that this was on a mound set within two circles of grass and in 1650 it was surrounded by six lilac trees. The description matches the drawing in the Lumley Inventory exactly, but Watson must have been less observant than the Inventory draughtsman for the nymph's hair is crowned by a crescent-moon. In other words, this garden is presided over by a tutelary deity, Diana, the chaste goddess of the moon and of the hunt.

To the east there was a more mysterious ornament, a prancing horse on a column. No drawing of this is included in the Inventory, although it is unlikely that an equestrian statue was erected in the reign of Henry VIII; the engraving, unfortunately, tells us too little. The statue led to the eastern, smaller privy garden, laid out in knots in the same way as the main one. To the west, beyond the obelisk, there was a maze or labyrinth, which could, like the topiary figures,

65

have been an early Tudor feature. Platter, in 1599, tells us that the hedges were high enough to prevent the visitor seeing through; this is not a feature typical of early mazes, so that it could equally have been later.

So far the gardens evoke Kenilworth with its strong heraldic overlay in terms of coats of arms, badges and obelisks. But the Diana fountain and the pelican suggest something else, for both are well-known images associated with the complex mythology of Elizabeth I. We are here touching the vital clue which will take us through the remainder of what must have been the first large-scale symbolic garden in the Italian Mannerist style to have been attempted in England. The pelican celebrates the Queen (oddly, coming from a Roman Catholic) as the nursing mother of the *Ecclesia Anglicana*. This was an accepted symbol; she wears, for example, pelican jewels in a number of her portraits.[41] Her role as Diana or Cynthia, the moon-goddess, belongs to a cult which began in the eighties, when the garden was created, and was particularly associated with Raleigh. In her portraits it takes the simple form of a crescent-moon-shaped jewel placed in her hair.[42] In the garden at Nonsuch, Lumley is surely celebrating Elizabeth, in the words of Ben Jonson's famous lyric, as 'Queen and huntress, chaste and fair' and the topiary animals of the chase are appropriately in attendance. The Lumley Inventory contains a drawing for another Nonsuch fountain, for which we have no description or location but which clinches this association. It is again of the basin type with lions' heads spurting water into the bowl, above which arises a nymph supporting a mushroom shape upon which sits a royal crown topped by a crescent-moon.

It is less in the formal gardens, however, that the allegory takes its most compelling form than in the informal or wild gardens beyond. These were planted, as in the case of the Villa d'Este or the Villa Lante, in groves of trees and shrubs, forming avenues and vistas to open spaces, and centring on some architectural or sculptural feature, directly in the Italian manner. This is the only instance of such a treatment recorded in Elizabethan England and its most important complex was the Grove of Diana, which lay beyond the labyrinth on the western side of the palace. Thomas Platter, in 1599, provides what is perhaps the most detailed description. There is, he writes:

> ... a grove [*lucus*] called after Diana, the goddess, from here we came to a rock out of which natural water springs into a basin, and on this was portrayed with great art and life-like execution the story of how the three goddesses took their bath naked and sprayed Actaeon with water, causing antlers to grow upon his head, and of how his own hounds tore him to pieces.[43]

The other accounts round out this description. No picture, however, survives of the ensemble which is referred to in the accounts as a fountain but which a 1613 visitor alludes to as a 'grotto or cavern'. The same source tells us that the figures were polychrome, that Diana was attended by two nymphs and stood in what must have been an assemblage of rocks in the grotto manner with water tumbling into a basin. All this was railed and Actaeon stood 'fifteen paces away' with antlers already sprouted on his head, attended by two dogs.[44] At the entrance to the grove there was a Latin inscription. Its theme was that man should abjure the example of the lustful Actaeon and lay low the fires of the passions. In other words we have here for the first time the kind of emblematic tableau which was a standard feature of the Italian Mannerist garden. In its simplest form it was to be read as a morality extolling youth to the path of

66

Homage to the Queen at Nonsuch

33 The Diana Fountain
in the Privy Garden

34 Fountain surmounted
by a royal crown and a
crescent-moon

virtue, Actaeon being a standard symbol for the senses unbridled.[45] At the same time, but on a different level, the Grove of Diana was also sacred to Elizabeth-Virgo.

It was complemented by two further items. The first was a Temple or Bower of Diana, evidently a wooden banqueting house. Platter describes it as being vaulted with a marble table within it. By 1610 it was so decayed that it had to be repaired and twelve years later had to be totally rebuilt.[46] Within it hung three further Latin verses, one praising the goddess of chastity and her chaste counsels as against the evil fruits of an unchaste mind, the second comparing the fountain to the mind from which, if impure, impurity will flow, and a third celebrating the pleasures of rest and contemplation. The final features of this area seem to have been an arch and a pyramid. Watson describes the arch thus: 'On a lofty arch is an eagle, a pinnacle is topped with a pelican, and on another pinnacle stands a phoenix'.[47] This led to an orchard where 'a handsome pyramid rises, set off with divers heads which, while counterfeiting dryness in the mouth, discharge small streams of water'.[48] The 1613 visitor describes these as being even more closely located together as a group:

> Nearby at [a distance of] 20 paces is a great wooden archway on which are many trees and other plants beneath, yet in the middle of the arch, embellished with small stones, [is] a Pyramis, from which water springs on all sides.[49]

It seems clear from this that the pyramid was a trick fountain which suddenly spurted the luckless visitor with water. Regarding the connection of all this with the Grove of Diana we have the evidence of the visitor's record that the following verses 'can be read on the walls there':

> *The fisherman who has been wounded, learns, though late, to beware;*
> *But the unfortunate Actaeon always presses on.*
> *The chaste virgin naturally pitied:*
> *But the powerful goddess revenged the wrong.*
> *Let Actaeon fall a prey to his dogs,*
> *An example to youth,*
> *A disgrace to those that belong to him!*[50]

Who built all this and what was its meaning? Perhaps we should begin with Watson's comment on the Latin verses which adorned the Grove. These, he writes, 'the hero Lumley caused . . . to be set up in praise of the goddess and as a warning to youths to avoid the fate of Actaeon'.[51] The story of Diana and Actaeon comes from the third book of Ovid's *Metamorphoses*. It reads like a scenario for a Renaissance garden grotto:

> There was a valley, thick set with pitch-trees and the sharp-pointed cypress; by name Gargaphie, sacred to the active Diana. In the extreme recess of this, there was a grotto in a grove, formed by no art; nature, by her ingenuity, had counterfeited art; for she had formed a natural arch, in the native pumice and the light sand-stones. A limpid fountain ran murmuring on the right hand with its little stream, having its spreading channels edged with a border of grass. Here, when wearied with hunting, the Goddess of the woods was wont to bathe her virgin limbs in the clear water.[52]

And we do not have to look far for the contemporary identity of this particular Diana: flanking the eagle over the arch described by Watson were the two personal emblems of Elizabeth Tudor, the phoenix and the pelican. An engraving of 1596 shows her flanked by them surmounting the 'imperial' pillars,[53] which we met at Wimbledon, in much the same relationship that they must have had at Nonsuch. Lumley's Nonsuch Grove might best be compared with Bess of Hardwick's celebration of Elizabeth as Diana in the High Great Chamber at Hardwick, where, in the plaster frieze above the chair of state, Diana sits surrounded by her nymphs and attended by virtuous symbols, such as the elephant and palm tree, while the Cavendish stag wards off the lion and the tiger.[54] In terms related to gardening, it finds its closest parallel in the Elvetham entertainment of 1591 when the host, Lord Hertford, had a vast crescent-moon-shaped lake dug in his park in tribute to Cynthia, 'the wide ocean's empresse'.[55] The cult of the Queen could as legitimately find its expression in emblematic gardening as it could in other more conventional forms of compliment.

Whereas the Privy Garden under Lumley was an extension of the principles of Whitehall and Hampton Court, that is of the garden as a vehicle for heraldic and genealogical display in the same way as the vanes on the exterior of the building or on the plaster ceiling within, the Grove has taken us on a slightly different path. Nature has been tamed by art to form a moral tableau which the visitor is asked to read on more than one level, in exactly the same way that he was meant to understand an allegorical painting or the allusions in a court entertainment. Lumley, in his re-creation of Ovid's Vale of Gargaphie, not only provides food for moral contemplation by his use of the Actaeon story but also pays homage to the Queen. She it is who is the presiding goddess of the gardens of Nonsuch and the focal point of its symbolic programme. With Nonsuch we have arrived in the world of the Mannerist garden.

Two lost gardens: Lord Zouche's Hackney and Lord Cobham's Cobham

Two other gardens were famous in their day, that of Edward la Zouche, 11th Baron Zouche, and that of William Brooke, 7th Lord Cobham. Very little is known about either of them, but they were so celebrated that we must put together what little we do. Zouche was a friend of the great herbalist John Gerard, and the celebrated botanist L'Obel supervised his garden at Hackney. Zouche seems essentially to have been obsessed by plants and indeed is said to have lost his patrimony because of his passion for horticulture. In 1586 he left England 'to live cheaply' abroad and did not return until 1593.[56]

Much more is known about Lord Cobham's garden at Cobham Hall in Kent. Francis Thynne, in his continuation of Holinshed's *Chronicles*, records

> . . . a rare garden there, in which no varietie of strange flowers and trees do want, which praise or price maie obtaine from the furthest part of Europe or from other strange Countries, whereby it is not inferior to the garden of Serimamis [*sic*].[57]

William Harrison, writing in 1586, listed Cobham Hall along with Hampton Court, Theobalds and Nonsuch as one of the great garden spectacles of the age. As late as 1629 John Parkinson, in his *Paradisi in sole: Paradisus terrestris*, records one of the garden's most astounding features, 'the goodliest spectacle mine eyes euer beheld for one tree to carry'. This particular tree was a lime whose branches were plashed to form an arbour. Then, after a further space of eight feet up the trunk, its branches were bent yet again:

... round about so orderly, as if it were done by art, and brought to compasse that middle Arbour: And from those boughes the body was bare againe for eight or nine foote (wherein might bee placed halfe an hundred men at the least, as ther might be likewise in that vnderneath this) & another rowe of branches in that encompasse a third Arbour, with stayres made for the purpose to this and that vnderneath it: vpon the boughes were laid boards to tread vpon . . .[58]

What Parkinson is describing is a tree trained into a two-storey banqueting house. The contemporary eulogies of Cobham Hall would suggest that it may have been a highly influential garden.

To these lost gardens we may add glimpses of ones that we occasionally get in contemporary pictures. The miniature oil portrait of Elizabeth I at Welbeck Abbey (*c.* 1580) has an inset scene of a garden enclosed within a wall and loggia, with square beds edged with hedges.[59] There is a view of a similar garden in Rowland Lockey's updated group of the family of Sir Thomas More (*c.* 1595), where a walled garden is followed by an inner hedge and within that knots edged with hedges.[60] Isaac Oliver's miniature of a melancholy young man seeking the solace of the greenwood tree (*c.* 1595) is more interesting.[61] In the background within a walled enclosure there is a garden of the type seen in the engravings by de Vries, enclosed by an arcade and with grass laid out in complicated geometrical patterns with paths between. This probably gives us a clear idea of what some at least of Burghley's Theobalds must have looked like. More mysterious is the allegorical enclosure in which Henry, 9th Earl of Northumberland, reclines (*c.* 1595). It is on an eminence and lies between two rectangular hedges, while from a tree the globe of the world balances a feather with the motto: 'TANTI'.[62]

The Elizabethan aesthetic

Our knowledge of the great gardens of Elizabethan England is, therefore, at the most fragmentary. Deprived of the central impetus of the Crown the effect is isolated and scattered. Perhaps of all the achievements, that which can be appreciated least today but which at the same time characterizes them most precisely, is pattern. Sixteenth-century gardening depended on geometrical pattern for its spectacular effects, the square knots being laid out in a seemingly inexhaustible variety of shapes. Our best approach to this is perhaps by means of contemporary painting and the applied arts, above all that of embroidery.[63] The aesthetic that dominated the age is epitomized by the work of the court miniaturist, Nicholas Hilliard.[64] His is a flat, two-dimensional world lit by an even, brilliant light. There is no understanding of the picture surface as a separate, enclosed world governed by its own optical principles, any more than garden planning suggests any application of scientific perspective. Everywhere in an Elizabethan painting there is pattern: on the carpet on which a sitter stands, all over the chair upon which he rests his arm, encrusted on every article of dress – gloves, ruffs, cuffs, doublets, shoes, hose, head-dress, bodice, sleeves, petticoat, cloak and farthingale. And this pattern was created by the art of the embroiderer, whose vocabulary depended on fruit, flower and foliage forms.

As we have discussed already, our only certain designer of knot gardens, Thomas Trevelyon, also provided designs for embroidery. This is surely a vital clue for our visualization of the Elizabethan garden; it is best understood by looking at one of the formalized icons of Elizabeth I – compilations of pattern in the form of jewels, lace, fabric and embroidery. Judging from these sources and from the few published ones, Elizabethan knots and mazes must have been of outstanding inventiveness in terms of design.

By the last decade of the reign that aesthetic was already outmoded in European terms. The image of the garden as Gloriana's glass was shortly to be destroyed. Among the architectural plans and elevations of John Thorpe, there is one of the palace and part of the garden of St Germain-en-Laye. Thorpe must have obtained it from Sir Henry Neville, who was ambassador in 1600 to the new French king, Henry IV. It shows the gardens that he was creating, not in the old-fashioned, flat style of Francis I's Fontainebleau or of Catherine de Medici's Tuileries, but in the grand Italian Mannerist idiom of the Villa d'Este, with the terrain sculpted into terraces, one descending to the next and connected by flights of steps. Beneath these, Thorpe wrote, 'is an Ile vawlted very faire with 3 rockes made very arteficially with byrds, stones & organs going with water, &c'.[65] The description is of mysterious grottos with mechanical singing birds and organs. From Paris news was arriving of the revolution which within a decade was to transform the Elizabethan emblematic into the Jacobean Mannerist garden.

35 Portrait of Salomon de
Caus by an unknown
artist (1619)

CHAPTER IV

THE MANNERIST GARDEN I
Salomon de Caus

By 1603, when Elizabeth I died, the visual arts in England had drifted sharply into almost total isolation from developments on the mainland of Europe. The accession of James VI of Scotland as king coincided with the re-establishment, more or less, of a peace in Europe which was to last until the outbreak of the Thirty Years War on the Continent in 1619 and until the advent of the Civil War in England in 1642. In 1598 Spain and France came to terms at the Treaty of Vervins, in 1604 England followed suit and in 1609 the Twelve Years Truce brought a lull to the struggle in the Low Countries. Simultaneously the opening decade of the seventeenth century witnesses a re-creation of court life after thirty years or more of religious war and in every instance that re-creation was to stem from a renewed acquaintance with the achievements of Renaissance Italy and, in particular, developments during the years when, because of civil war and religious persecution, the north had been cut off from the south. Everywhere as we move into the age of absolutism there is a cult of the sovereign's residence, including the introduction on a huge scale and at vast expense of elaborate gardens, fountains and water effects. In the case of England this took the form of a new dynasty and a new court of prodigal extravagance after half a century of regal impoverishment and frugality. And for the first time since the reign of Henry VIII the court took a decisively active role in setting fashion in the world of the arts. In the case of the garden all this can conveniently be focused on a single figure, one of international importance in the history of gardening north of the Alps: Salomon de Caus.

Salomon de Caus   Salomon de Caus was born in 1576 in the Pays de Caux in Normandy, probably in Dieppe.[1] The family was Huguenot and may even have spent some time in England during the period of the religious wars. We know that there were English connections because by 1600 several of the de Caus family are listed as members of the French Protestant Church in London. Little is known of Salomon's formal education other than what we can deduce from his own writings. He had studied the works of Hero of Alexandria, Vitruvius, Pliny, Diodorus Siculus, Diogenes Laertius and Euclid; he was also familiar with the writings of Jacob Besson and Ramelli. All these, as we shall see, place him within a particular Renaissance thought context, one which we shall examine shortly. Some time between about 1595 and 1598 he visited Italy and, in particular, the famous garden created by the Grand Dukes of Tuscany at Pratolino outside Florence. He was also acquainted with the Villa d'Este and Frascati. And this experience, like his reading, must be regarded as central to an understanding of his contribution to garden design.

The next established fact is that de Caus was in Brussels in July 1601 in the service of the archdukes Albert and Isabella. De Caus was for almost a decade in the employ of this new and highly civilized court. It was not until 1599 that the archduke had arrived in the Low Countries and begun to set about re-creating a court life of the type which had vanished thirty years before. Its main flowering lay in the future with the arrival of Wencel Cobergher in 1605 and the return of Rubens from Italy in 1608. Mary of Hungary's palace at Mariemont had to be restored and its gardens relaid out; the same applied to the palace in Brussels. Both had to be in the new style which de Caus had learnt about in Italy, with elaborate fountains and grottos. In 1603–4 he supervised the transformation of an old mill into a hydraulic machine for bringing water to the gardens of the Brussels palace. The following year he was appointed engineer to the archdukes. His work for them has yet to be disentangled because he was first of all subject to a certain Leonard d'Aymery and subsequently to Wencel Cobergher. We know that he was responsible for an 'artificielle fonteyne' in the great gallery of the Brussels palace and presumably for grottos and fountains in the gardens. One was a rustic house with five entrances with a triumph of Parnassus in the centre. While he was in the Low Countries he married and had a child and is said to have come to England in a fit of pique because the Prince de Condé defaced his grotto and left it 'rompu et gasté'.

De Caus was in England from 1607–8 to 1613. Initially he was in the service of the new queen, Anne of Denmark, around whom centred this revival of activity in the visual arts, and for whom he laid out gardens both at Somerset House and Greenwich. Subsequent to Anne's eldest son Henry being created Prince of Wales in June 1610, when he was given his own household, de Caus became 'Ingenieur du Serenissime Prince de Galles', as he described himself in the dedication to his *La Perspective avec la raison des ombres et miroirs*, published in London in 1612. The dedication is actually dated 1 October 1611 and written as from the Prince's palace at Richmond;[2] in it he states that he had been giving lessons on perspective to the young Prince for two or three years. De Caus was occupied during this period with creating elaborate gardens and waterworks in the grounds of Richmond Palace in association with Inigo Jones and a Florentine architect, Constantino dei Servi, a project which came to an abrupt end in November 1612 when the Prince died. De Caus was still in England in July of the following year, when he petitioned 'to returne into his owne Countrey',[3] but from France he promptly wended his way to the court of Heidelberg where he designed and supervised the construction of the famous Hortus Palatinus for Prince Henry's sister, Elizabeth, and her husband Frederick, the Elector Palatine. This was to last until 1619, when the election of this legendary couple as King and Queen of Bohemia was to precipitate the outbreak of the Thirty Years War.

At this moment there is no necessity to take the story of de Caus any further. We need instead to turn back and construct his intellectual biography, because from this stems the garden revolution of early Jacobean England. We need secondly to study the two gardening traditions, French and Italian, with which he was most familiar, for out of all these constituents was to spring the development of the Mannerist garden during the opening decade of James I's reign.

The revolution embodied in the elusive figure of Salomon de Caus has to be placed within a European perspective; it was through him that the arrival in England was signalled of the Renaissance engineer. No one who has written about the history of garden design in Britain seems ever to have grasped the enormous role played in its development by the engineer. Garden history, like so many subjects, has been the victim of misleading compartmentalization of a sort totally alien to the Renaissance mind. De Caus belongs firmly to a group of polymaths whose preoccupations embraced hydraulics and who find their most famous exemplar in Leonardo da Vinci.

The Renaissance engineer was an artist and an artisan, a military man, an organizer of court festivities, a man whose mind was of such complexity and genius that no effect was beyond his powers.[4] This typically Renaissance phenomenon not only drew upon existing mechanical and technical traditions from the Middle Ages but was more especially born of the Humanist 'rediscovery' and study of the engineering literature of antiquity: Archimedes, Ctesibius and Hero of Alexandria and Vitruvius. The knowledge gained from these, often only by means of secondary texts, created an orbit of activity which embraced the sciences of the measurement of surfaces (geodesy), of moving machines (automata), of the traction of heavy weights (baralcus, after the work by Hero), of weights and balances, of measuring instruments (metrology) and of lenses and mirrors. When we come to examine the writings of de Caus these are precisely his subjects, ones which would strike us, devoid of the knowledge of the tradition to which he belongs, as an extraordinary assortment. His prototype already existed in fifteenth-century Italy in figures such as Brunelleschi, an architect who was also an inventor of machines, of optical instruments and a designer of décor for festivities, and Leonardo, who was only incidentally a painter and primarily a military engineer, an architect, an expert on hydraulics, a geometrician preoccupied with the new art of scientific perspective and a designer of automata for Sforza court fêtes. This alliance of science and Humanism made the engineer not merely a practical man whose discoveries facilitated this or that particular mechanical effect, but something much more. His exploration of the universe through his discoveries was devoted to revealing and confirming the organizational schema of a universal order of things. But primarily the thread to follow is the Renaissance revival and study of the mechanics and engineering of classical antiquity.

Salomon de Caus's magical, mechanical wonders, which were to be the focal points of the gardens of Anne of Denmark and her son, Henry, Prince of Wales, bring us into contact, therefore, with a tradition central to late Renaissance garden making, that of automata.[5] De Caus's gardens, which feature giants and grottos, speaking statues and water organs, mobile sculptures and startling hydraulic effects, belong to the Renaissance rediscovery of the mechanics of the School of Alexandria.

The School of Alexandria was at its apogee in the three centuries before the birth of Christ and its central figures were Ctesibius, Philo of Byzantium and, above all, Hero of Alexandria.[6] Ctesibius was a Greek doctor who lived in the third century BC, all of whose works have disappeared; we know of them through Vitruvius, who describes Ctesibius's use of air pressure, hydraulic machines, including a water clock, and the construction of automata. The second, Philo of Byzantium, lived about 200 BC and the fragments of his work which have survived are of the same kind, basically what we would think of as using scientific principles for frivolous effects, self-lighting lamps or elaborate water tricks. This approach was indeed central to the method of the Alexandrian School and nowhere is it better illustrated than in the key text for the Renaissance cult of automata, the *Pneumatics* of Hero of Alexandria.

This book is essentially a series of sixty-seven theorems concerning mechanics and hydraulics, which he then proceeds to demonstrate, but always by constructing moving machines with human and animal forms. Deliberately clothing the scientific aspect in this manner made it easier, by means of a retention of the images in the mind of the reader, to deal with the problems and behaviour of gas, steam, air pressure and the movement of liquids. Let us take an example. Theorem XXXVII tells the reader how to build a temple with an altar in front of it which, when a fire is lit on the altar, will cause the temple doors to open automatically, the motive force being the expansion and contraction of air.

This approach is continued in a second work, also known to the Renaissance, on the use of automata in the theatre. In this, Hero describes both moving, three-dimensional automata (of the type used in alfresco court festivals) and those which required a fixed viewpoint for the onlooker. The book includes instructions on how to make a mechanical apotheosis of Bacchus and on the changes in décor necessary for a five-act play using automata.

These works were to have an immense influence not only on the development of Renaissance science and theatre but also on the evolution of the garden and the grotto. The works of Hero were known to the fifteenth century through Latin and Arabic translations, but in 1501 the known fragments were published for the first time (again in Latin) by Lorenzo Valla. Other editions followed but without doubt the most important was the Italian translation by Aleotti which appeared in 1589, the same year as Baldi's translation of the work on theatrical automata. Aleotti's publication is illustrated and is the direct ancestor of de Caus's most important book, *Les Raisons des forces mouvantes*. A glance at one or two of the theorems is sufficient to establish that the mechanical marvels of the Renaissance grotto were in one aspect a re-creation by the Renaissance architect engineer of the scientific principles of Hero of Alexandria.

Theorem XXXVII is the one we described in which temple doors were made to open mechanically when a fire was lit on an altar before it. The altar is connected by a tube (G) to a globe of water (H). When the fire is lit, the heat causes the water to expand; it rises and passes into the suspended cauldron (M), which then descends owing to the weight of the water, thus operating a simple turning winch connected to the hinges of the door, which swings open. Theorem XL depicts Hercules slaying the dragon and seizing the golden apple of the Hesperides which lies between them. A pedestal is constructed (AB) which is divided into an upper and a lower section (CD), the upper one of which is filled with water. The dramatic action is precipitated by lifting the golden apple (K), which raises the cone (E) within the upper section; this, in turn, by means of the pulley (X), causes Hercules to draw his bow (R). Meanwhile, water has passed via the cone (E) into the lower part of the pedestal causing the air there to produce a hissing noise, which is emitted from the dragon's mouth via

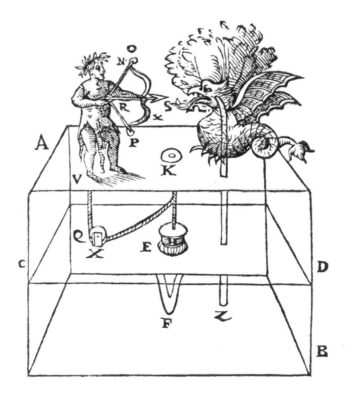

Two theorems from Aleotti's translation (1589) of the *Pneumatics* of Hero of Alexandria

36 Theorem XXXVII. A fire on an altar before a temple causes its doors to open

37 Theorem XL. By lifting the golden apple (K) of the Hesperides, a tableau of Hercules and the Hydra comes alive: the hero draws his bow and the beast hisses.

tube z. Once these principles had been grasped, the paraphernalia of suction, compressed air, water pressure, of winches, pulleys and weights were enthusiastically taken up and developed. And, as in classical antiquity, the most obsessive and dramatic use of this rediscovered art was in court festivals and in automata for grottos.

Within the wider context of late Renaissance thought, the phenomenon of the grotto belongs to the emergent science, or rather pseudo-science, of the seventeenth century. These mechanical figures simultaneously demonstrated a physical theorem and illustrated a myth, itself with an allegorical significance for the educated onlooker. The links with the progressive trends from which experimental science was to spring are obvious, but that is to anticipate. The world of the automata, which arrives in full force in the gardens of Jacobean and Caroline England, is that of late Renaissance occultism.

All this might seem a somewhat weird approach to garden history but it can be placed in context by examining the one garden which de Caus had studied in depth in Italy and which to the north epitomized the new ideals, that of Pratolino. It is not Bramante's Belvedere, nor Ligorio's Villa d'Este, nor the garden arrangements of Palladio's villas along the Brenta which the courts of the north wished to imitate and emulate. It is the fantastic world of Pratolino with its strange and spectacular fountains, its mysterious moving statues, its use of simulated natural and musical sounds, its amazing metamorphoses and sudden startling effects which stirred their passions. Pratolino *is* the Mannerist garden.

Pratolino and the Mannerist garden

Pratolino is so important that I shall begin by quoting a description of it by the Elizabethan traveller Fynes Moryson, written in the middle of the 1590s, when Italy was once more opening up to foreign visitors:

> Early in the morning we went out by the plaine lying on the west side [of Florence], & came to Pratoline, the Dukes famous garden, seven miles from the City. . . . This garden is divided into two inclosures, compassed with stone walls. In the upper inclosure is a statua of a Giant, with a curled beard, like a Monster, some forty six els high, whose great belly will receive many men at once, and by the same are the Images of many Nimphes, all which cast out water abundantly. Neere the same are many pleasant fish-ponds, and there is a Cave under the earth leading three miles to the Fountaine of water, from whence by many pipes the waters are brought to serve the workes of these Gardens. There is a Fountaine which hath the name of a Laberinth close by it. And a Fountaine of Jupiter & Iris distilling water; the Fountaine of the Beare; the Fountaine of Bersia. I call these by the name of Fountaines, vulgarly called Fontana, which are buildings of stone, adorned with many carved Images distilling water, and such are placed in most parts of Italy in the market places, open and uncovered: but in this and like Gardens, these Fountaines are wrought within little houses, which house is vulgarly called grotta, that is, Cave (or Den) yet they are not built under the earth but above in the manner of a Cave.[7]

In this way Moryson introduces his reader to one of the fundamental features of the Renaissance garden, the grotto.

The grotto was a revival of an antique form and is dwelt on in some detail by Alberti where he describes how the ancients had constructed caves in their gardens 'covering the surface with rough and rocky things putting there little bits of pumice, spongy stone and travertine'.[8] As part of the Renaissance garden in Italy it was later to become the quintessential expression of Mannerism. The *grottocina* (*c.* 1553–4) in the Boboli gardens was one of the earliest examples of the pan-naturalistic architectural resolution of the grotto as a form in which pastoral elements combine with stalactites, 'sponges' and cascades of water to make a fantastic display. In the grotto the natural forms of the material are deliberately stressed and put together to suggest bizarre, exotic and often frightening shapes. The grotto reflected the late Renaissance preoccupation with the exploration of the natural world's phenomena and through it its hidden occult meaning.

Moryson then proceeds to describe the lower garden and the palace, beneath which there was a famous series of grottos with automata.

> . . . there is a Cave, vulgarly called la grotta Maggiore. . . . In the said Cave, a head of marble distelleth water; and two trees by the turning of a cocke shed waters abundantly, and a little globe is turned about by Cupid, where the Images of Duckes dabble in the water, and then looke round about them; and in the middest of a marble table is an instrument, which with great art and force, driveth water into any furthest part of the Cave. . . .[9]

He continues to describe, one after another, a whole series of grottos of this type, one in which 'certaine images of Nimphes are carried by the water out of the Cave, and in againe, as if they had life', another in which 'unseene waters cause a noise like thunder, and presently a shower of rain fals' and, that which impressed him most of all, in which 'the Image of Fame doth loudly sound a Trumpet, while the Image of a Clowne putteth a dish into the water, and taking up water, presents it to the Image of a Tyger, which drinketh the same up, and then moves his head and lookes around about with his eyes. . . .' He concludes thus: 'I know not any place in the World affoords such rare sights in this kind'.

For those who see a garden in terms of trees, plants and flowers, Moryson's eulogy of what amounts to a series of hydraulic *tableaux vivants* might seem somewhat extraordinary. This in itself is an important fact. For Moryson, as he experiences the gardens of late Renaissance Italy, they have become a setting first and foremost for sudden and miraculous mechanical metamorphoses.

Pratolino was created by an architect–engineer of the type de Caus was to emulate, Bernardo Buontalenti, who worked on the palace and its gardens, initiated by the Grand Duke Francesco between 1569 and 1584.[10] Today only the giant described by Moryson survives, the rest having been swept away at the beginning of the nineteenth century to create *un jardin anglais*. Pratolino, in its spectacular manipulation of water, was deliberately designed to excel the effects at the Villa d'Este, but it was also an expression of the Grand Duke's interest in scientific experiment. Buontalenti was re-creating in these hydraulic grotto devices the automata of the Alexandrian School and like them they were not only conceived to have an allegorical significance embodied in the myths they depicted but, at the same time, demonstrated a scientific theorem.

In its planning, Pratolino was, of course, a Renaissance re-creation of a garden of classical antiquity. Its aim was to present 'Art and Nature together in one composition' by following the description of Pliny's Tusculan villa with its formal garden and meadow, 'the natural beauty of which is as great as the artificial beauty just described'. The disposition of the grounds followed Alberti's instructions that areas should be architectural, planted in 'circles and semi–circles', that trees should be set in lines and that there should be grottos.

Pratolino   *The most influential of all Italian gardens on
the Mannerist courts of northern Europe at
the opening of the 17th century*

facing page:
38 View of the gardens of Pratolino in 1599. Its most
famous grottos were in the basement of the villa. The
garden was planted geometrically in the Renaissance style,
linking it axially to the villa, with architectural features,
statuary, automata and water combined to produce a highly
esoteric artificial environment.

39 Stefano della Bella's engraving of one of the most
celebrated of the grottos in which Fame, in praise of the
Medici, sounded her trumpet and ascended heavenwards.

The last are the most important for, as Baldinucci wrote, the ones at Pratolino were studied by 'all those who afterwards have worked in similar things throughout Europe'.[11]

Pratolino was also meant to be read in the same way as any late Renaissance allegorical painting or court festival. What the exact reading of Pratolino is may be open to discussion but in 1586 Francesco de Vieri published what he held to be an allegorical commentary on the meaning of the gardens.[12] He begins with rudimentary statements of the garden as the earthly paradise, as an expression of princely magnificence and as a means whereby philosophers were able to express the truths of the universe. Vieri is saturated in late Renaissance hermetic philosophy, in which the universe is pervaded by occult influences and correspondences. The garden for him is like the famous *intermezzi* (also designed by Buontalenti with elaborate machinery and transformation effects), a profound expression of man's power to control the physical universe, to create artificial facsimiles of it and to demonstrate arcane truths by means of symbolic images. He then proceeds to provide a gloss on the 'meaning' of Pratolino. Two instances will suffice to illustrate his method. The famous giant is Mount Apennine, one of the fallen Titans that had attempted to overthrow Jove. This symbolized that anything without God's aid was destined to disaster. Within the giant the cave of precious metals spoke of God's munificence to man through the natural resources of the earth. Nearby the labyrinth of laurel with its temple in the midst told of man's search for virtue.

Gardens with such elaborate and often comprehensive, if diffuse and ambiguous, allegorical programmes were standard in the late Renaissance. The Villa d'Este was conceived by Pirro Ligorio as a celebration of the two Greek heroes, Hercules and Hippolytus. That of the latter alluded to the creator of the garden, Ippolito d'Este, Cardinal of Ferrara, that of the former to the patron deity of Tivoli and of the Este family.[13] Bomarzo, with its amazing monsters, used in honour of its duke the myths of Mars – Hercules and Ceres – Proserpina, so it has been argued, to expound the union of the dead with the forces of nature which yet triumphed in the life reborn each spring.[14] So far in England we have only seen isolated emblematic tableaux such as the Grove of Diana at Nonsuch.

The exegesis by Vieri of Pratolino provides a key as to how it was intended that these Mannerist gardens should be read. Vieri sees the whole garden as an emulation of all the mechanical marvels of antiquity gathered into one place. Like the *intermezzi*, he dwells on the stupendous effect that such things have on the onlookers, leaving their minds overcome by the occult mysteries revealed by means of these marvels and delights and yet clothed in fable and allegory. And when he writes of this he appeals inevitably to both Boccaccio and Ficino. Pratolino, therefore, made the garden into something else, a setting in which late Renaissance man could rival the marvels which in the past he had only read about. Here he could not only experience them but try to surpass them. De Caus belongs to this late Renaissance world, when magic and science have not as yet taken their separate paths. Technical advance did not always relate to rational function but rather to demonstrating some mythical or symbolic truth. It is the technicians within the Vitruvian architect–engineer tradition who, as Eugenio Battisti has written, challenge the philosophers, whom they accuse of ignorance by taking to its furthest limits man's imitation of the effects of the natural world. This above all is epitomized in the late Renaissance world by the emergence of the picture frame stage and by the grotto. Both were completely artificially controlled environments in which the onlooker or visitor was subjected to 'closed', dramatic, and isolated happenings, often violent and sudden in nature. In England, therefore, it should come as no surprise that de Caus should introduce symbolic fountains, grottos and automata simultaneously with Inigo Jones's introduction of the proscenium arch and the perspective transformation scenes of the Stuart court masque.

The gardens of Henry IV

Although Pratolino was the ultimate inspiration of the Mannerist fountain and grotto mania which occurred in early Jacobean England, the influences also came, as usual, from a source which de Caus must have known even better, the gardens of Henry IV and Marie de Medici. In France in the aftermath of the wars of the Catholic League, Henry IV began to create a new court life. Fynes Moryson describes the gardens at Fontainebleau in 1595 as 'wild and unmanured' and in that year work began on their restoration.[15] The team under which this was carried out consisted of Claude Mollet, whose family was to dominate gardening in France until the advent of Le Nôtre and who were also to work in the Low Countries, Sweden and England, and the Italian hydraulic engineers, fountain and grotto designers, Tommaso and Alessandro Francini, whom Henry IV had summoned from the court of the Grand Duke of Tuscany in 1598 to construct fountains and grottos of the Pratolino variety.[16]

These improvements are best studied in the aerial view made by one of the Francini of the palace and its gardens, dated 1614. The most important innovations were the island garden in the lake and the Grand Parterre or King's Garden to the south-east. The latter centred on a huge rectangular fountain surrounded by balustrading. A vast, recumbent River Tiber holds a cornucopia, from which jets arise and beneath which two swans, two dragons and four vases also spout water. The Fontaine du Tibre was famous and formed the focal point of the whole area, which was dominated by a new canal of which the fountain occupied the intersection. Claude Mollet was responsible for devising a new type of design for garden beds, vast and intricately articulated parterre surfaces. At Fontainebleau this was introduced some time after 1600 and was complete by 1614 when Francini made his view. The beds are in groups of four, diagonally partitioned, those on the north side having circular centres. Although the garden is too far from the palace to be architecturally related to it, it is conceived in broad terms and Mollet's linking of the beds into groups of four is an important step towards monumentality of conception. In a plan of *c.* 1600 these parterres are still geometrical in form but by 1614 they have been replaced with embroidery-like scroll forms in box. The island garden in the lake also has elegant parterres in the same manner. We are witnessing the emergence of a major feature of the seventeenth-century garden, the *parterre de broderie*.

St Germain-en-Laye was built in the mid-sixteenth century for Henry II by Philibert de L'Orme.[17] Here Henry IV, aided by Etienne du Pérac, created a mighty series of terraced gardens linked by ramps and flights of steps to the River Seine; it was directly Italian in manner and, in particular, derived from the Villa Lante at Bagnaia. The garden at the top had an embroidered parterre in the style of those Mollet did at Fontainebleau, articulated by concentric walks. In Francini's view of 1614 we can see the letter H for Henry IV still in some of the parterres but in others it has already been replaced by L for Louis XIII. Unlike those at Fontainebleau there is an important new element: they are surrounded on three sides by terraces terminating at the furthest points with pavilions. This enabled the visitor to view the pattern of the parterres. The next terrace had a wilderness with circular walks in the usual Mollet style. Finally there was a water parterre directly lifted from the Villa Lante but interspersed with further parterres embellished with 'lettres et devises'.

However, St Germain-en-Laye was even more famous for its grottos (which had been built in France from the 1540s onwards) and automata by the Francini; they were in the tradition of Pratolino and housed in the arcading of the terraces.[18] In one, Perseus descended and vanquished the Dragon, which

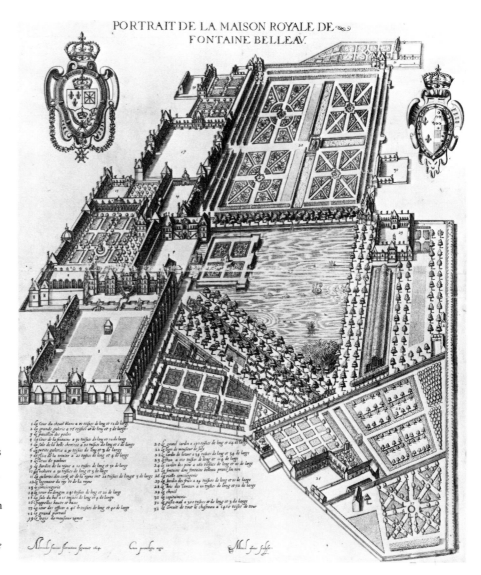

40 Fontainebleau as it was laid out for Henry IV by the hydraulic engineers Tommaso and Alessandro Francini and the gardener Claude Mollet. At the top is the King's Garden, with its canal centring on the Fontaine du Tibre surrounded by *parterres de broderie*.

84

disappeared beneath the waters. In another, there was a hydraulic organ played by a lady in a farthingale, recalling the huge organ at the Villa d'Este. There were grottos of Neptune, Orpheus and of the Dragon (all mythological allegories celebrating Henry IV), but the most astounding was the Grotte des Flambeaux. In this, the visitor was subjected to a series of transformation scenes parallel to those in a *ballet de cour*. The sun rose, a storm followed and then subsided to reveal a view of the palace with the royal family strolling in front of it and the Dauphin descending from the clouds in a chariot supported by angels.

De Caus must have been familiar at first or second hand with a lot of this and, as we shall see, his designs are related to those by the Francini. Even more important was the interest of the Jacobean court in what was happening across the Channel. In spite of his conversion to Catholicism, Henry IV remained the

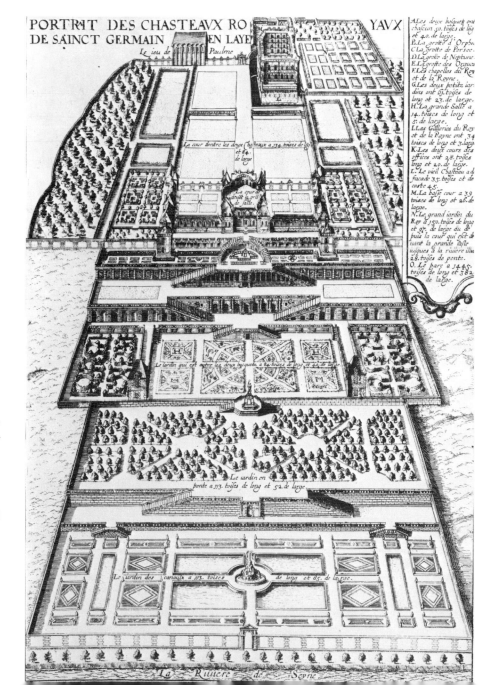

41 St Germain-en-Laye as laid out for Henry IV. The rectangular terraces descending from formal parterre to tree-lined walks to water parterre had great influence in England. The celebrated grottos were beneath the arcades, close to the palace.

C'y est La Grote dOrphee qui est au Chau de S' Germain en Laÿe
laquelle n'est que la fasale ou sont les Mouuemens estant en la Sconde Gallerie
au lieu Marque. F. aüd portrait de S' Germain

Francini Inuen .   N. Bosse Sculp

42 The Grotto of
Orpheus at St Germain-
en-Laye. An instance of
the highly elaborate
symbolic grottos devised
by the Francini using
hydraulic automata and
sound effects

focal point of Protestant and liberal conciliatory Europe. After his assassination
in 1610, Henry, Prince of Wales, seems to have tried to take upon himself that
role and to have deliberately modelled himself on the deceased French king.
Terracing, islands, embroidered parterres, grottos and fountains are the
features which cross the Channel in the opening decade of James I's reign and
which create the era of the Mannerist garden.

De Caus's initial work in England was for Anne of Denmark, whose lively interest in the arts is mostly known through her patronage of Ben Jonson and Inigo Jones, in the creation of the Stuart court masques. These were undoubtedly her most significant contributions to the development of the visual arts. Building and gardening came four years after the first masque, in 1609, when she began to remodel her London palace, Somerset House.[19] This 'large and goodly house', as Stow described it in 1598, had been built by Lord Protector Somerset and was a milestone in mid-Tudor classicism, heavily influenced by France. On Somerset's fall from power it became Crown property.

The creation of the garden here was Anne's most elaborate manifestation of the new style epitomized by de Caus. The garden lay by the riverside and fell into two areas. Kip's engraving, which dates from the early eighteenth century, enables us to get our bearings. This records Inigo Jones's refacing of the south front in 1638 and the new river frontage of 1661. The raised walk around the west garden remains as a token of de Caus's work, which is recorded in its initial stages by Robert Smythson in a drawing probably made by him during his visit to London in 1609 while work was in progress.[20] It depicts the west garden with a raised walk around it and flights of steps down into it, both from the terrace by the house and at the sides. The garden itself is symmetrical with a quatrefoil laid onto a square, the patterns accentuated by trees and with a central walk down the middle from north to south to a water-gate. Another walk running on the same axis divides the west from the east garden and also leads to a landing stage. Within the east garden there is a large circular feature with something octagonal within it. This must have been the garden's most striking feature, a huge grotto fountain depicting Mount Parnassus.

More important perhaps than either of these, however, is the view in the background of Marcus Gheeraerts's portrait of Anne at Woburn Abbey. This picture was almost certainly painted for one of the Queen's closest friends and the creator of a number of major gardens in the new style, Lucy Harington, Countess of Bedford. Another version of this portrait bears the date 1614 which effectively gives a *terminus ad quem* for the Woburn picture.[21] This glimpse records the west garden presumably as it was finally completed, with the raised walks faced by pilasters and niches in the classical style. The pattern of the parterre is different from that recorded by Smythson, indicating changes probably during construction. That the garden was included at all in the background of a major royal portrait is an index of the importance attached to it by Anne as a symbol of royal power and regal munificence.

Before adding to our visual evidence the descriptions by visitors, there is the information provided by the Works Accounts. As usual these are slightly confusing. Already by May 1609 payments had been made for building walls around the garden, for 'making of the new Terrass . . . with the railes and ballesters of stone' and 'the making of a Force with divers brass workes (and a new House for it) to bring water to the garden'.[22] In other words de Caus had designed a pump house to supply water from the Thames. The accounts would indicate that a certain William Goodrowse, the Sergeant-Surgeon, was responsible for laying out the west garden in 1609, for which he received the large sum of £400.[23] Smythson's drawing indicates that this was 203 by 176 feet and that the walk which surrounded it on the south, east and west sides was

43 Portrait of Anne of Denmark with a garden view, probably of Somerset House in its final form. It shows a garden surrounded by a terrace supported by arcading in the classical style looking down onto parterres of turf cut in patterns and trees.

44 Robert Smythson's plan of the garden in 1609 while it was still in the making. The layout of the parterres in the west garden may not have been finally in this form. The octagonal object in the east garden is the Parnassus within a pond.

facing page:
45 The river frontage at the opening of the 18th century. Elements of de Caus's arrangements remain: the terracing around the west garden, the tree-lined walk to the water-gate, and the area to the east where the Parnassus once stood.

46 Sketch by a German visitor of the Parnassus in the garden at Pratolino

47 Design by de Caus for a Parnassus, from his *Les Raisons des forces mouvantes*. This, with the addition of four figures representing the rivers of Great Britain at the base, is identical to what he constructed at Somerset House.

Somerset House

Salomon de Caus's most fully documented work in England, begun in 1609

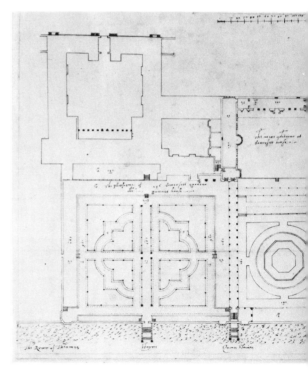

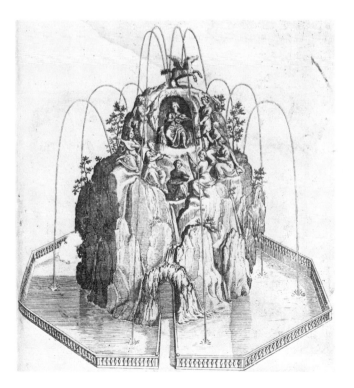

22 feet wide. Whether or not it was laid out as in the drawing and then altered to the formation in the Gheeraerts painting it is impossible to know. The layout for the quarters as recorded in the portrait of Anne is virtually identical to one recorded in 'Problesme XI' of *Les Raisons*, which would seem to confirm de Caus as its designer. In neither plan of the parterre is it of the new embroidered variety but of the kind included in *Les Raisons*, geometrical and punctuated by fir or cypress trees. Parterres of this type can be seen in the garden of Nicholas Houel's House of Charity in Paris in the middle of the 1580s.[24]

The exact extent of de Caus's supervision is therefore unclear. All that is certain is that the west garden in its final form is closely related to what we know of his work. As far as the Works Accounts are concerned his orbit is summed up in the words: 'Works about [the] fountaine in the Garden and building a house towards the Thames for Mounzer to Coie to make the Rocke in for the ffountaine'.[25] This was the marvellous Parnassus and there is no evidence to suggest that there was a second fountain in the west garden. The little 'house' can probably be identified with the house by the river in the east garden drawn by Smythson, in which de Caus presumably worked at his 'Rocke'. De Caus must also have devised the pump by which water was raised from the Thames to feed the Parnassus. 'Problesme Premiere' in the second book of his *Les Raisons* depicts a machine designed specifically for doing that job.

The Works Accounts go on to tell us of two other features in the Somerset House garden, 'a house for orange trees' and, a traditional feature, a banqueting house.[26] Whether de Caus was also responsible for these we do not know, but 'Problesme XI' has a grotto with a water-house above it approached by walks lined with orange and lemon trees in tubs with a vault beneath in which they passed the winter. This could reflect a projected arrangement for Somerset House. *Les Raisons* is after all a collection of designs he executed, so he states, for Prince Henry, many out of pure fancy and out of the fertility of his own invention. We shall have further evidence when we come to his involvement in Hatfield.

So much for the visual and documentary evidence. By far the most evocative, however, comes from two written accounts, one by the German escort, Neumayr, of the young Duke of Saxony in 1613, the second by a Frenchman, the Sieur de Mandelslo in 1640.[27] The earlier is the fuller and more suggestive:

> Farther Your Grace came down into the garden. It is next to the Palace and extends as far as the river. It is very well laid out, and is divided into diverse beautiful plats of curious shapes.[28]

Neumayr is describing the west garden, entering it from the loggia onto the terrace. It is the garden we see in the Gheeraerts portrait.

He then continues to describe what is 'to one side' or 'At one side' of the west garden. Then follows a long account of what surely must be the object for which Smythson gives some sort of ground-plan and which dominated the east garden:

> To one side stands a Mount Parnassus: the mountain or rock is made of sea-stones, all sorts of mussels, snails, and other curious plants put together: all kinds of herbs and flowers grow out of the rock which are a great pleasure to behold. On the side

facing the palace it is made like a cavern. Inside it sit the Muses, and have all sorts of instruments in [their] hands. Uppermost at the top stands Pegasus, a golden horse with wings. On the mountain are built four small arches, in each rests a naked statue of marble. They have cornucopiae in [their] hands and under their arms jugs from which water flows into the basin about four good paces wide, and is all around the mountain. They are supposed to represent four rivers. Among others there stands above such a female figure in black marble in gold letters *Tamesis*. It is the river on which London lies, and [which] flows next to this garden. Next beneath [is] this distich:

> *Me penes imperium, emporium sunt classis & artes*
> *Et schola bene fluens, florida prata rigo.*

Similar lines stand over the other three statues also. They let the water play. [It] sprang up to the very top of the rock thick as an arm and besides here and there out of the mountain. It is thus a beautiful work and far surpasses the Mount Parnassus in the Pratolino near Florence.[29]

Neumayr is describing a vast grotto fountain standing in a basin. The description is exact: it was a mountain around which reclined four river gods, representing the principal rivers of Great Britain headed by the Thames, each of which as in antique representation rested on an urn from which water flowed and each of which held a vase from which a jet arose to the top of the mount. On the mount itself, on the side facing Somerset House, sat the nine muses (there is no mention of Apollo, although he was probably there) with a golden Pegasus at the top.

As in the case of the rest of the garden, we can pursue this further in the illustrations to *Les Raisons*. 'Problesme XXIII' depicts exactly what this German visitor saw excepting the reclining river goddesses. De Caus writes that this huge Parnassus fountain was to be at least 80 feet in diameter and was designed 'pour orner un Iardin Royal'. The east garden area in the Smythson drawing is 140 feet square so that the diameter of the fountain basin in the middle must have been about 100 feet. If we want to add the river goddesses we can get some impression from the illustration to 'Problesme XXXVII' of the first book, which depicts a male river god at the bottom of a similar mount.

The model, as the German visitor noted, was Pratolino. Another German traveller gives us a rough sketch of what that looked like when he visited it in 1600[30] and this corroborates the view that de Caus's version far exceeded the original in terms of size and spectacle. Whether de Caus had a hydraulic organ within it as at Pratolino we do not know although he would have been capable of adding one. More interesting is the significance of the Parnassus. Francesco de Vieri, who describes the symbolism of the one at Pratolino, states that it celebrated men whose lives were dedicated to the pursuit of virtue by service to the Muses. Pegasus embodied 'la loro volontà al bene' whose wings recalled 'l'intelligenze perfetta di essa virtù, & L'ardentissimo Amore ad essa'.[31]

Turning to the Somerset House Parnassus we seem close to the world of the court masque and this indeed is the best clue to its symbolic function, for it expressed in permanent form an iconographic programme typical of Anne of Denmark. It is a celebration of Anne as 'Tethys, Queen of Nymphs and rivers', the subject of Samuel Daniel's masque presented by the Queen to mark the creation of her son Prince of Wales in 1610 during the laying out of the garden. The theme was Anne as Tethys, Queen of the Ocean, and wife to Neptune (James I), attended by a bevy of great ladies as the rivers of the newly created

Empire of Great Britain come to pay homage to the king. Her chief attendant on that occasion was her daughter, the Lady Elizabeth, who played the role of the nymph of the Thames. The costumes and scenery were by Inigo Jones, who designed for Anne a head-dress of shells and coral entwined with floating veils.[32] And the ladies were revealed enthroned within a grotto directly in the de Caus manner:

> On the midst of this was a triangular basement formed of scrolls and leaves . . . with a frieze of fishes and a battle of tritons, out of whose mouths sprang water into the bowl beneath. On the top of this was a round globe full of holes, out of which issued abundance of water, some falling into the receipt below, some into the oval vase borne up by the dolphins; and indeed there was no place in this great aquatic throne that was not filled with the sprinkling of these two natural-seeming waters. . . . In the middle . . . was a bowl or fountain made of four great scallops . . . above this were three great cherubins' heads, spouting water into the bowl. . . . The rest of the ornaments consisted of mask-heads spouting water.[33]

The Stuart court masque was always a visual progression from disorder to order and here the grotto, the second scene, with its mingling of art subjecting nature, prepared the way for the final tableau in which the queen and masquers appeared in their natural guise 'in a most pleasant and artificial grove'. As in all court masques the garden is always symbolic of wild nature tamed and, by inference, tamed by virtue of the peace and harmony ushered in by the rule of a monarch by Divine Right.

Behind both de Caus's Parnassus and the rocky grotto of 'Tethys' Festival' stretches a vigorous tradition with which de Caus must have been familiar. One would have been from the fêtes of the Valois court. In 1573 Catherine de Medici staged in the famous gardens of the Tuileries palace an entertainment in honour of the Polish ambassadors. 'The Ballet of the Provinces of France' was a landmark in the evolution of the *ballet de cour*. Sixteen court ladies representing the provinces arrived on a rock; so too did the musicians whom we can see in Antoine Caron's drawing attired as Apollo and the Muses, silhouetted against the parquets of the formal gardens.[34] Perhaps de Caus would have been more familiar with the mounts his 'master' Buontalenti created for the Florentine *intermezzi*. In those of 1589, which celebrated the marriage of Catherine's niece to the Grand Duke Ferdinand, Mount Helicon arose from beneath the stage in the midst of a garden of orange and lemon trees.[35] In 1600, as a prologue to Caccini's *Il rapimento di Cefalo*, which celebrated the marriage of Marie de Medici to Henry IV, Mount Helicon was some twenty ells high and topped by Pegasus with a stream trickling from his hoof down the mountainside on which sat Apollo and the Muses shaded by bushes of laurel and myrtle.[36] Nor should we forget such traditions within Elizabethan court entertainments. In January 1595 the gentlemen of Gray's Inn presented a masque at court, in which the magical powers of the queen were seen to vanquish those of the Adamantine Rock which opened to release its imprisoned knights.[37]

What are we to make of the Somerset House garden? As far as our knowledge of it goes it must have been one of the most striking garden ensembles in the new manner in early Jacobean England, although Prince Henry's works at Richmond would no doubt have far oustripped it had they been finished. Although the nature of the existing building eliminated any

48 Festival sources for de Caus's Parnassus. The musicians in 'The Ballet of the Provinces of France' in 1573, disguised as Apollo and the Muses seated on a rock. Behind stretch the gardens of Catherine de Medici's Tuileries palace.

possibility of the two being totally related, nonetheless a considerable effort was made to unify them. The loggia on the south front formed as it were a proscenium arch through which the visitor entered onto the terrace and instead of separate parquets, the whole west garden was thrown together as a single entity, the four quarters being absolutely identical. This was, of course, an enormous advance in planning, anticipating the boldness which was the essential principle of the Baroque garden. There was also the inclusion of a raised walk from which to view the pattern of the parterre and, above all, the startling introduction of elaborate waterworks in the vast Parnassus, in which Apollo and the Muses, accompanied by the rivers of Great Britain, sang the praises of the mistress of the place in perpetuity. Also new, and introduced in a forceful way, was the idea of a symbolic programme.

Simultaneously with the major work at Somerset House, de Caus was employed to relay out the gardens at Greenwich, the palace by the Thames assigned to Anne by James I. Very little is known about the old Tudor palace

93

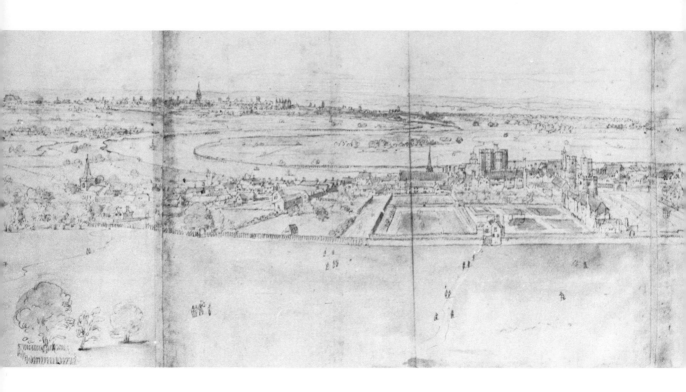

Greenwich

Salomon de Caus's second garden for Anne of Denmark

facing page:
49 View, *c.* 1555, showing the palace and the old Tudor gardens

50 Design by de Caus for a grotto aviary, from his *Les Raisons*. The one at Greenwich was similar, with three arches, but the water effects within related to figures that included a female centaur in the centre arch

51 Design by de Caus for a river goddess fountain, from his *Les Raisons*. Contemporary descriptions of the one at Greenwich match this closely.

52 The Fontaine du Tibre at Fontainebleau. One of the most ambitious additions by the Francini and a direct source for de Caus

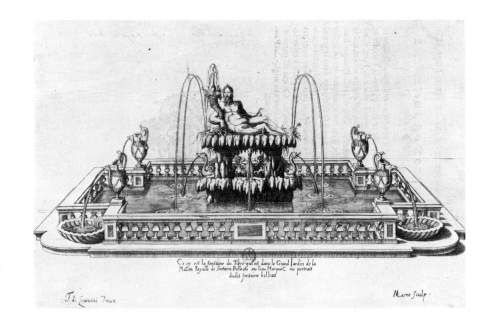

which is depicted in Wyngaerde's drawing of *c*. 1555 as a rambling red-brick building in the manner of Whitehall, or Hampton Court, although smaller. The tilt-yard can be seen to the right, while to the left, seemingly laid out in simple parquets with paths between, there is the first garden. A further wall divides it from a second to the west. Neither has any feature of note.[38]

De Caus's work lay in the reordering of this area. The two gardens were thrown into one and laid out as at Somerset House, presumably in walks and geometrical parterres centring on a fountain.[39] Our German visitor of 1613 describes it as follows:

> After this Your Grace was shown the garden: in the middle of the same is a large fountain. [It] is a female figure [which] gives water out of a cornucopia [and] was gilded all over. [It] has several lovely garden plats around.[40]

Nearly forty years later the Sieur de Mandelslo gives virtually the same description, adding that it stood in the midst of a great basin.[41] The Works Accounts record that this fountain cost the very large sum of £542 15s 10d.[42]

There is little difficulty in identifying this fountain with 'Problesme v' in *Les Raisons*: 'Autre desseing de fontaine pour representer vn Fleuue ou Riuiere, par vne figure'. With appeals to the ancient Egyptians, the Greeks and Romans who represented river gods as recumbent figures with vases from which cascaded their waters, he goes on to warn against placing this particular fountain anywhere where its fine jets would be impeded by gusts of wind. The basin, which has balustrading all around it, is twenty feet square. De Caus's inspiration must surely have been the Tiber fountain at Fontainebleau, an antique figure which was placed on rocks in the midst of a basin bordered by balustrading in the centre of the king's new garden. The elongated Mannerist formula of the de Caus river goddess recalls directly the tradition of the School of Fontainebleau. Gilded and with its jets plashing into the waters around it, the fountain at Greenwich must have been an impressive centrepiece for the garden.

De Caus's second construction was a grotto aviary. Mandelslo describes this as 'une des plus jolie que j'aye jamais vues'. Neumayr's description is more detailed, however:

> Farther on one comes to a grotto. [It] is a small house from the front and on both sides mostly open, with great iron railings there [i.e. where it was open]. On the wall are three different arches, thus all along the whole wall embellished with snails, mussels, mother-of-pearl and all kinds of curious sea plants; in some places flowers, grass and all sorts of lovely herbs grow out. In the middle arch stands a figure, half a woman and half a horse in the right size, also made from shells and mussels; it gave water from itself unto the ground. In the other two arches were other figures, from which water also sprang: on the ground sea stones were put together like rock. In some places there grew also flowers and small shrubs out of wood. There was also something of grass therein: on the wall sat on a branch a cuckoo, such [a cry] the gardener makes calling across the water. This house was also in the roof open in several places, although protected by wire grating, so that the birds, of which a great number were flying around inside could not get out.[43]

What Neumayr is describing is a typical de Caus structure, a building outside like 'a small house', arcaded at the front and sides, with openings in the roof to the sky, all of which were covered with protective grating. Inside, three arches repeated the façade arches: the centre one had a female centaur fountain and was flanked by two other fountains with unnamed figures. The wall at the back was completely encrusted with the usual shells, stones and plants.[44]

Nothing exactly like this appears in *Les Raisons* but elements of a number of 'Problesmes' combine to evoke Queen Anne's aviary. 'Problesme VII' has a design for 'une volière' eighty by twenty feet with five arches opening into a grotto, each opening coinciding with an opening in the roof. The wall is exactly as recorded in the descriptions but the centre fountain shows a ball balanced on a jet.

Both Somerset House and Greenwich place de Caus's work firmly in the perspective of Italian and above all Florentine gardens overlaid by France. The various works and projects for Anne and for Prince Henry are closest in spirit to what had happened in France when the team of Claude Mollet and Tommaso Francini, the hydraulic engineer, had laid out St Germain-en-Laye and Fontainebleau.

De Caus and Henry, Prince of Wales: Richmond

Henry, Prince of Wales, is such a lost figure in British history that it is difficult for us to recapture the ferment of optimism which surrounded the heir to the throne during the three years when, as Prince of Wales, he had his own court.[45] From 1610 to 1612 the hopes of England focused on this secretive youth, who seemed to embody the aspirations of those who, disillusioned with James I's policy of appeasement towards Spain and disgusted at the degeneration of court morals, saw in Henry a return to the ideals and policies of the England of Elizabeth I. Sir Charles Cornwallis describes the Prince in the following terms:

> He loved and did mightily strive to do somewhat of everything, and to excel in the most excelent; he greatly delighted in all Kinds of Engines belonging both to the Wars, both by Sea and Land: In the Bravery and Number of great Horses; in shooting and levelling of great Pieces of Ordinance; in the Ordering and Marshalling of Armies, in Building and Gardening, and in all Sorts of rare Musik, chiefly the Trumpet and Drum; in Limning, Painting, and Carving, in all Sorts of excellent and rare Pictures, which he had brought unto him from all Countries.[46]

The artistic programme, as revealed through his accounts, embraced engravers, musicians, painters, architects, engineers and equestrian experts. It included collecting Italian Renaissance pictures, antique coins and medals, establishing a riding academy and excelling in all chivalrous feats of arms and in the courtly compliment of the masque. It also embraced building and, of course, gardening.

As the Venetian ambassador wrote: 'His Highness ... attends to the disposition of his house, having ordered many gardens, fountains and some new buildings.'[47] Or, as this was recalled in retrospect:

> *To plant and build he had a great delight,*
> *Old ruins his sole presence did repair;*
> *Orchards and gardens forthwith at his sight*
> *Began to sprout and spring, to flourish fair:*
> *Ask of fair* Richmond *standing by the Thames,*
> *If this be true, or yet of his* S. Iames.[48]

The gardens in question were those at the riverside palace assigned to him by the King at Richmond. The palace had been built by Henry VII and was regularly used by all the Tudor kings and queens. Elizabeth I had in fact died there in 1603. As a building, however, we know very little about it. Completed in 1501, years before the more domestic style of Wolsey's Hampton Court, it was a palace–castle built around a courtyard which, from afar, judging from illustrations, was a forest of crocketed turrets topped by gilded vanes.[49] It was here that de Caus was commissioned to create a major garden.

Unfortunately we know tantalizingly little about what these gardens looked like; although unfinished at the Prince's death, they must have constituted a remarkable spectacle, conceived as they seem to have been on a vast scale. The extent of de Caus's role is difficult to measure because we know that Robert Cecil's gardener, who carried out elaborate naturalistic water effects at Theobalds, was involved and drew plans.[50] The issue is further complicated by the fact that in the year 1611 a Medicean architect, Constantino dei Servi, was summoned from Florence to make for the Prince designs for 'fountains, summerhouses, galleries and other things on a site in which his Highness is most interested'.[51] Dei Servi was in England by August of that year and was given an annual stipend double that of de Caus. The reference in the letter must be to Richmond, which could suggest that by that date de Caus was gradually to be replaced by an architect–engineer of the type the Grand Duke had sent to Henry IV, who could be capable of creating the fabulous gardens the Prince demanded. Dei Servi's arrival might also explain two things which occurred on the death of the Prince. The new architect must have made Inigo Jones and de Caus feel inadequate. Jones left for Italy with the Arundels, with the express purpose of learning in depth about the principles of Renaissance architecture. De Caus left for Germany and found service with Henry's sister, Elizabeth, the Electress Palatine. The irony of all this is that dei Servi's only court masque, that for the Somerset wedding in December 1613, was a disaster as the stage machinery failed to work. Campion, the author of the masque, tartly refers to dei Servi as 'being too much of himself'.[52] He left shortly after.

Following the Florentine's arrival, there is mention of the work going on at Richmond, including specifically the erection of a 'great figure . . . three times as large as the one at Pratolino, with rooms inside, a dove-cot in the head and grottoes in the base'.[53] The reference, of course, is to the famous Mount Apennine; in other words the one at Richmond would have been gargantuan in size. Nothing like it can ever have been seen in England. Was it by de Caus or dei Servi?

All the Works Accounts connected with Richmond make it clear that de Caus was in charge. And if we turn to *Les Raisons*, 'Problesme XIV' is a 'Desseing d'vne figure representante le Mont Tmollus', which had within it a grotto with automata depicting the contest of Pan and Apollo before Midas ('Problesme XV'). In his description of this object de Caus refers to the Apennine at Pratolino. 'Problesme XVI' is a second giant, 'vne grande figure rustique pour representer vn flueue', this time reclining and with a grotto of Orpheus taming wild beasts by the magic of his music within it ('Problesme XVII'). This second giant is an enormous island with a vast waterfall falling from the vase upon which he rests his arm.

The Works Accounts take this a little further because they refer to the making of three islands; islands are a feature which we shall meet again in de Caus's work at Hatfield.[54] Perhaps one of them was this vast reclining river

Richmond Palace

The gardens at Richmond, under construction from 1610 to 1612, remain one of the enigmas of the Jacobean garden revolution: they were never completed, being abandoned on the death of the Prince of Wales. One certain feature was the huge figure of a giant.

above left:
53 Design by de Caus for a giant in the form of an island, from his *Les Raisons.* Islands were a known feature of the Richmond project.

above right:
54 Giambologna's giant at Pratolino, the source and inspiration for that at Richmond

55 Design by de Caus for a giant with a grotto inside, from *Les Raisons*

Richmond Palace

56 View from a landing place towards water and islands, presumably at Richmond Palace. Detail from a portrait of Henry, Prince of Wales

57 An artificial mountain with an aviary within it and a pathway leading up to a re-creation of the speaking statue of Memnon. Project, probably for Richmond Palace, by de Caus in his *Les Raisons*

god. Otherwise the accounts are cryptic, with references being made to the 'rockhouse' and 'glass stuff for the rock at Richmond'.[55] We might, however, go a stage further, atmospherically, by looking through the window in the portrait of the Prince, which is now in the National Portrait Gallery, but which must almost certainly have belonged to his sister, the Princess Elizabeth.[56] The vista shows a path coming from the left leading to a strange pair of what appear to be seats beneath a canopy attached to a brick wall. We are at a landing, for the path forks away from the canopy towards balustrading, flanking stairs which lead down to the waterside. In the distance, beyond these, is what might perhaps be one of the islands, for it is surrounded on three sides by water.

All this seems to indicate works on a far larger and more adventurous scale than those for the Queen, a man-made landscape in which stone and earth was moulded and planted to resemble a Mannerist fantasy by Arcimboldo. We can only speculate as to what the garden must have looked like for there are no descriptions and a pall of silence falls after the Prince's death. De Caus dedicates the second book of his *Les Raisons* to the Princess Elizabeth in 1615,

in tribute to the memory of her brother and he goes on to say: 'i'ay representé icy quelques desseins que i'ay autrefois faits, estant à son seruice, aucuns pour servir d'ornement en sa maison de Richemont, & les autres pour satisfaire a sa gentille curiosité qui desiroit touriours voir & coignoistre quelque chose nouueau'. In other words, the book is a mixture of executed designs and ones made to satisfy what Cornwallis describes as the Prince's delight 'in all Kinds of rare Inventions and Arts'.

We have already disentangled from amongst its plates designs for the giant. There is only one other, however, which must have a specifically Richmond connotation, 'Problesme XIX', a design for a simple fountain covered in Tudor roses with jets falling into an octagonal basin. This is confirmed by its appearance in de Caus's *La Perspective, avec la raison des ombres et miroirs*, which was dedicated to the Prince and published in London in 1612.[57] The others are infinitely more bizarre: a vast mountain eighty-four feet square by fifty-five high to be built in the middle of a garden which has a walkway up to its summit, on which stands a re-creation of the Alexandrian speaking statue of

58 Grotto into palace. Inigo Jones's design for the palace of Oberon in *Oberon, the Fairy Prince*, Prince Henry's masque of 1611

Memnon and within which there was an aviary and grottos; a nymph playing a hydraulic organ in a cave with an echo nearby; a tempietto for the centre of a garden or daedalus (labyrinth) with a fountain inside it; a fountain with a ball balanced on a jet of water or a fountain of Cupid.

The imagery is, however, consistent. It is of wild nature tamed by art, of the music of Orpheus subjecting the animals with harmony, of Apollo's melodies vanquishing those of Pan, of the fount of Cupid, god of Love. It is sufficient to evoke the mood of the gardens which must have related closely to the themes pursued by Jonson in the Prince's masque of 1611, *Oberon, the Fairy Prince*. In this Silenus and a band of satyrs, symbols of untamed passions, await the arrival of Oberon and his fairy attendants before the rude nature of a rocky escarpment. This subsequently parts to reveal 'a bright and glorious palace', a visual sequence evocative of a de Caus grotto but in reverse. The palace is medieval, having battlements and towers with pinnacles on the top, deliberately evocative, it seems, of early Tudor Richmond but with an appropriate overlay of details in the new style derived from Serlio. The wanton and intemperate satyrs are silenced into rendering homage to the prowess and truth embodied in the Prince of Wales and his companions, who issue from the palace to pay 'homage to the British court'. In its fusion of Tudor mythology, Spenserian fairyland and Elizabethan chivalry, together with the demands of late Renaissance classical scholarship and the new Italianate taste within the visual arts, *Oberon* is a touchstone for the world of Henry, Prince of Wales.[58] It also evokes what must have been the 'meaning' of the Richmond gardens as created by de Caus.

When Prince Henry died on 6 November 1612, that world came to an abrupt end. For those who were part of it there is no doubt that strong memories lingered, amongst which some of the gardens were present. Six years later Inigo Jones designed the scenery for Jonson's *Pleasure Reconciled to Virtue*, in which a new Prince of Wales danced. It opened as follows:

> The scene was the mountain Atlas, who had his top ending in the figure of an old man, his head and beard all hoary and frost as if his shoulders were covered with snow; the rest wood and rock.[59]

Was this perhaps a reminiscence of the great mountain giant he had seen de Caus create at Richmond? More elusive still, perhaps, is *The Tempest*, which suggests, with its magical island, its monsters and strange happenings, that Shakespeare might in one aspect have been thinking of late Mannerist garden marvels.

We know that a play called *The Tempest* was performed at court in 1611 which must have been Shakespeare's, and it was certainly acted before the Princess Elizabeth and her betrothed, the Elector Palatine, in 1612. The central figure in *The Tempest* is Prospero, the late Renaissance magus working within the tradition of Cornelius Agrippa's *Occultia philosophia*, who exercises through his powers a discipline of virtuous knowledge and practices; as Frances Yates writes, 'the high intellectual and virtuous magic'. He purges the enchanted island of evil magic and uses his magico-scientific powers to effect peace and reconciliation.[60] But *The Tempest* is also a Mannerist fantasy in the visual sense. Its figures and phenomena are just such as could be found in the royal gardens in the years when the play was written: water nymphs, the monstrous Caliban ('A man or a fish ... his fins like arms'), the 'strange shapes', simulated thunder and lightning, vanishing tables and spirits in the shape of dogs and hounds. We seem, in fact, at times, to be wandering through a garden by de Caus where we are suddenly confronted by dreamlike monsters, or entering a wild grotto to be struck suddenly, at the turn of a stopcock, with surprise and wonder at moving statues and magical music, as gods and goddesses spring to life and enact an *intermezzo*.

De Caus and the gardens of Hatfield House

De Caus's only other known major work in England was for Robert Cecil, Earl of Salisbury, who had inherited his father's passion for gardening. As a young man he had created, as we have already seen, a remarkable emblematic garden at his house at Pymms in honour of Elizabeth I, and soon after he came into Theobalds, on Lord Burghley's death, he commissioned (in 1602) a naturalistic river and stream at that place.[61] This was carried out by his gardener, Mountain Jennings, who also plays the central role in the Hatfield gardens. James I loved Theobalds and, as part of the price of being the King's first minister, Cecil handed the house over to the Crown in 1607 in exchange for, amongst other things, the old Tudor palace at Hatfield.

The building of Hatfield House, in Hertfordshire, and the laying out of its gardens took place between the years 1607 and 1612 and without doubt is the most completely documented of all Jacobean building enterprises.[62] The documentation is as complex as the changes of mind that attended the planning of both house and garden. I have tried to put together here what seems to be the history of the evolution of the garden plan but this is hampered by a total absence of contemporary descriptions or views. As a house it was never designed to be on the vast scale of Theobalds which, in its use of red brick with stone facings, it re-echoed, but, of course, from the start it was conceived as a total *mise-en-scène* fit to receive the court on one of its ceremonial summer progresses. Although the building of the house proceeded under the direction of Robert Lyming no single person, as Lawrence Stone points out, was its architect. Cecil himself supervised the building programme in all its details at every juncture, not hesitating to bring in the King's Surveyor, Simon Basil, as a consultant or, in the final stages, call on Inigo Jones to recast the south front and design the clock tower. The arrival of Jones, which was more or less to coincide with that of de Caus, indicates how sharply aware the Earl was of changes in fashion. The building story, which is one of stops and starts, sudden alterations and retrenchments, followed by bursts of extravagance, parallels exactly that of the garden.

Hatfield House still stands on the site Cecil had chosen for it in April 1607 when, attended by the earls of Suffolk, Worcester and Southampton, he visited Hatfield. It is on an eminence facing south with a magnificent façade to which an approach was made by means of a new road and an inner and outer courtyard. The approach today is from the north. Although there was a garden to the west with two banqueting houses within it, the main formal gardens were to the east where the ground fell away from the house down to a river. The east wing housed the private apartments. Evelyn wrote of it in 1643: 'the more considerable rarity besides the house (inferior to few then in England for its architecture) was the garden and vineyard, well watered and planted'.[63]

Who did the garden? Like the building it was piecemeal but undoubtedly the central figure was Cecil's Theobalds gardener, Mountain Jennings. In September 1609 he, together with Robert Bell, a London merchant and garden expert, drew up the first plans. Efforts were made to persuade a certain 'Bartholomew the gardener' to come to Hatfield but he declined on account of age, agreeing to act as a consultant. The plans of these three were submitted to Cecil in November: 'wee did determine', Bell wrote, 'of a plott to bee drawne, shewed unto my lord, which I thinke will doe very well, & after may be chaunged or alltred at my lords pleasure'.[64] This puts in a nutshell the piecemeal sequence of events. Alteration happened almost immediately, for Cecil brought in a certain Thomas Chaundler.

Although Chaundler was paid for making several plots of the gardens, without doubt his work was confined to the layout of the splendid East Garden.[65] On 7 January 1610 he was paid £15 'towards makeinge of the East Garden' and he was still working on it at the end of August 1611. The East Garden was the most important of all, and may have proceeded under Chaundler's direction for almost two years. Its plan was as follows: a terrace next to the house led down to an upper garden which, in turn, led down into a lower one. Between the two there seems to have been a fountain from which ran a stream through the garden eventually returning into the River Lea below from which the water came. These waterworks were the work of a Dutchman,

Simon Sturtevant, and were advanced far enough by May 1611 for the water to be let into the little stream and for turfing to begin.[66] The fountain was a rock upon which stood the statue of Neptune in polychrome,[67] all of which seems to have been in working order in time for James I's visit in July, for which the rock was altered no less than twice.[68]

It was the King's visit, perhaps, that led to Chaundler's dismissal, for by November de Caus had taken over the supervision of a complete reworking of the East Garden. Perhaps also, Cecil had been inspired by seeing the Frenchman's fountains at Greenwich and Somerset House. Whatever the reason, the first payments to de Caus begin on 9 November and continue until the middle of the following May when the final bill for a fountain was settled.[69] In a long letter by Cecil's man, Thomas Wilson, dated 25 November he describes de Caus's visit, wearily writing that 'Every iorney brings newe designes'. Wilson scribbles in the margin a plan of what these were to be: a new cistern to feed two new fountains in the upper garden and a large new central fountain in the lower.[70] Only the new cistern and the last of the fountains in fact proceeded and were incorporated into the existing garden arrangement. Chaundler's terracing remained, as did his fountain; also remaining were the wooden flights of steps which connected the various levels with their painted posts and rails topped by carved cups and lions holding coats of arms. The two furthest corners of the garden had pavilions with arched façades flanked by niches and these de Caus raised substantially in height. He also greatly enlarged the cistern in order to supply the new great fountain and the river was remade shallower in January 1612 to resemble the one at Lord Exeter's at Burghley House.[71]

The fountain cost £112 19s and had a marble basin carved by Garrett Jonson containing the inevitable rock upon which stood a 'figure' by Garrett Christmas,[72] painted by Rowland Buckett to resemble copper.[73] There are payments for 'leaves, snakes, fishes &c.' for both it and the river[74] and John Tradescant transported one chest and eight boxes of shells back from France.[75] There is scarcely enough for us to identify this fountain from amongst those engraved in *Les Raisons* but it must have looked something like 'Problesme XXXVII' in the first book, which is a huge rock with a reclining river god and the figure of Fame on the top, who sounded her trumpet by means of a hydraulic organ within the rock operated by solar energy.

How far did de Caus affect the design of the rest of the garden? Very little probably. Certainly it is unlikely that he had any hand in the layout of the West Garden, which was on the kitchen side. More problematic are the two features below the East Garden, the Island and the Dell. The first was formed in May 1611 when the water was let into it from the river to make the Island. The creation of the Island was part of the whole hydraulics system worked out by Sturtevant; it emanated from a force within what was referred to as the conduit grove. A planting of whitethorn, sweet-briar and osiers was well in hand in the spring of 1611 so that we can discount de Caus for the Island, a project which resembles very much Mountain Jennings's river at Theobalds in 1602. The Dell was a second, more elaborate island, almost a kind of water parterre. It is first alluded to in January 1611, when there was an estimate by Sturtevant for bringing water to it for Mountain Jennings's 'workes, and devises about the fontaynes'.[76] Surely the primitive drawing, or rather diagram, still preserved amongst the state papers is one by Jennings of the Dell?[77] Jennings was, like Thomas Chaundler, paid on several occasions for drawing up plots. This looks like one of them and is totally devoid of the sophistication of a drawing by de Caus. The Dell in this plan is a diamond-shaped island with a stream running right through the middle of it. Formal walks radiate out from a pavilion built over the central stream, the pavilion being flanked by sea-monster fountains. Most of this work went on during January 1612. The pavilion must surely be the 'standing' referred to in the accounts; it was painted in June by Buckett. The two arches, with their elaborate excrescences, which are at two of the points of the diamond, must be those for which orders were given 'to garnish the two arches in some slight maner according to a plott drawne for they are ill favored'.[78] Arbours were to be built at 'the waterworkes', which are presumably the monsters floating in the stream. Jennings's geometrical island with its pavilion floating above the waters must have been one of the most delightful of all the features of the Hatfield gardens.

The Hatfield papers preserve one other drawing which should relate to the gardens.[79] It is of a large formal garden laid out in quarters and surrounded by elaborate walks at more than one level, with balustrading and probably a central fountain with access provided by steps. The elaborate knots are directly in the manner of those in the pattern books of Thomas Trevelyon. Could this perhaps be one of Chaundler's plots, of which we know that he prepared many? Further research may one day establish the identity of this important drawing.

The planting at Hatfield was enormous and went on for over three years. This was the task of someone whose fame lay in the future, John Tradescant, who undertook journeys to Holland, Flanders and France, bringing back shiploads of rare trees, fruits, flowers, plants and seeds.[80] Tradescant was to be to Hatfield what John Gerard had been to Theobalds. The garden was to be horticulturally famous. From those who sought Cecil's favour came mighty gifts of stock: five hundred fruit trees from Marie de Medici, who also sent over two of her gardeners to supervise the planting,[81] and thirty thousand vines from Madame de la Broderie, wife of the French ambassador, for the vineyard.[82] In 1609 Lady Tresham wrote a touching letter offering fifty fruit trees from Lyveden: 'Because I think no one can furnish you with more and better trees and of a fitter growth than this ground, for my late husband, as he did take great delight, so did he come to great experience and judgement therein'.[83]

Hatfield is by no means central to de Caus's work, but it must have been heavily influenced by everything that was going on in the royal gardens at the time. The islands at Richmond and at Hatfield cannot be a coincidence. As in the case of the other gardens, new elements are being grafted onto old, much in the same way that Inigo Jones was adding porticoes in the Italian taste, lifted from Serlio, onto the front of Jacobean houses in the neo-Gothic romantic manner. The garden at Hatfield belongs to this phase. There is no unity as yet between house and garden, although there are steps in this direction. The gardens did not lie far away from the house. The formal East and West Gardens were married to their respective wings and the East with its descending terraces must have had a decidedly Italianate flavour. Each part was still, however, a separate unit, although again there were efforts to marry them by means of the river which ran through one into the other. Unlike the gardens of the royal palaces Hatfield was created from nothing, thus giving us a unique insight into garden planning in early seventeenth-century England.

Robert Cecil died on 24 May 1612 and never lived to enjoy his great house and magnificent garden. We have to wait forty years for a description, the only one with any detail, of what these marvellous gardens looked like. In 1663 they and the house were described by a visiting Frenchman, Monsieur de Sorbière:

> It stands very advantageously, from which you have a Prospect of nothing but Woods and Meadows, Hills and Dales, which are very agreeable Objects that present themselves to us at all Sorts of Distances: Our Nobility . . . would have made Use of the Waters here, for some Excellent Uses and Inventions; and more especially of a small River, which as it were forms the Compartments of a large *Parterre*, and rises and secretly loses itself in an Hundred Places, and whose Banks are all Lined or Boarded [presumably the Island and Dell]. . . . When you come through the Chief Avenue to the Park Side, and when the Gates of the lower Courts are open, there are Walks present themselves to your View, that reach to the further end of the Park, and make you lose your Sight. . . . We Dined in a Hall that looked into a Greenplot with Two Fountains in it [Chaundler's and de Caus's], and having Espaliers on the Sides, but a Balister before it, upon which are Flower-Pots and Statues: From this Pa[r]terre there is a way down by Two Pair of Stairs, of about Twelve or Fifteen Steps to another, and from the Second to the Third [this seems to be a muddled account of terrace, upper and lower garden]: From this Terrass you have a Prospect of the great Water Parterre I have spoke of [the Island and Dell]. . . . I ought not to forget the vineyard, nor the several small buildings on the side of it, some of which serve for a Retreat to several sorts of Birds, which are very tame. There are also Arbours or Summer-Houses, like *Turkish* Chiosks, upon some of the Eminences, which have a Gallery round, and are erected in the most Beautiful Places [e.g. standing in the Dell], in order to the Enjoying of the Diversified Prospects of this Charming Country: You have also in those Places, where the River enters into and comes out of the Parterre, open Sort of Boxes, with Seats round, where you may see a vast Number of Fish pass to and fro in the Water, which is exceeding clear; and they seem to come in Shoals to enjoy all the Pleasures of the Place; and quitting their own Element by jumping sometimes out of the Water, this they do as it were to observe all the things I have describ'd to you.[84]

In this description a Frenchman pays tribute to the gardens of what he defines as 'this Enchanted Castle'. Through it we are able to conjure up in the mind's eye an impression of one of the greatest of English Renaissance gardens, one of the few to survive the Civil War and live on into the Baroque age.

Hatfield, with its walled, terraced gardens falling away from the house, was new in 1612 and destined to have probably a very considerable influence on the development of a particular garden type which was to run on into the post-Restoration period. The traditional setting of the Elizabethan and Jacobean great house on a prominence lent itself naturally to an adaptation of the Italianate terrace system. For what is a reflection of the influence of Hatfield, we should study a view painted in 1662 of Massey's Court, Llanerch, in Denbighshire (now Clwyd).[85] This picture records a typical provincial Jacobean house perched on a hill with the land sloping sharply away from it down to a river at the bottom, in exactly the same way as Hatfield. The sequence is identical. It begins with a terrace with summer houses at each end.

Hatfield

*Robert Cecil's Hatfield, planted between 1607
and 1612, is the most fully documented of all
Jacobean gardens. Like the house itself, it was the
result of many influences, including that of de Caus.*

59 Design, probably by Mountain Jennings,
for the Dell, a diamond-shaped island with
formal tree-lined walks, highly decorated
wooden arches and a pavilion astride a central
stream

facing page:
60 Design for a walled garden with terraces
and probably a central fountain, possibly a
project for Hatfield

facing page, right:
61 Design for a fountain of the type de Caus
made for Hatfield from his *Les Raisons*

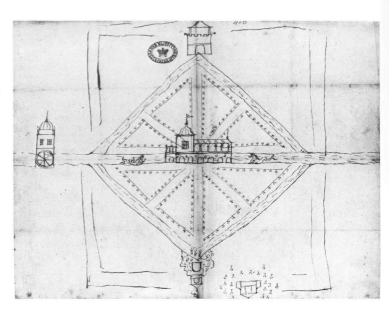

62 Aerial view of Hatfield House today. The main gardens lay to the east side of the house,
where the land was terraced and then sloped down to the Island and the Dell. The
present terracing is a Victorian echo of the original Jacobean arrangement.

63 A garden in the manner of Hatfield: Massey's Court, Llanerch, in 1662. The Jacobean manor house has two terraced gardens falling away from one side of the house down to a river. An ornamental effect is achieved in the same way as at Hatfield.

In the centre is a double curved staircase around a grotto with Mercury on the top of it; this is certainly a later introduction in the manner of the engravings in Falda's *Fontane*. The staircase leads to the upper part of the formal garden, of which the walls are covered with espaliered fruit trees, and which in its turn leads down by two flights of steps to a lower part with wooden arbours in the corners, a fountain and a Jacobean stone-built gazebo. This opens out to other elaborations, an Italianate double staircase which leads to a formally planted wilderness with a tiny grotto and cascade beyond, and a circular amphitheatre with a fountain of Neptune enclosed by hedges and cypress trees. Beyond this the path continues to the river over which there are pretty painted bridges. In spite of the overlay of Caroline and later details the layout is basically Jacobean and must capture exactly in miniature that of its grander progenitor, Hatfield.

De Caus: Heidelberg and after

The remainder of Salomon de Caus's career was spent on the Continent, in Germany and France. In July 1614 he was officially appointed engineer and architect to the Elector Palatine. During the years up to the outbreak of the Thirty Years War he created his most famous garden, the Hortus Palatinus.

The Hortus Palatinus belongs in a sense to the history of garden design in England because it shows us what a complete de Caus garden actually looked like. It was, in one sense, Richmond transported from the banks of the Thames to those of the Rhine. That this was so is reinforced by the fact that the court under Frederick and James I's daughter, Elizabeth, retained the ethos and intellectual preoccupations of Prince Henry's circle.[86] As a garden design de Caus's Hortus Palatinus[87] draws, in particular, on his knowledge of the Villa d'Este, for the hillside outside the castle was blasted away to build a spectacular series of terraces connected by flights of steps. And, as in the case of his work in England other than Hatfield, there was no chance of relating house and garden in the complete Italian style. The garden is monumental in concept and executed in the grand manner but it remains essentially a collection of separate entities and these run through the entire de Caus repertory. There are knots and parterres in the usual French style and ones in the new embroidered fashion. There is a river god fountain and an aviary on the lines of Greenwich, an orangery as at Somerset House, a Pratolino-style grotto, a water parterre in the manner of St Germain-en-Laye, a speaking statue of Hercules–Memnon directly derived from Hero of Alexandria. Detailed research would establish also that it was the vehicle for an allegorical programme. In its time the garden was one of the wonders of the civilized world. De Caus never quite completed it, owing to the outbreak of hostilities and in the war that followed the garden was to be devastated beyond recall. De Caus left for France where he passed the last six years of his life and became engineer to the young Louis XIII. He was buried, in his fiftieth year, on 28 February 1626 in the Protestant cemetery of the Eglise de la Trinité.

Twenty years earlier he had been married in a Catholic church in Brussels. Does this suggest some form of religious ambiguity? Perhaps it gives us some sort of clue by which we can place de Caus in the context of developments within the arts during the opening two decades of the seventeenth century. Although religion was central to his make-up the exact outward form that it took may have been less so. On this we can only speculate but de Caus belongs firmly to that group of savants whose exploration of the natural phenomena of the physical world was dedicated to leading to a knowledge of the divine. He is one of that generation which had grown up in a period of extreme religious intolerance, which had witnessed the demise of the old world picture, but which now, through an intense analysis of the visible universe, hoped to re-establish a new order of things. With the outbreak of the Thirty Years War hopes for a return to the unity of the Old Europe were to be forever shattered.

De Caus had immense influence through his numerous publications. The earliest of these, as already mentioned, appeared in England, *La Perspective, avec la raison des ombres et miroirs* (1612), dedicated to Henry, Prince of Wales. In it he casts himself decisively, as he does in all his works, as a Renaissance architect–engineer, whose sphere of activity spanned not only building (he built a picture gallery for Henry at Richmond[88] and a wing at Heidelberg for the Elector Frederick) but also the study of music, geometry, mathematics, perspective, painting, science, mechanics and hydraulics. *La Perspective* is the earliest full–length treatise to appear in England on perspective and included a plate depicting a garden, revealing that de Caus was at least thinking in terms of optics in relation to his garden designs.

His next work, *Les Raisons des forces mouvantes*, which appeared in 1615, with a German edition in 1620 and a French one in 1624, was dedicated to Elizabeth of Bohemia and later partly to Louis XIII. It opens with a definition of what a machine is, based on Vitruvius, and goes on to cite the Bible, Archimedes, Diodorus Siculus and Hero of Alexandria on the effects of air and water in the making of moving machines and automata. He next places himself in a line of descent which includes Dürer, Michelangelo, Raphael, Ramus, Besson and Ramelli. The first book then follows as a series of *problesmes* which demonstrate the basic principles of hydraulics. One of these is justly famous for it includes

64 The Hortus Palatinus. De Caus's most celebrated garden, attached to the castle at Heidelberg; laid out 1613–19

the earliest exposition of the steam engine, marking de Caus as a precursor of the Industrial Revolution. After this come the grottos and fountains.

Institution harmonique (1615) was dedicated to Anne of Denmark and is a typical exposition, derived from Zarlino, of the Renaissance belief in music as the chief of the sciences because it had its basis in number. In particular it deals with the construction of a water organ as described by Vitruvius and as reconstructed at the Villa d'Este and St Germain-en-Laye. In 1624 he produced a book on sun-dials, another subject of intense interest during this period, *La Pratique et demonstration des horloges solaires*, and at the same time he was engaged on a translation of the first book of Vitruvius into French; the translation still exists in manuscript.

De Caus in context   De Caus was not a unique phenomenon at the Jacobean court. Robert Fludd, the philosopher, was a similar, if only armchair, magical technologist, whose works, taking up from those of the great Elizabethan magus, John Dee, deal extensively with machines and mechanical devices of the Alexandrian School.[89] So, too, was another figure, Cornelius Drebbel, who presented James I with a famous perpetual motion machine which became one of the sights of the day, but whose inventions included things as varied as forerunners of the submarine and the magic lantern.[90] The Mannerist courts took a deep interest in all forms of technical advance.

All this is essential for grasping just how complex the new garden development was in the opening decade of James I's reign. The Mannerist garden revolution has many threads to it, of which only one was the introduction of new forms and layouts as they had been developed first in Italy and later in France. To de Caus and his generation, the garden was an expression of something much more profound. It became in one aspect the demonstration laboratory of the Renaissance architect–engineer. These waterworks, grottos, automata, canals and curiosities demanded an immense advance in technical ingenuity. Out of that came a second stage when it was all integrated in the form of abstract scientific concepts and principles. So when we walk in a de Caus garden we are strolling in an atmosphere of magic and nascent science, at that brief moment when it seemed that through these technical triumphs anything was possible. The plashing fountains, the chirping birds, the ordered walks, the geometric parterres, the exotic plants and the menageries of the Mannerist garden spoke of an effort to re-establish the unity of Europe. These gardens were created above all at courts which looked to a middle way against the polarized extremes: the Medici Grand Dukes, Rudolf II, Henry IV and James I. All, regardless of religious belief, could share in the mysteries of art and nature which seemed through occultism, a belief in the spirit world and the triumph of machines, about to reveal some new universal order of things.[91] The development of elaborate gardens around the palace and the great house was a manifestation of this desire to create a tangible encyclopaedia of the visible world. And yet within its component parts were all the tensions of the age. It was at the same time practically scientific and technical but also magical and hermetic. The new machines harnessed the magical properties of nature to startling effect and yet that effect was unfolded in the form of symbolic images. In this way de Caus partakes of the nature of a late Renaissance magus.

CHAPTER V

THE MANNERIST GARDEN II
Francis Bacon and others

Simultaneously with Somerset House, Greenwich, Richmond and Hatfield there was an unprecedented creation of new gardens during the Jacobean period. This craze for the elaboration and extension in size of the garden is vividly reflected in the anonymous *Masque of Flowers* presented by Gray's Inn at court on Twelfth Night 1614, in honour of the marriage of the King's favourite, Somerset, to the notorious Frances Howard.[1] The masquers came as flowers and the setting was a garden surrounded by a brick wall with espaliered fruit trees, within which there was balustrading on the lines of Hatfield with pedestals topped by 'personages of gold, lions of gold, and unicorns of silver'. The garden itself was

> . . . cast into four quarters, with a cross-walk and alleys compassing each quarter. In the middle of the cross-walk stood a goodly fountain raised on four columns of silver; on the tops whereof stood four statues of silver, which supported a bowl, in circuit containing four and twenty foot, and was raised from the ground nine foot in height; in the middle whereof, upon scrolls of silver and gold, was placed a globe garnished with four gold mask-heads, out of which issued water into the bowl; above stood a golden Neptune, in height three foot, holding in his hand a trident, and riding on a dolphin so cunningly framed that a river seemed to stream from his mouth.[2]

The quarters were bordered with a hedge of cypress and juniper and laid out in knots with herbs. In the two nearest the audience stood obelisks in the manner of Kenilworth, in the two others were tulips.

At the back was an elaborate mount with an arbour of honeysuckle and eglantine on top of it. It was thirty-three feet long and twenty-one feet high, adorned with turrets and faced with arcading which revealed the flower masquers in embroidered costumes. Spring, evoked by the sunshine of monarchy in the midst of winter, is the masque's symbolic message:

> *Flowers of honour, Flowers of beauty*
> *Are your own; we only bring*
> *Flowers of affection, Flowers of duty.*[3]

In this way the garden was presented not only as a new ideal of aristocratic life but also as a symbol of the King's peace.

At this point we must turn to examine in greater detail other aspects of the Jacobean garden mania. That it was such is caught in the report on England of a Venetian in 1618, in which he describes what he thought were the country's salient features of garden layout and design.

65 Unknown lady of the
Hampden family
(*c.* 1610–15), standing on
the terrace of a walled
garden. The balustrading
is wooden while below,
the garden is laid out in
knots.

What struck me as worthy of note is the mode of varying the plan of the gardens and even of the orchards. Thus for instance, in the midst of a large space they raise a circular mound four feet high, placing a column in its centre for the sundial. From this mound four walks diverge cross wise, terminating so as to form a square. They are made to slope, the sods being covered with very close grass. The walks at the end are beautifully laid out and one ascends to them by wooden stairs adorned with pyramids and balls on the balustrades all around. Sometimes they make the steps of turf, surrounding the walks and the space with privet or thorns or any other plant, in lieu of the balustrade. Others merely make a raised walk all around the square, serving as a causeway, and ornamenting it in one of the ways mentioned above. Walking on this terrace one has a good view of the general arrangement, the fountains and all the designs.[4]

This is basically the same as the garden in the *Masque of Flowers* and the same as that to be seen in the portrait of an exotic lady beneath an emblematic palm tree. She stands on a terrace with wooden balustrading behind her. These gardens can also be equated with those of Oxford and Cambridge colleges as engraved by Loggan in the 1670s, both universities being notoriously conservative in the arts. Sidney Sussex, Cambridge, and Wadham, Oxford, match the Venetian's description exactly.[5] New College, Oxford, is the garden of the *Masque of Flowers*, although the mount was completed in the 1640s.[6] Terracing is one of the most important developments during the Jacobean period – the introduction of raised walks surrounding the garden on all or nearly all sides. This feature is accompanied by two others whose resolution was of extreme importance for the future, namely the increasing desire to marry house and garden as a single unit and the move towards bolder and more monumental planning of the whole.

There are, in addition, other major developments which we need to study: the geometric, symbolic garden and the use of water. Both are typical expressions of the esoteric Mannerist mind, the deployment of the garden as a vehicle for allegorical exposition and the obsession with the control of water for extraordinary artificial effects. In short, in this chapter we shall be going on to investigate the elements of the Mannerist garden already examined in the work of Salomon de Caus, as they were taken up and adapted by other members of the court.

Garden plans in the Smythson drawings

The Smythson drawings, which included the early plan of the Somerset House garden, contain further garden plans which directly reflect these developments. The first is that of Edward Somerset, 4th Earl of Worcester, for his house at Nonsuch in his capacity as Keeper of the Great Park and made by Robert Smythson probably during his London visit of 1609.[7] Worcester had succeeded Elizabeth's favourite Essex as her last Master of the Horse and in the new reign rose to greater heights. He was appointed Earl Marshal for the coronation, for James I's state entry into London in 1604, for the christening of the princess Mary in 1605 and for the creation of Henry as Prince of Wales in 1610. He was expert in all matters of court ceremonial and in his private capacity had remodelled Raglan Castle on the Welsh Borders to conform with contemporary taste, a remodelling which included a walk beneath the walls lined with busts of Roman emperors.[8] Worcester Lodge is therefore in the latest fashion, following directly the arrangement at Somerset House, a large walled enclosure 180 feet square with raised walks on three sides 20 feet in

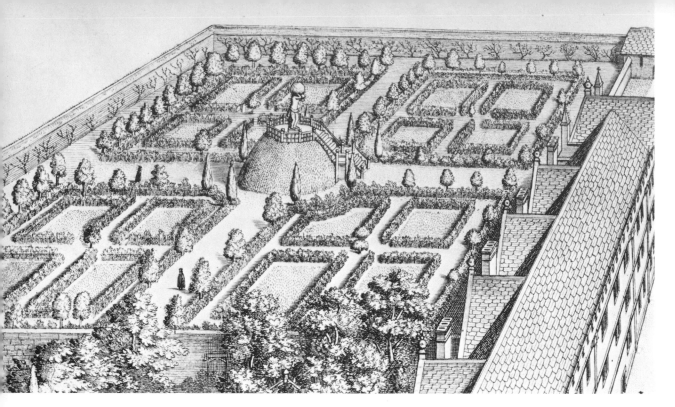

Oxford college gardens   *These, as recorded by David Loggan in the 1670s, were Jacobean in style.*

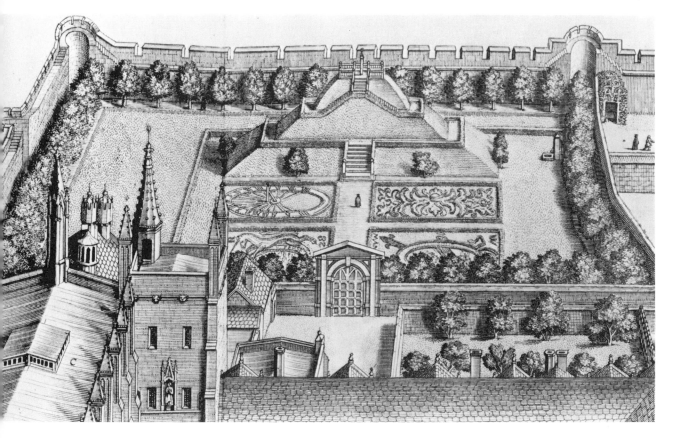

width, the one nearest the house being lower. The placing of the garden, however, bears no relationship to the architecture of the house. The walks are set with fruit trees and short flights of steps lead down to the lower walks encompassing flower-beds boldly laid out in a quatrefoil pattern.

The second plan is of Sir Thomas Vavasour's Ham House at Petersham near Richmond.[9] Vavasour was a soldier, a courtier and 'a person very agreeable to her Majesty'. Under Elizabeth he had been a Gentleman Pensioner, taking part in all the ceremonial tilts in her honour each Accession Day. He became James I's Knight Marshal, another ceremonial role, and built Ham House in 1610.[10] Although Smythson gives no plan for the Principal Garden to the left of the Inner Court, he provides striking information about the orchard and gardens at the rear. Here again there are raised terraces, the main one across the façade 436 feet in length, dividing the space into three areas, two gardens and a central orchard. Of these, by far the most important from our point of view is the orchard, which has a central axis and walk based on the house. Two oval circles of trees form the centre, followed by two hexagonal ones with triangles in the spandrels. This planning of a broad central parterre or wilderness or orchard with oval or circular plantings of trees intersected by walks and flanked by smaller rectangular gardens could only come from a knowledge of Claude Mollet's St Germain-en-Laye.

Even more than at Somerset House, which has some indications of an attempt to relate the building and garden, the relationship between house and garden is emphatically made in terms of actual planning and optical effect. And this is new. The eye could look either way, to or from the back of the house down an avenue of fruit trees through what can only have been designed to be a perspective effect. The flower-beds are banished to one side and do not occupy the position that was normally theirs, beneath the windows of the house. Smythson's plan of Ham is the first instance we have of house and garden integrated geometrically as one. That this was possible was due to the fact that, unlike Somerset House, both house and garden were new.

Ham House is closely related to the garden arrangement of Northampton House in the Strand, built by Henry Howard, Earl of Northampton, between 1605 and 1609.[11] This has a long rectangular garden which in its arrangement anticipates by a decade the Chelsea garden of Sir John Danvers, which John Aubrey cites as the earliest one in the Italian manner. Northampton is supposed to have travelled in Italy in the eighties. The garden is exactly the width of the façade of the house. It has a terrace with steps leading down, and a broad central avenue leading to another flight of steps up to a riverside terrace. The squares flanking the walk look as though they were typically Elizabethan knots. There is an absence of statuary or fountains but the overall arrangement looks forward to a whole series of Italianate gardens in the thirties. In its perspective axial treatment it is exactly contemporary with Ham and both exhibit the architectural relationship between house and garden last used at Wollaton a generation before.

One other house comes into this group so definitely concerned with the union of house and garden: a drawing of a ground-plan by John Thorpe for Sir William Rigdon of Dowsby, Lincolnshire.[12] More even than Northampton House this recalls Wollaton in its totally symmetrical layout, in which house and garden are conceived as a complete square divided into sixteen equal

66 Wadham College. A garden cast into quarters with a mount in the centre

67 New College. A garden cast into quarters with knots laid out in the form of the royal and college arms and a sundial with a large mount at one end

units. On it is the inscription 'nothing out of square' and this is the only instance where the draughtsman has gone on to indicate the patterns of the knots and trees in the orchards. The planting is again old-fashioned. Sir William was knighted in 1603 and died in 1610, which presumably dates the drawing and the building of Dowsby Hall. All three drawings indicate an increasing concern with marrying house and garden as a totality during the opening decade of the seventeenth century.

The final drawing is later in date and by Robert's son John Smythson. It is of the new orchard planted by Sir Percival Willoughby at Wollaton in 1618.[13] There is no plan of the house with this drawing so that it is impossible to know whether the two were closely related or not. The garden entailed the creation of a vast terrace over 450 feet in length with steps down at each end leading to walks laid out in the same broad format as Worcester Lodge and Ham but with a fountain or mount in the centre.

These gardens must certainly have been heavily influenced by what was going on in the royal palaces under de Caus's direction during the vital years 1609–12. The adoption of terrace walks looking down onto formal parterres is unanimous, as is the breadth of the scale of the planting. The garden is no longer a series of isolated enclosures dotted at random and fenced around. Planning is bolder, grander and more monumental, although it is still to a degree piecemeal. There is a definite stirring of an intention to relate house and garden as a unit and this contains the seeds of a revolutionary attitude. Above all there is a realisation of the nature of the laws of perspective.

The Jacobean garden was an artifice based on the cultivation of nature according to, amongst other things, prevailing optical principles. That radiating walks and vistas begin to appear at the same time as single point perspective on the stage in England cannot be a coincidence. Inigo Jones's stage sets, which in 1605 in the *Masque of Blackness* first used Renaissance scientific perspective with a seascape which caught the eye from afar with 'a wandering beauty', are the touchstone for what was simultaneously happening in all the visual arts in early Jacobean England, namely the birth of pictorial space in the Renaissance sense of the word. That de Caus's own first book dedicated to Henry, Prince of Wales, was on perspective, *La Perspective, avec la raison des ombres et miroirs*, is symptomatic of this. As in gardening, perspective arrives by fits and starts in the masques. Jones was initially concerned with creating moving emblematic tableaux. Perspective was employed in these pre-Italian years to strengthen the myth and fable and less as an optical doctrine in itself. It was used to give added power to the allegory unfolding on stage, deliberately controlling the eye and leading it to contemplate some new platonic mystery, above all that embodied in the figures of queen, prince and great ones of the court revealed as the stars, seasons, signs of the zodiac or other heroic exemplars. The situation is exactly the same when applied to the garden. Here, too, perspective arrives hesitantly.[14] It is not as yet a principle from which to work but a 'device' to be used for occasional optical effect, to enhance the grandeur of a house, as in the case of Ham. This combination, however, of breadth of composition, the linking of house and garden in planning and the new set of optical principles based on Renaissance single point perspective was ultimately to lead in the second half of the century to the Baroque gardens of Chatsworth, Bretby or Badminton.

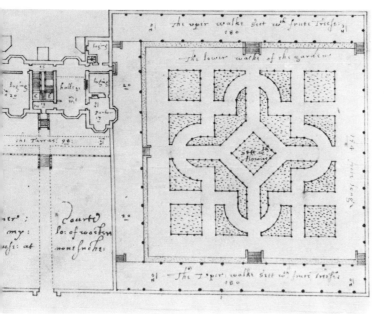

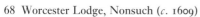

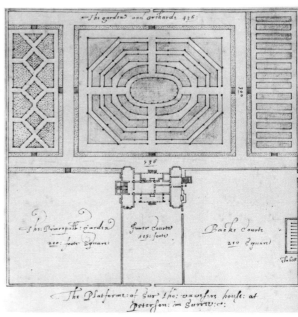

68 Worcester Lodge, Nonsuch (*c.* 1609)

69 Ham House, Petersham (*c.* 1609)

Four Jacobean garden plans

All four record the enormous growth in scale of gardens during the opening decade of the 17th century.

70 Dowsby, Lincolnshire (*c.* 1603–10)

71 Northampton House, London (*c.* 1609)

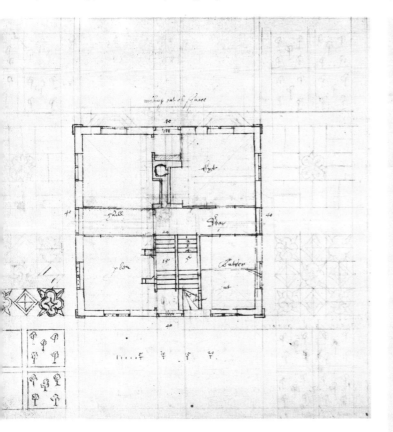

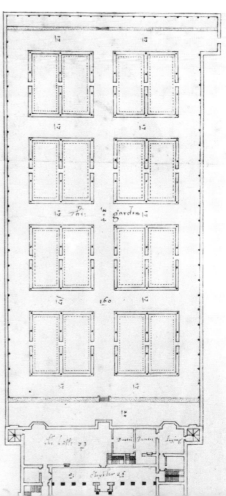

Amongst the great ladies who sat in tableau in Jones's evocation of a grotto by de Caus, one was missing, Lucy Harington, Countess of Bedford. Lady Bedford had appeared in all the Queen's masques prior to 'Tethys Festival' and was aptly described by Lady Anne Clifford as 'so great a woman with the queen, as that everybody much respected her'.[15] She was also a great gardener. And in the same year that de Caus was working on Greenwich and Somerset House, Lady Bedford was busy creating the first of her two celebrated gardens, that at Twickenham Park, just north of Hampton Court.

Lucy Harington was both a cultivated and an extravagant woman. As the eventual sole heiress of Sir John Harington of Exton she was immensely rich in her own right. To this she was able to add the rank of a countess by dint of her marriage to Edward Russell, 3rd Earl of Bedford, in 1594. The Earl, in marked contrast to his wife, had no taste for public life and after a disastrous fall from his horse retired altogether from court to live a life of solitude. Lady Bedford, however, was both lively and ambitious and became the centre of a circle of poets and men of letters that included Samuel Daniel, John Donne, Michael Drayton, Thomas May and Ben Jonson. Donne records reading his poems to her in the garden at Twickenham and indeed one of his *Songs and Sonnets* is entitled 'Twickenham Park', in which the young lovelorn poet seeks the solace of her garden:

> *Blasted with sighs, and surrounded with tears,*
> *Hither I come to seek the spring,*
> *And at mine eyes, and at mine ears,*
> *Receive such balms, as else cure everything . . .*[16]

That Lucy Harington was also in the vanguard of visual taste we know from a letter by Sir Thomas Roe, who speaks of her knowledge of antique medals.[17] She also had a passion for collecting pictures. In 1617 she described herself as 'a very diligent gatherer of all I can get of Holbein's or any other excellent master's hand'.[18]

Twickenham Park had been let in 1594 on a twenty-one-year lease to Francis Bacon who, 'found the situation of that place much convenient for the trial of my philosophical conclusions'.[19] Twelve years later Bacon was forced to sell it to Lucy Harington, who lived there until 1618, planting the garden which Robert Smythson records, probably on his visit to London in 1609. The garden is 321 feet square, bounded at its perimeter by a wall. Within this it is encompassed by a series of hedges: an outer one of quickthorn, one of 'trees cut into Beastes', a third of rosemary and a fourth of fruit trees. Set into this enclosure there is what on first glance would seem to be a daedalus on the lines of the oft-printed plan which appears in the numerous works of Thomas Hill. But Hill's daedalus can never have been on this scale as his was to be planted with thyme or hyssop whereas Lady Bedford's is of trees and walks with mounts in the spandrels. It is also not a maze: paths lead in and out of it from four sides. In the middle there is a circle, probably of grass (Smythson does not indicate what), followed by concentric circles, three of birch and two of lime with an outer circle of fruit trees. Flights of steps at each of the corners lead up to what must have been raised vantage-points planted with trees, perhaps even topped by pavilions, though these are not indicated. From these the visitor was able to contemplate this extraordinary plan, for Lucy Harington's garden is

Two geometric
gardens

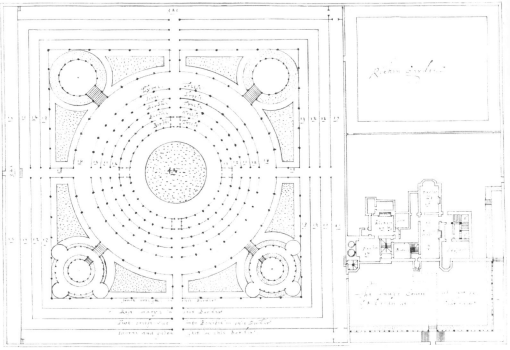

72 Plan of the Countess of Bedford's garden at Twickenham Park (*c.* 1609). The garden dwarfs the house, being laid out in circles based on the plan of the pre-Copernican universe inset into a series of squares. In the spandrels, steps lead up mounts probably to banqueting or summer houses.

73 Pre-Copernican universe showing the Earth in the centre encompassed by the spheres of the planets

74 The garden of Chastleton House, originally created *c.* 1602–14, was replanted in 1828. It nonetheless seems to have preserved elements of its Mannerist geometry.

surely an emblematic one based on the familiar plan of the pre-Copernican universe, the circle in the centre being Earth followed by Luna, Mercury and Venus (birch circles), Sol and Mars (lime circles), Jove (fruit trees circle) and Saturn (beyond). That such an interpretation is not too fanciful is confirmed by similar celestial configurations in the gardens of Rudolf II in Prague as described by Fynes Moryson:

> the trees are planted in the figure of starres, and a little faire house therein is likewise built, with six corners in forme of a starre.[20]

In this way the Twickenham garden reflected admirably its creator, whom Jonson hailed as the 'brightness of our sphere', for she literally reigned over one.[21]

The garden at Twickenham Park, as Mark Girouard has observed, is reminiscent of a surviving garden whose original layout is of the same date. Chastleton House in Oxfordshire was built by Walter Jones, a rich wool merchant from Witney, on land purchased from one of the Gunpowder Plot conspirators in 1602.[22] The house was finished in 1614 and the garden is an enclosure, almost square (170 feet by 145), and placed to one side of the house in exactly the same manner as Twickenham and Worcester Lodge. Today it centres on a sun-dial encircled by rose beds, twenty-four whimsical topiary figures in box, a circular yew hedge with entrances at the cross axes and further flower-beds beyond. The shapes could be a distant reflection of the original layout as the house was an extremely conservative one, the family being royalist and then Jacobite. No one knows the precise date of the present planting although Inigo Triggs states that there was a replanting in 1828 on the lines of an earlier arrangement. This seems highly likely although the garden is also reflective of the Romantic movement's revival of the formal garden and the cult of 'The Mansions of England in the Olden Time'. What strikes the visitor as right is not the planting but the geometry. At Chastleton we are as near as we can get to a surviving geometrical Mannerist garden from the Jacobean age.

Twickenham relates to yet another garden, a forgotten one, about which we know even less. It is the one created by William Herbert, 3rd Earl of Pembroke, at Wilton, near Salisbury, in Wiltshire. In 1623 John Taylor, the Water Poet, paid a visit and left the following account:

> Amongst the rest, the pains and industry of an ancient gentleman, Mr. Adrian Gilbert, must not be forgotten: for there he (much to my Lord's cost and his own pains) used such a deal of intricate setting, grafting, planting, inoculating, railing, hedging, plashing, turning, winding, returning, circular, triangular, quadrangular, orbicular, oval, and every way curiously and chargeably conceited: there hath he made walks, hedges and arbours, of all manner of most delicate fruit trees, planting them and placing them in such admirable art-like fashions, resembling both divine and moral remembrances, as three arbours standing in a triangle, having each a recourse to a greater arbour in the midst, resemble three in one and one in three; and he hath there planted certain walks and arbours all with fruit trees, so pleasing and ravishing to the sense, that he calls it 'Paradise', in which he plays the part of a true Adamist, continually toiling and tilling.
>
> Moreover, he hath made his walks most rarely round and spaceous, one walk without another (as the rinds of an onion are greatest without, and less towards the centre), and withal the hedges betwixt each walk are so thickly set one cannot see through from one walk who walks in the other; that, in conclusion, the work seems

endless; and I think that in England it is not to be followed, or in haste will be followed.[23]

Taylor is telling us that prior to the even more celebrated garden created by the Earl's brother in the 1630s there was a famous Jacobean garden at Wilton of a heavily geometric and symbolic nature.

William Herbert, Earl of Pembroke, inherited Wilton in 1601 and married Mary Talbot, daughter of the 7th Earl of Shrewsbury, three years later. John Aubrey hailed him as 'the greatest Maecenas to learned men of any of his time or since' and with Pembroke we find ourselves back again in the world of literary patronage, of George Herbert, Samuel Daniel (who was his tutor), Philip Massinger and Ben Jonson. He also found favour with James I, who visited Wilton twice, in 1620 and 1623. Pembroke, like Lucy Harington, was learned and literary and the garden description (for we have no plan) sounds very much of the Twickenham Park type. Taylor makes it clear that it was geometrical and emblematic with references to circles, triangles, quadrangles, orbs and ovals in which it was possible to read 'both divine and moral remembrances'. Of these he cites two. One is an arbour emblematic of the Trinity, a diagrammatic arrangement in garden terms similar to the Triangular Lodge at Rushton or Longford Castle, both buildings based on a symbolic exposition of the Trinity.[24] The second was an arrangement of a great circular walk or labyrinth with high hedges which gradually led to the centre, though what to we are not told.

Perhaps the best clue as to how Pembroke's symbolic garden would have been viewed at the time is the geometrical patterns of dances in court masques and in the French *ballet de cour*. The famous *Balet Comique de la Reyne*, performed at the French court in 1581, had as its climax a grand ballet of no fewer than forty symbolic geometrical figures. In 1610 a ballet danced the 'alphabet of the ancient Druids' in which, for example, a square within a square meant Virtuous Design or three tangential circles The Truth Known.[25] In the case of Wilton it would have been a personal iconographical programme based on symbolic geometry.

Another symbolic garden created during the same period was that of Sir Henry Fanshawe at Ware Park in Hertfordshire. Sir Henry was 'the favourite of Prince Henry' and equipped with all those attributes we associate with the early Stuart gentleman virtuoso: a collector of pictures, prints, drawings, medals, engraved stones, books and musical instruments, besides being proficient in the Italian tongue and in the equestrian arts. He was 'as handsome and as fine a gentleman as England then had'.[26] Fanshawe came into Ware Park on the death of his father in 1601. Five years later work began on the garden. John Chamberlain, the letter writer, gives a lively description of its creation in October 1606:

> . . . for the new garden is wholy translated, new levelled, and in a manner transplanted, because most of the first trees were dead with being set too deep, and in the middest of yt, in steede of a knot he is making a fort, in perfect proportion, with his rampars, bulwarkes, counterscarpes, and all other appertenances, so that when yt is finished, yt is like to prove an invincible peece of work.[27]

The garden plan based on fortifications was not unique. Andrew Marvell's description of the gardens laid out by Sir Thomas Fairfax (d. 1599) at Appleton

House suggests that they were on the same theme:

> *Who, when retired here to Peace,*
> *His warlike studies would not cease;*
> *But laid these Gardens out in sport*
> *In the just Figure of a Fort;*
> *And with five Bastions it did fence,*
> *As aiming one for ev'ry Sense.*[28]

What was the significance of Sir Henry Fanshawe's garden? It could have been, like Sir Thomas Fairfax's, apparently symbolic of the five senses, but it could have been, like Lucy Harington's, of cosmological significance. The most popular form of Renaissance fort was a five-pointed star which one scholar has argued, citing Cornelius Agrippa's *Occulta philosophia*, was taken up 'for magical reasons or as homage to the mystical or Pythagorean "perfection" of the pentagram'.[29] That this should be the motivating reason for the shape of sixteenth-century fortresses and citadels seems highly unlikely but transported into a garden in miniature it would surely take on a symbolic role beyond that of being a mere conceit. Sir Henry Fanshawe's garden clearly had a meaning although what it was, devoid as we are of either views or plans, must remain forever elusive.

Seven years later there had been a change of plan. Again the irascible Chamberlain is our source. On 1 August 1613 he wrote from Ware Park:

> where I am as yt were planted for this vocation, and where we are busied about new workes, and bringing of waters into the gardens, which have succeded so well that we have a fine fountaine with a pond in the lower garden where the fort was, (yf you remember the place) and a running streame (from the river) in the upper garden, between the knotts and the rancks of trees in the brode walke or alley, wherein we hope to have plentie of troutes fed by hand; these workes with industrie and cost are brought almost to perfection, and when they are well and come to the highest, I wold there might be an end, for els there is no end of new inventions: for hither came yesterday, Signor Fabritio . . . and as he is ignorant in nothing, so he takes upon him to propound many new devices, and wold faine be a director where there is no need of his helpe.[30]

The interfering Signor Fabritio was Sir Henry Wotton, twice ambassador to Venice and a virtuoso in the arts. Wotton in his *The Elements of Architecture* describes how Fanshawe graduated the colours of the flowers so that the darkest would always be in the centre of any bed, lightening gradually outwards.[31] More to the point, by 1613 the whole garden had been altered away from the conceit of a fort into one devised in terms of water; this must surely be a direct reflection of de Caus's work for the royal palaces but perhaps, also, of the fountains and streams of nearby Hatfield. Ware Park was, in its brief heyday, a famous garden. Camden sings its praises: 'none excelling it in flowers, physic herbs and fruit'.[32] Three years later Fanshawe died at the age of forty-eight and we hear no more of the garden.

All these Jacobean gardens so far indicate that between *c*. 1600 and *c*. 1620 there was an immense fashion for the large-scale geometric garden, often laid out with deliberate symbolic intent. Ware Park, however, catches something else, the abandonment of this in favour of the introduction of sizeable, elaborate water effects. The development in the use of water is one of the most striking features in garden making in the years leading up to 1642. And it is to this that we must now turn our attention.

Ponds, rivers and islands: Francis Bacon's Gorhambury

Fanshawe's Ware Park, Cecil's Hatfield and Prince Henry's Richmond belong also to this development in the use of water for large-scale naturalistic effects such as artificial rivers, streams, lakes and islands, which is such a marked characteristic of the opening decade of James I's reign. For this handling of water on a massive scale we shall have to pursue our enquiry back in time.

The use of water within a garden as part of the *jardin de plaisir*, apart from the fountain, has its roots necessarily in the moat and the fish-pond or a combination of both. These were inheritances, from the Middle Ages, part of the scheme of the medieval house guaranteeing protection and a source of fish in particular for the observance of Lent. We have already discussed the French use of canals in gardens and their appearance as a feature of Burghley's planning of the formal gardens at Theobalds, but water on a larger scale has a slightly different history. We start within the context of its use in Elizabethan court festivals. The moat becomes a setting for spectacle and drama and therefore, by implication, is something other than a purely utilitarian feature. Perhaps the earliest example of this occurs in the 'Princely Pleasures of Kenilworth' in 1575, when Leicester dazzled Elizabeth and her court with his lavish entertainment. In this instance the castle moat became the home of the Lady of the Lake. As Elizabeth, returning from the chase, crossed over the castle bridge, a triton appeared on the waters sounding his trump and haranguing the Queen on the sad fate of the Lady who, because she had imprisoned Merlin beneath a huge rock, was vengefully pursued by the wicked Sir Bruse sans Pitie. Through Neptune's benign intervention she had been environed with waves where she would remain until, fulfilling Merlin's prophecy, she was rescued by 'a better maid than herself'. At this point, inevitably, the Lady and her nymphs floated across the moat to pay homage and Arion sang astride a dolphin's back.[33]

The next spectacular use of water comes sixteen years later. Instead of a moat or fish-pond being overlaid by drama, a lake was deliberately dug to receive it. The famous Elvetham entertainment given by Lord Hertford in September 1591 belongs to the history of the development of the pleasure garden as much as it does to that of the court masque.[34] For the second day's entertainment a vast crescent-moon-shaped lake set with islands had been excavated in the park. We have an illustration of this lake and it is interesting to contemplate that here we are looking at perhaps the source in British landscape gardening from which were ultimately to stem the conceptions of Capability Brown. Thus the lake has its birth within the thought context of the Elizabethan emblematic garden. Elizabeth is the moon goddess, Cynthia, Diana or Belphoebe, who rules over this watery empire. Its shape

> *. . . figures the rich increase*
> *Of all that sweet* Eliza *holdeth deare.*

It is symbolic of Elizabeth in the post-Armada era, when prophets and seers hailed her with messianic fervour as being destined to world domination. Within this lake were three islands: one with trees on it arrayed like ships' masts, a second on which stood a fort built by Neptune in defence of England,

and the third a huge mount forty feet in diameter and twenty feet high, in which the circles of privet ascending it assumed the guise of

> *Yon ugly monster creeping from the South,*
> *To spoyle these blessed fields of Albion . . .*

In other words the monster was the might of Catholic Spain and the papacy. This *mise-en-scène* became the setting for an elaborate little drama in which Elizabeth's naval war against Spain was prophesied to come to a victorious conclusion, a theme carried to its end on the following evening when the lake became the setting for a great firework display in which Neptune's fort vanquished the wicked monster mount.

Elvetham was a deliberately created lake conceived in emblematic terms. Before we take this theme further we should pause and examine its most likely roots. And these are, of course, on the other side of the Channel. It was at Fontainebleau in 1564 that that most French feature of the garden, the canal, was used as a setting for a little drama by Ronsard, when King Charles IX was met by sirens singing of the golden age he was about to bring the war-scarred country. Later Neptune appeared riding along the canal on a chariot drawn by four sea-horses and a nymph was seen on a rock.[35] As in the case of Kenilworth but a decade earlier it used an existing water feature as a setting for a spectacle cast in symbolic terms.

At Bayonne on the Franco-Spanish frontier the following year, the water festival was developed to its most elaborate pitch. On this occasion the entertainment made use of an island reached by canals. The court voyaged to it in fantastic boats, viewing *en route* a series of incidents: an attack on a whale, musicians dressed as tritons floating on the back of a sea-tortoise, Neptune as at Fontainebleau coming to pay homage and Arion, along with the inevitable sirens. On landing, the voyagers were greeted by dancers as shepherds attired in the costumes of the provinces of France and there followed a banquet and a ballet.[36] Although this was utilizing the natural features of the landscape it could as easily have taken place within the contrived waters of a château.

That this was so can be seen from a drawing for an unknown water tourney on the lake at Fontainebleau some time in the reign of Henry III, presumably in the late seventies. In this, boat-loads of warriors in fancy dress of all sorts are attacking an island in the middle defended by savages.[37] In other words the lake at Fontainebleau was not only for fish; it also had an ornamental purpose and was a suitable setting for courtly masquerades. Perhaps the most famous instance of this in permanent form was Charles de Bourbon's extraordinary canal and lakes which he added to the already elaborate gardens at Gaillon *c.* 1550. At one end of the canal, linked by a bridge to the land, stood the Maison Blanche, while at the other there was a chapel and, within a square pond, a vast rock with a hermitage.[38]

Apart from the emblematic lake for the Elvetham entertainment, which recalls vividly the watery fêtes of the last Valois, the development of ponds and rivers as part of the garden is not taken up until the second half of the first decade of the seventeenth century, when large-scale water effects were central to the concept of both Prince Henry's Richmond and Robert Cecil's Hatfield. They were also the fundamental feature for a third garden begun at the same period, Francis Bacon's Gorhambury.

In July 1608 Bacon wrote a 'platt' for an island in a lake, which looks back to Elvetham and connects with both Richmond and Hatfield, all of which were progressing simultaneously. That he wrote in his journal 'to speak of this to my lord of Salsbury' confirms the fact that Cecil's views on garden design were to be respected.[39] The lake as a whole sat within a square, walled enclosure which on the exterior was bordered by birch and lime trees. Within it there was a walk all the way round, twenty-five feet in width. Then came a naturalistic little stream followed by a bank and a second walk of the same width as the upper one but bordered with lilies. Within this was a square lake enclosed within gilt balustrading underplanted with flowers and strawberries. A bridge spanned the water to the large central island, a hundred feet in breadth, on which stood a house with a gallery, a supper room, a bedroom, a cabinet, a music room and a garden. The lake was scattered with some six more projected smaller islands: one 'where the fayre hornbeam' was, another with a rock, another with a grotto, another with 'flowres in ascents' and yet another 'with an arbor of Musk roses sett with double violetts for scent in the Autumn', each of which was to be adorned with a statue of an appropriate nymph or triton.

John Aubrey saw Bacon's garden at Gorhambury in 1656. The walks 'were most ingeniousely designed' and the elegant summer houses in the classical style were 'yet standing, but defaced'. Next to the transitory architecture of the court masque these garden buildings must have been some of the earliest instances of purely classical architecture in England. But it was the ponds which struck Aubrey most of all. He guessed that they covered no less than four acres and that, as at Hatfield, the bottoms were lined with coloured pebbles carefully selected by Bacon. 'In the middle of the middlemost pond', he wrote, 'in the Island, is a curious banquetting-house of Roman architecture, paved with black and white marble; covered with Cornish slatts, and neatly wainscotted'.[40] As a young man, during the seventies, Bacon had been in France at the English embassy in Paris. The lake and islands at Gorhambury reminded one of Gaillon and Fontainebleau.

Bacon died in 1626, ironically at the very time his gardens were being copied by James I at Theobalds. Robert Cecil had already begun something of this sort in 1602–3, when he created a naturalistic river outside the formal gardens, probably inspired directly by the demands of a classical villa garden as described by Pliny, with its contrast between the formal and informal. All this was taken much further in 1625–6, when two new ponds were created, one of which was large enough to have an island and the second a mount at one end of it. As at Gorhambury the great pond was bordered by palisading, suggesting that it must have had a formal shape with an underplanting of strawberries, primroses and violets. The planting was of cherry, plum and other fruit trees and there was an artificial river, perhaps connecting the ponds, over which were placed several wooden bridges. At the lower smaller pond there was 'a new stand about a tree' and here and there were decorative pyramids. A barge house was added in 1626–7.[41]

We can end this account of lakes, islands and rivers with two more examples. An aerial view in Kip contains a lake and an island of the type we have been discussing. Its central feature is an island with a spiralling mount in the Elvetham manner. The boscage includes a pleached tunnel for hunting wild duck, which were driven along into nets.

Ponds and rivers

75 The emblematic lake dug for Lord Hertford's 1591 entertainment celebrating Elizabeth I at Elvetham. Its crescent-moon shape represented the Queen as Cynthia and the islands within it included (*front centre*) Neptune's Fort and (*right*) the Snail Mount.

76 Water festival at Bayonne (1565). An instance of an existing river and island given an allegorical meaning by becoming the setting for a court fête

facing page:
top:
77 Water spectacle at Fontainebleau (*c.* 1570). An artificial lake used as a symbolic setting for an attack on a man-made island defended by savages

centre:
78 Ponds and islands at Gaillon (*c.* 1550). *From right to left*: the 'Maison Blanche' in a pond leading to a canal; a square lake with a rock in the middle of it; a hermitage

bottom:
79 Decoy for hunting duck in the form of a geometric lake, islands and a mount at Haughton, Nottinghamshire

right:
80 Diagram based on Francis Bacon's description of a pond with islands and a house at Gorhambury (1608)

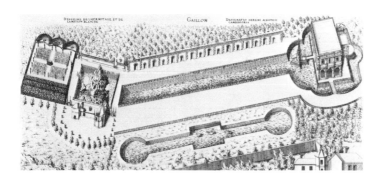

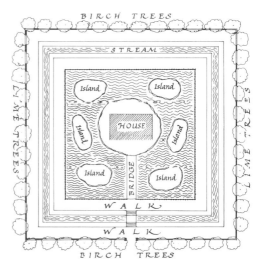

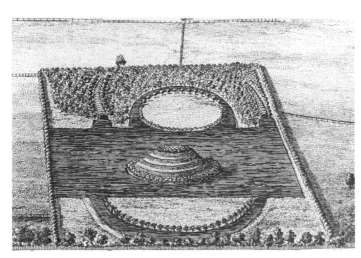

The house, Haughton, belonged to Sir John Holles, who was highly esteemed by Henry, Prince of Wales, who visited it. Is this perhaps a provincial echo of de Caus's Richmond schemes? Stukeley (1724) illustrates a similar decoy in Lincolnshire in the form of a cinquefoil. Even in the case of the hunt, water is reduced characteristically to a geometric or emblematic form.

Thomas Bushell and the Enstone Marvels

The most extraordinary expression of this preoccupation with water in Stuart England appears in the work of Francis Bacon's servant Thomas Bushell at the close of the 1620s in Oxfordshire.[42] The Enstone Marvels, as they were called, are also important because they highlight the very real interconnection that existed between the development of garden delights and scientific advance in seventeenth-century England.

Bushell had an extremely bizarre life. Born in 1594, he became a servant to Francis Bacon, who shared with him his 'experimental studies' and in particular those concerning metallurgy. On Bacon's disgrace Bushell fled London and for two years became a poor fisherman on the Isle of Wight. Eventually he returned to the Earl's service but Bacon died in 1626. There then follows the strangest period of all. He retired to the Isle of Lundy to live the life of a hermit for a period of three years 'in obedience to my dead lord's philosophical advice' and the hut he occupied on a remote height was still visible at the close of the last century. There he made 'a perfect experiment' upon himself for obtaining a long and happy life, as instructed by Bacon, living 'most like that our long liv'd fathers before the flood'. In all this, with its accent on contemplation in solitude, its preoccupation with experiment and its examination of natural phenomena, we are in the world of the late Renaissance magus. On his return to England in 1628 this Prospero-like figure was to bring his knowledge of the secrets of nature to spectacular fulfilment at the little estate he inherited at Enstone.

This work occupied Bushell for seven years and its completion was marked by a visit from Charles I and Henrietta Maria on 23 August 1636, when the hermit of Enstone arranged an entertainment with music by Simon Ives in which he presented his Rock, as it was known, to the Queen, who bestowed her own name upon it.[43] Bushell's creation was achieved by harnessing natural springs by means of pipes and conduits to form a grotto, which included most of the effects de Caus describes in his *Les Raisons*. By 1636 this complex was famous and in 1635, the year in which Charles I had paid a private visit, a visitor wrote a long description of its watery marvels:

> On the side of a hill is a Rocke of some 11 or 12 Foote high, from the bottome wherof (by turning of a Cocke) riseth and spouts vp about 9. foote high, a Streame which raiseth vp on her top a Siluer Ball, and as the sayd Streame riseth or falleth to any pitch or distance, so doth the Ball, with playing, tossing and keeping continually at the top of the sayd ascending Streame . . .

In other words it is the familiar fountain device illustrated by de Caus of a ball rising and falling on a single jet of water. This was followed by a wall of jets which could spring up suddenly as in the approach to the grotto at Wilton:

> . . . like a plash'd Fence, whereby sometimes faire ladies cannot fence the crossing, flashing and dashing their smooth, soft and tender thighs and knees, by a sudden inclosing them in it.

TAB.12.   ad pag: 240.

To the most Illustrious Lady, the Lady
CHARLOTTE
Countess of Lichfield Viscountess Quarrendon &
Baroness of Spelsbury &c.
This 12. Table
Shewing the interior Prospect of ENSTON Water
works, with the greatest devotion is humbly Consecrated
by R.P. LLD.

The Enstone Marvels

The hermitage and grotto built between 1628 and 1635 by Thomas Bushell

81 The interior of the grotto showing the elaborate water effects including, to the right, a water curtain over the entrance

82 The approach and exterior of the hermitage as it was in 1677. The grotto was in the basement and Bushell lived above.

This famous Rock was enclosed within a house which we can see in the illustration in Robert Plot's *Natural History of Oxfordshire* (1677), built in what can only be described as the artisan Gothic style. In the engraving it is recorded as it was restored in the 1670s with a gabled roof, but in 1635 this was 'flatt with Battlements about . . . and a neat Garden adioyning to itt'. The Rock and grotto were in the basement and the engraving of this is carefully marked with all the effects. Over the entrance a curtain of water can be seen descending and the Rock with its great central jet is at the end. On the occasion of Charles I's 1635 visit the effects were elaborate:

> . . . many strange formes of Beasts, Fishes and Fowles doth appeare; and with the pretty murmuring of the Springs; the gentle running, falling and playing of the waters; the beating of a Drum; the chirping of a Nightingale, and many other strange, rare and audible sounds and noyses doth highly worke vpon any Mans Fancy . . .

In other words the effects are again those described by de Caus but without the introduction of automata.

Over this extraordinary grotto the hermit lived in three rooms. The central one was painted with biblical stories concerning water: the Woman of Samaria; Hagar, Ishmael and the Angels; and Susanna and the Elders. This room, too, had its strange effects:

> . . . in this Chamber is a naturall Rocke, like vnto the Head of a Beare; on the top thereof, the water rises and spouts forth, falling in the Rocke . . . from about the middle of this Chamber, they make a Canopy of Raine, which . . . a man . . . may stand dry, which with the reflection of the Sunn at high Noone, makes appeare to our fancies Rainbowes and flashing like Lightening.

In other words Bushell made use of the refraction of light to produce rainbows in the same manner that Isaac de Caus was later to do at Wilton, as recorded by Aubrey.

On either side of this was a further chamber, one a hermit's cell hung with black, 'representing a melancholy retyr'd life', the other a bedchamber with the story of Christ in wall hangings. The little house stood on a hillside and was approached by terraces interconnected with flights of steps and planted with fruit trees. On the other side of the house were flower gardens and at the bottom of the hill there appear to have been more pools and 'a curious Walke, with neatly contriu'd Arbours'. Our 1635 visitor ends his account with this verdict on poor Bushell: 'A mad gim-crack yet heriditary to these Hermeticall and Proiecticall Vndertakers'.

Work began on all this in 1628, the year after the publication of Bacon's *New Atlantis* with its description of a house in which natural phenomena of this sort were imitated:

> We have also great and spacious houses, where we imitate and demonstrate meteors; as snow, hail, rain, some artificial rains of bodies and not of water, thunders, lightenings . . .[44]

Bushell, as a result of royal favour soon after, became the King's farmer of minerals in Wales. He recovered the silver mines in Cardiganshire (now part of Dyfed) and re-established and ran the Royal Mint at Aberystwyth. Later he fought as a royalist in the Civil War and lived on into the Restoration period.

132

Bushell is a strange figure in the history of gardens in England but an essential touchstone for this obsession with water. Enstone with its miraculous effects belongs to the world of Renaissance hermeticism, with the magus Bushell reigning over it, harnessing the magic properties of one of the elements and leading a life of solitude and religious contemplation. He is closer in this respect to the studies of Elizabeth's astrologer Dr John Dee than to the practical exploration of the physical world expounded by Bacon. That came in the second half of his life, which takes us through to the foundation of the Royal Society.

As a footnote to Bushell there is John Bate's *The Mysteryes of Nature and Art*, which was published in 1634 and covers a wide range of strange topics including fireworks, drawing, painting, perspective and rudimentary scientific experiments.[45] The subject matter is reminiscent of Bushell but the book is in English and of a popularizing nature. It opens significantly with a section entitled 'Of Water-workes', which deals with the principles of hydraulics on the lines of de Caus and goes on to give instructions on how to make the kinds of machines which are described by Hero of Alexandria: 'How to make that a bird sitting on a basis, shall make a noise, and drink out of a cup of water, being held to the mouth of it', 'A device whereby the figure of man standing on a basis shall be made to sound a trumpet' or, his grand finale, 'How to compose a great or little piece of Water-worke', an amazing compilation of dragons, whales,

83 'How to make that a bird sitting on a basis, shall make a noise, and drink out of a cup of water, being held to the mouth of it'

84 'A device whereby the figure of a man standing on a basis shall be made to sound a trumpet'

Hydraulic automata from John Bate's *The Mysteryes of Nature and Art* (1634)

swans and marine deities. Appearing in English in the 1630s this book is immensely important and part of that movement in late Elizabethan and Jacobean England which John Dee had initiated and supported, to communicate practical information on the mechanical sciences in the vernacular.[46] Bate was a friend of John Babington, mathematician and gunner, who published in 1635 *A Short Treatise on Geometrie* with tables of logarithms.[47] All this is of consequence in understanding that garden hydraulics were part of that upsurge in experimentation at the beginning of the seventeenth century which was to lead from magic to science.

Two garden theorists: Wotton and Bacon

We can round off our survey of the development of the Jacobean pleasure garden by reference to two famous works that appeared within a year of each other, Sir Henry Wotton's *The Elements of Architecture* (1624) and Sir Francis Bacon's essay 'Of Gardens' which was published in 1625.

Wotton was ambassador to Venice from 1602 to 1612 and again from 1621 to 1624. He had, as we have seen, an intense interest in gardens. Because of its political stability and stoutly independent attitude towards the papacy, Venice was immensely attractive to the English. Its paintings and Palladian architecture were regarded as canons of taste according to the new classical ideals.[48] Wotton's attitude to gardens is an unusual one, however. He opens his discussion by stating:

> First, I must quote a certaine contrarietie betweene *building* and *gardening*: For as Fabriques should bee *regular*, so Gardens should bee *irregular*, or at least cast into a very wild *Regularitie*.[49]

This is a far cry from the immediate and taut relationship of building and garden typical of the villas along the Brenta. Wotton was obviously not drawn by them but by the Mannerist fantasies of Pratolino or the Villa d'Este with its vistas and planned surprises. In fact, the passage that follows could be an account of the general effects that would be had by a visitor to either of those places approaching the garden from the terrace next to the villa and about to descend the flights of steps:

> . . . [to] exemplifie my conceit; I have seen a *Garden* (for the maner perchance incomparable) into which the first Accesse was a high walke like a *Tarrace*, from whence might bee taken a generall view of the whole *Plott* below but rather in a delightfull confusion than with any plaine distinction of the pieces. From this the *Beholder* descending many steps, was afterwards conveyed againe, by severall *mountings* and *valings*, to various entertainments of his *sent*, and sight . . . every one of these diversities, was as if hee had beene *Magically* transported into a new *Garden*.[50]

This garden of successive sensuous entertainments unfolding as a series of surprises was certainly a more natural garden than the Italian style as it had so far reached England, which essentially aimed at achieving a single *coup d'œil* from the terrace of the house. His remaining observations are few but specific: he praises an arcade of water which excelled anything in the *Pneumatics* of Hero; he condemns grottos although he recommends the building of underground caverns from which to observe the movement of the stars by day; and he approves of large-scale aviaries.

Bacon's 'prince-like' garden is a mixture of old and new elements with also a strong but very different bias towards the natural garden, although his detailed specification for a royal garden is oddly surprising after his own at Gorhambury.[51] There is, as with Wotton, no mention of any relationship of the house to the garden as an architectural entity. Indeed, his essay 'Of Building' is totally separate. The garden, he writes, is to be not less than about thirty acres, four of green, twelve for the main garden in between and eighteen of heath surrounding it. The green is of short grass but with covered pleached alleys. The main garden is square and encompassed with a hedge upon a six-foot-high bank of flowers supported by arches of carpenter's work set with tiny aviaries above it and turrets or 'some other little figure, with broad plates of round coloured glass gilt, for the sun to play upon'.

Within this he leaves it 'to variety of device'. He dismisses knots of coloured earth to be seen from the windows of the house: 'you may see as good sights many times in tarts'. He states his dislike of topiary images: 'they be for children'. Instead, he commends broad walks, low hedges and pyramids, decorative wooden columns and a thirty-foot-high mount in the middle with a banqueting house on the top of it. In other words we are in a garden which looks backwards to Theobalds and Kenilworth.

The gestures to new fashion come in his eulogy of fountains: 'they are of great beauty and refreshment'. Oddly, in view of his own garden, he dismisses pools. They 'mar all, and make the garden unwholesome, and full of flies and frogs'. Neither can be effective unless the water be perpetually changed. The scornful description of the pond is in fact evocative of what he built at Gorhambury. The bottom and the sides of it should be lined 'with images' and 'withal embellished with coloured glass, and such things of lustre', the whole surrounded by balustrading with statues on the top. Unlike Wotton he seems to have no time for the delights of the School of Alexandria: 'they be pretty things to look on, but nothing to health and sweetness'.

But by far the most interesting part is his concern to create a horticultural *ver perpetuum* by deliberately planting for all seasons and in his account of the heath. This was to be a 'natural wilderness' without trees but with thickets of sweet-briar, honeysuckle and wild vine. Small hillocks like molehills were to be planted with thyme, violets, rosemary, strawberries, cowslips and so on. The heath on either side of the garden was to have broad gravelled walks flanked by fruit trees and hedges and against the far boundary walls mounts were to be thrown up from which 'to look abroad into the fields'. In this we are moving from the emblematic *hortus conclusus* towards the garden as an ally of experimental science.

The Mannerist garden There are no absolutely clear-cut phases in garden history. Less long-lasting than buildings, earlier gardens can live on or be swept away to be replaced by a new fashion. Right up to the Civil War, Henry VIII's Hampton Court, Whitehall and Nonsuch survived virtually untouched, for the most part refurbished as memorials to venerated monarchs of an earlier, more heroic age. So did Lord Burghley's Theobalds and doubtless many other gardens of great houses laid out in the previous century. Nonetheless, the reign of James I can be conveniently categorized as the age of the Mannerist garden. An unparalleled burst of activity occurred in garden making such as we have no evidence for from the previous century. In this, the court and a prodigal aristocracy led the way. As a result, gardens became much larger in scale, their ground-plan dwarfing that of the house itself. Gardens have embarked on that process which is the key theme for the whole century, of gradually swallowing up the countryside around until the landscape itself is made subject to the great house, a fundamental principle of the post-Restoration Baroque garden.

The Jacobean Mannerist garden essentially remains, however, the old *hortus conclusus*. It is a walled enclosure within which nature tamed by art is made to fulfil the wildest of Mannerist fantasies, above all by means of the new hydraulics. Like late Elizabethan and Jacobean houses they were intended from the start as 'conceits', as deliberately puzzling geometrical riddles of triangles, circles, squares and ovals. These were designed to be read symbolically both in terms of plan and planting. And, although there is a noticeable shift towards an understanding of the potential of the new science of perspective, it is seldom used. The Jacobean garden looks back to the garden of isolated incident, which is essentially Elizabethan, and only occasionally looks forward to the bold overall effect that was to come in those of the Caroline age. Distance and *point de vue* are not yet fundamental characteristics; nor is that presiding genius of the place, the garden statue. But all this was shortly to come in the changes to be wrought by Inigo Jones during the twenty-five years following his return from Italy.

85 Grotto architecture as stage scenery. Inigo Jones's design for the House of Oceanus in Ben Jonson's *The Fortunate Isles and their Union* (1625)

137

CHAPTER VI

THE ECLECTIC GARDEN I

Anne of Denmark died in 1619, the same year that the Thirty Years War broke out, an event which directly precipitated the climax of James I's political ambitions, the match of Prince Charles with the Infanta of Spain. As a result, the artistic policies of the court, particularly under the direction of the precocious Prince of Wales and the King's final favourite, George Villiers, Duke of Buckingham, turned in a new and revitalized direction. This phase was epitomized in a single building, Inigo Jones's Whitehall Banqueting House, the ceremonial hall in which James hoped he would receive the bride. By 1619 the French sculptor, Hubert le Sueur, is working in England; in 1620 payments to Daniel Mytens, the portrait painter, begin, Francis Cleyn opens the Mortlake Tapestry workshops and Van Dyck comes to England; and in 1621 we have the famous reference to Rubens being willing at the Prince's command to paint the ceiling of the new Banqueting House. In other words we are at the beginning of that vast renaissance in the visual arts which was to reach its flowering after Charles became king in 1625. In gardening, as in everything else, it had its most important and influential figure. In this case it was Salomon de Caus's brother Isaac, who was to dominate the art of the garden in England up until the outbreak of the Civil War.

Isaac de Caus and the Whitehall Banqueting House

The de Caus family must have been remarkable to have produced two such talented engineers as brothers. Isaac was younger, being born in 1590 but his preoccupations were exactly parallel with Salomon's.[1] He was a hydraulic engineer, an architect, and a designer of grottos and automata. There can, however, be no doubt that it was Salomon who was the more original and that Isaac's position was fundamentally a derivative one. Our earliest glimpse of him occurs in 1617 when, on the occasion of a state visit by Louis XIII to Normandy, he devised a hydraulic automaton across the main façade of the town hall to welcome the King.[2] This included not only the usual mechanical singing birds but also jets of water upon which a ball and crown arose and fell in the air, effects familiar from *Les Raisons* and which Isaac was to re-create himself in his masterpiece of the 1630s, the garden of Wilton House in Wiltshire.

In the Works Accounts for 1623–4 Mr de Caus appears for the first time, being paid 'for making a Rocke in the vaulte under the banquetting house'. The materials for its construction included 'rocke stuffe' and 'shells' and in 1625 he made an addition to its exterior of 'Shellworke'.[3] What the Works Accounts are recording is the decoration of the King's Privy Cellar, James I's *private* cellar, a room into which he could retreat together with his cronies and favourites to tipple and converse for the evening. Ben Jonson's *The Dedication of the King's New Cellar* celebrates this grotto and its royal master:

> *Since,* Bacchus, *thou art father*
> *Of Wines, to thee the rather*
> *We dedicate this Cellar,*
> *Where now, thou art made Dweller;*
> *And seale thee thy Commission:*
> *But 'tis with a condition,*
> *That thou remaine here taster*
> *Of all to the great Master.*[4]

That it was regarded as desirable to have a grotto *à la* Pratolino beneath Inigo Jones's revolutionary Palladian building is deeply revealing of court taste in the early 1620s.

Jonson's poem ends by widening the horizons beyond the activities which were pursued immediately within de Caus's grotto and taking them into the outer world symbolized by the events which took place in the room above, prophecies above all of the festivals to come:

> *When with his royal shipping*
> *The narrow Seas are shadie,*
> *And* Charles *brings home the Ladie.*[5]

The lady, of course, never came in the end, but Jonson commemorated the return of Charles and the Duke of Buckingham in two masques, *Neptune's Triumph for the Return of Albion* and *The Fortunate Isles and their Union*. The first was never performed owing to the usual squabbles over ambassadorial precedence, but the second, a revised version of the first and using the same scenery, took place on 9 January 1625. *The Fortunate Isles*, like 'Tethys' Festival', belongs in one of its aspects to the history of gardening in England. Inigo Jones, whose emblematic visions always so exactly reflected the artistic preoccupations of the avant garde at court, conjured up for its climax 'a maritime palace, or the house of Oceanus'.[6] This rustic palazzo, with its pillars of bound slaves and its parapets adorned with conch-trumpeting tritons, is very much in the vein of the grottos which Salomon de Caus had built for Prince Henry and Anne of Denmark and which Isaac, in a new wave of grotto mania, was shortly to erect elsewhere.

Isaac de Caus and Lucy Harington, Countess of Bedford: Woburn and Moor Park

The arrival of de Caus may have other connotations about which we shall never know because of the loss of evidence. One of these involves the exuberant figure of Lucy Harington, Countess of Bedford, whom we have already met in connection with Twickenham Park. We know Isaac worked for the Bedfords in the thirties when they were laying out the Covent Garden[7] but from our point of view there is something much more important, a unique survival, namely the grotto he designed for the basement of Woburn Abbey in Bedfordshire. This room, the oldest in the abbey, was built when the 3rd Earl of Bedford decided to make Woburn his home and bears his arms, thus dating it before his death in 1627. Like the Whitehall Banqueting House it was an indoor basement room.

86 Isaac de Caus's grotto
for Lucy Harington,
Countess of Bedford, at
Woburn Abbey, before
1627

The grotto at Woburn alone remains to conjure up the marvels of those
Salomon had made at Richmond and Heidelberg and that Isaac was to make at
Wilton. It gives the substance of reality to the engravings in *Les Raisons* and in
the *Hortus Palatinus*, providing a northern interpretation of the grotto
repertory of Pratolino: a vaulted room, the ceiling decorated with ornate
arabesques in shells, the walls of simulated rock and coral formations with a
frieze at the top directly related to that in the great grotto at Heidelberg
showing *putti* riding on dolphins and sea gods drawn along on shell chariots.
Niches in the walls must once have had statuary, certainly fountains, possibly

140

even automata. At Woburn we are witnessing a startling survival of the magical world of the late Renaissance.[8]

This grotto at Woburn has given us a highly important clue. De Caus must have been greatly in demand but he did not begin on his most famous work at Wilton until 1632. What was this astounding man doing during the preceding decade? In the first place he must have designed other grottos in the Woburn manner. The style is so very idiosyncratic – quaint might be almost a better word for it – that he must surely be the author of a design for a Grotto of Callisto long unattributed in the Victoria and Albert Museum. In arrangement it is a direct repetition of Woburn: the ribs of the vault are clearly accentuated and the ceiling between ornamented with characteristic arabesque patterns; the walls are divided into arches and small niches for fountains and statuary. In the centre of the ceiling four *putti* bear crowns, conceivably a hydraulic mechanism which could rise and descend. The sources of the grotto would seem to prove beyond a doubt that Isaac, like Salomon, had studied in Italy and at Pratolino in particular. The group of Diana's nymphs discovering Callisto's unchastity is derived from an engraving after Titian's famous painting of the subject, while the satyr herms which bear up the vault borrow Buontalenti's use of Michelangelo's Slaves to support the corners of the Grotto Grande in the Boboli Gardens. And overall it directly reflects a grotto on the same subject at Pratolino itself.

The Diana and Callisto grotto is one of three designs in the Victoria and Albert Museum which must be by Isaac de Caus dating from this period. One depicts a female Bacchus surrounded by wild animals perched on rocks, holding a bunch of grapes from which water falls into a pool below. On either side there is another pool, each fed by descending *putti*, one bearing a torch of Hymen, the other a garland. The second grotto design includes Mercury as its presiding deity playing the pipes, presumably a sound produced hydraulically, while below a machine bears Europa astride her bull through an archway. On the wall on either side there is a panorama of the countryside. De Caus must surely have worked for other people in the 1620s, so that we must imagine weird grotto rooms of this sort, with rusticated stonework, shell-work, trickling water and symbolic automata, becoming a feature in the more avant garde houses and gardens of the 1620s and 1630s.

De Caus's Woburn grotto gives us another clue, for his patroness, the extravagant Lucy Harington, was celebrated for another garden which had a 'grotto embellished with figures of shell-work, fountains, and water-works': Moor Park, Hertfordshire. Writing in the 1670s Sir William Temple, a garden connoisseur, regarded this as 'the perfectest figure of a garden I ever saw' but no one as far as I know has ever connected it with Isaac de Caus. And yet surely it must be de Caus's earliest masterpiece and the precursor of Wilton? As such Moor Park deserves examination in some detail.

In 1617 Lucy Harington parted with Twickenham Park when James I granted her Moor Park,[9] where during the decade 1617–27 she created what was to be a celebrated garden 'with very great care, excellent contrivance and', absolutely in character, 'much cost'. Temple is so specific that the garden was her creation that it is surprising to read in the contract of the sale of the house to Robert Cary, Earl of Monmouth, in 1631: 'all that great house or lodge, lately built wherein the Earl and Countess of Bedford lately dwelt; also all that new

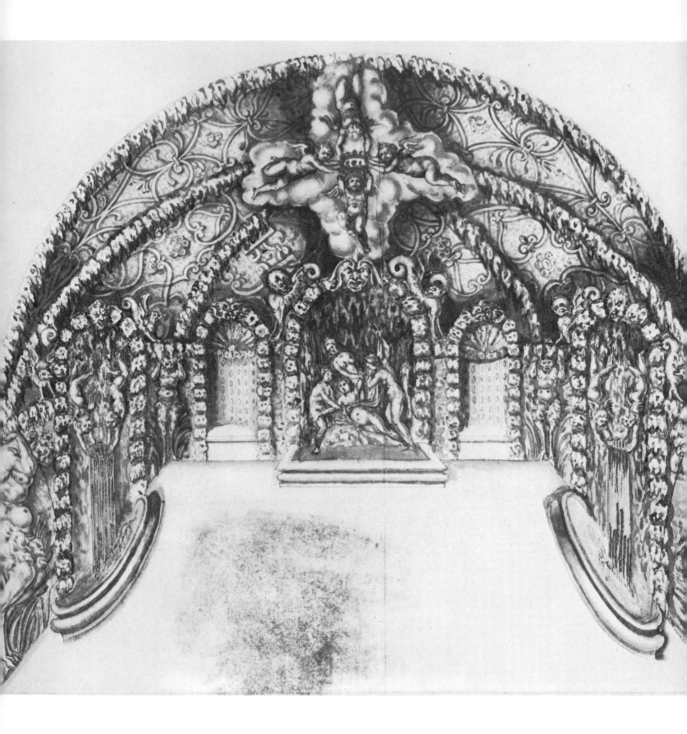

Two grotto designs by Isaac de Caus

87 Grotto depicting Diana and Callisto, inspired by one at Pratolino. The cherubs supporting the coronet above may have been operable by a hydraulic machine.

88 Grotto with Mercury and Europa. Mercury's pipe would have
warbled by means of hydraulics and Europa would have moved
through the arches by means of a machine of the type illustrated
in Salomon de Caus's *Les Raisons des forces mouvantes*.

garden adjoining to the said house eastward made by William Earl of Pembroke . . .'. These two sources are at total variance one with the other. Both the Countess and Pembroke were great gardeners; both were directly or indirectly connected with de Caus. Pembroke had Moor Park after the Countess's death in 1627 until his own in 1630. This question-mark must, therefore, hang over any discussion of Moor Park. No doubt exists, however, about its significance in the history of garden design.

Temple's description written in 1685 in his essay 'Upon the Gardens of Epicurus' is the most detailed evocation we have of a Jacobean garden.

> Because I take the garden I have named to have been in all kinds the most beautiful and perfect, at least in the figure and disposition, that I have ever seen, I will describe it for a model to those that meet with such a situation, and are above the regards of expence. It lies on the sides of a hill (upon which the house stands) but not very steep. The length of the house, where the best rooms and of most use or pleasure are, lies upon the breadth of the garden, the great parlour opens into the middle of a terras gravel walk that lies even with it, and which may be, as I remember, about three hundred paces long, and broad in proportion; the border set with standard laurels, and at large distances, which have the beauty of orange-trees, out of flower and fruit: from this walk are three descents by many stone steps, in the middle and at each end, into a very large parterre. This is divided into quarters by gravel walks, and adorned with two fountains and eight statues in the several quarters; at the end of the terras-walk are two summer-houses, and the sides of the parterre are ranged with two large cloisters, open to the garden, upon arches of stone, and ending with two other summer-houses even with the cloisters, which are paved with stone, and designed for walks of shade, there being none other in the whole parterre. Over these two cloisters are two terrasses covered with lead, and fenced with balusters; and the passage into these airy walks is out of the two summer-houses, at the end of the first terras-walk. The cloister facing the south is covered with vines, and would have been proper for an orange-house, and the other for myrtles, or other more common greens. . . .
>
> From the middle of the parterre is a descent by many steps flying on each side of a grotto that lies between them (covered with lead, and flat) into the lower garden, which is all fruit-trees, ranged about the several quarters of a wilderness, which is very shady; the walks here are all green, the grotto embellished with figures of shell rock-work, fountains, and water-works. If the hill had not ended with the lower garden, and the wall were not bounded by a common way that goes through the park, they might have added a third quarter of all greens; but this want is supplied by a garden on the other side of the house, which is all of that sort, very wild, shady, and adorned with rock-work and fountains.
>
> This was Moor-Park when I was acquainted with it, and the sweetest place, I think, that I have ever seen in my life, either before or since, at home or abroad.[10]

What in fact is Temple describing? The word picture is so precise that it can easily be translated into diagrammatic terms. The house opened out onto a broad terrace with summer houses at each end; from these it was possible to walk along the top of cloisters flanking the parterre garden below to two more summer houses. In other words the arrangement is that of Henry IV's St Germain-en-Laye, with walks and summer houses above formal patterned parterres. It is a formula we have seen already, in probably more modest form, at Somerset House in 1609. The garden onto which the terrace and walks overlooked was in the usual quarters but adorned with fountains and statuary,

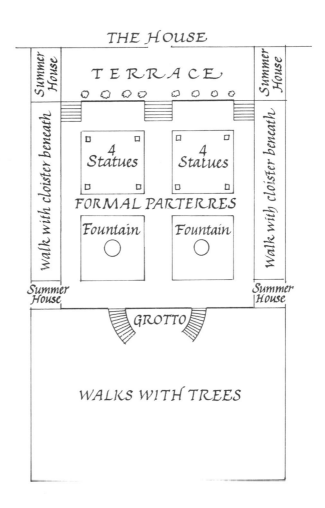

THE HOUSE

TERRACE

Summer House

Summer House

Walk with cloister beneath

Walk with cloister beneath

4 Statues

4 Statues

FORMAL PARTERRES

Fountain

Fountain

Summer House

Summer House

GROTTO

WALKS WITH TREES

89 Diagram of the layout
of Moor Park

that is to say like the parterres at Heidelberg, although whether the beds were
newly invented *parterres de broderie* is not altogether clear. From this formal
element, which could also be looked down upon from the upper floors of the
house, steps descended either side of a de Caus grotto into a formalized orchard
having walks planted with fruit trees. Perhaps this descent from one level to
another encircling a grotto was inspired by the arrangement at Pratolino,
encompassing the Fontana del Mugnone. The orchard with its geometrical
walks is a feature we have already met in the plan amongst the Smythson
drawings for Ham. Above all the terrace system is directly Italianate: terrace
descending to parterre, parterre to orchard. We have seen it already at Hatfield
but Moor Park seems more definitely Italianate. In plan it appears to have been
based on St Germain-en-Laye but without the water parterre.

The least elaborated description is that of the third part of the garden on the
far side of the house (not shown on the diagram), the wilderness of evergreens
with rockwork and fountains. This, too, must have been Italianate. There is no
mount, no daedalus, no separate little gardens with banqueting houses in the
middle. Moor Park must have been the earliest, most spectacular evidence of

90 View of the gardens of
Bedford House, London,
as seen from the piazza in
Covent Garden (*c.* 1649).
Behind the wall there is a
raised, balustraded terrace
terminating in a summer
house.

Italian Renaissance gardening in England. It made extensive use of terraces, of
the grotto, of statuary, of fountains and probably of automata. Its terrain
descending a hillside must have made it infinitely more Italianate than de
Caus's visually documented masterpiece, Wilton. And it was created in
England by Isaac de Caus simultaneously with his brother's grander
counterpart, the Hortus Palatinus. Nothing remains of Moor Park: it was
swept away by Capability Brown.

Lucy Harington had one other house, her London one, Bedford House on
the north side of the Strand, which had been built for her husband *c.* 1586 with
a garden which occupied part of the site of a former convent garden.[11] What
little we know of this also suggests the hand of Isaac de Caus. A bird's eye view
of Covent Garden by Wenceslas Hollar shows a large garden to the north laid
out in quarters with a central feature, probably a fountain. On the north side
there was a terrace overlooking the piazza with flights of steps down on either
side of the central doorway and pavilions at each end. We can get a clearer
impression of these from a painting of *c.* 1649 of the piazza which shows one in
rusticated style and indicates that the garden was laid out in a more
complicated manner than Hollar would suggest. To the east there was a grove
or wilderness in the manner of Moor Park. More significantly, to the south
there was a grotto which was demolished in 1705. This was in what by that date

146

was referred to as the 'evidence' house, the repository for family and estate papers. Near it there was a 'great' cistern. This, combined with the knowledge that de Caus worked for the Bedfords on laying out the Covent Garden estate in the 1630s, would seem to clinch the connection.[12]

De Caus and Philip Herbert, 4th Earl of Pembroke: Wilton

The creator of the garden at Wilton was forty-eight in 1632, an advanced age in seventeenth-century terms for embarking on a garden. Philip Herbert, 4th Earl of Pembroke, inherited Wilton in 1630 on the death of his brother William, who died without male issue.[13] Together the two Herbert brothers are remembered by history as the 'incomparable brethren' to whom the First Folio of Shakespeare was dedicated. Philip was the second son of Henry, 2nd Earl of Pembroke, and Mary Sidney. He was born on 10 October 1584 and christened Philip after his famous uncle whose mantle as England's chivalrous hero was seen to descend upon the shoulders of the child. In 1600 Philip first appeared at court, where his forwardness was immediately cause for comment but it was not until the new reign that 'the comeliness of his person' and his skill in all field sports made him his fortune. He is described as 'the first who drew the king's eyes towards him with affection'. James rewarded him lavishly. In 1603 he was made Knight of the Bath and a Gentleman of the Privy Chamber, in 1605 a Gentleman of the Bedchamber and Earl of Montgomery, with a lavish gift of lands from the King. By then he had married Susan de Vere, one of the Earl of Oxford's daughters. In 1608 he was made a Knight of the Garter, in 1615 High Steward of Oxford, in 1617 Keeper of Westminster Palace, Spring Gardens and St James's, in 1624 a Privy Councillor. He made a point of cultivating the old king's last favourite, Buckingham, and the new king remained faithful to him in the new reign. In 1626 he succeeded his brother as Lord Chamberlain, in 1630 as Earl and as Lord Warden of the Stanneries and he only narrowly missed being made Chancellor of Oxford in favour of Laud.

His career at court was nothing if not dazzling and it brought him vast financial rewards. But what kind of man was he? Like all the Herberts he was intensely cultivated. And the intellectual world he belongs to is that of the generation of Henry, Prince of Wales. For thirty years Pembroke as Montgomery led the court in masques and exercises of chivalry in all of which he shone. Even at the age of forty-seven and as the holder of the grave office of Lord Chamberlain he danced in Jonson's *Love's Triumph through Callipolis*. That he was essentially associated with the tradition of Elizabethan and Jacobean romance can be demonstrated by the translations from the French which were dedicated to him of the *Amadis de Gaule* (1619), of *Ariana* (1636), of Honoré d'Urfé's *L'Astrée* (1620) and Saulnier du Verdier's *Romant des Romans* (1640). Like all his family he attracted a steady stream of dedications revealing him as a man far removed from the image of illiteracy he tried to adopt. His authors hymn him as a 'Nobleminded lover of learning', a 'Patrone of Vertue', as 'heir' to Henry, Prince of Wales, in his prowess in 'feates of Armes'.[14] Courtly hyperbole it may be but these descriptions surely also reflect that beneath his courtier's cunning and ignorant buffoonery he was a man of taste and discernment.

The only documentation to survive on the laying out of the garden is contained in a single warrant Pembroke issued in his capacity as Lord

147

Chamberlain. This orders the demolition of the old south front of the house and its rebuilding:

> And likewise to take down ye Gardeners litle house & the Tenis Courte & sett up convenient houseing for ye Gardner in ye new kitchen garden which Garden Mr. De Caux is to lay out in fitt proportions, walks & Quarters to bee planted with fruits, hearbes & rootes by Dominick Pile who is to have ye Custody there of & to receaue his direccions from Mr. De Caux & the officers for that which shall bee for his Lordship's service.[15]

The warrant is dated 14 March 1635/6, by which time the main garden was virtually complete because we have a detailed description of it by a visitor who saw it the previous summer. The Estate Accounts provide two further pieces of information: that £200 was spent on constructing the garden in 1632–3 and that the grand total for the 'construction of the lord earl's new garden and house' during the years 1634–5 was £1,292. From these we can conclude that de Caus's work lasted in all some three years. It included the rebuilding of the whole south front along the lines recorded in a drawing at Worcester College depicting the finished garden, a scheme which architectural historians regard as having been carried out by de Caus but under the supervision of Inigo Jones. According to Aubrey this monumental extravagance originated with the king who 'did love Wilton above all places, and came thither every summer'.[16]

There is more evidence about the Wilton garden than for any other prior to the outbreak of civil war.[17] De Caus himself issued a series of plans and view of it entitled *Le Jardin de Wilton* (*c.* 1645),[18] it was visited by a Lieutenant Hammond in 1635,[19] by Lodewijk Huygens in 1652,[20] by Celia Fiennes after 1686[21] and it is later described and illustrated in Colin Campbell's *Vitruvius Britannicus*[22] and in a painting by an unknown artist, still at Wilton.[23]

John Aubrey, when he came to categorize the garden, states that it was the third to be made in England in the Italian manner, the first two being those created by Sir John Danvers at Chelsea and Lavington.[24] Aubrey's explanation is perhaps too simple. The importance of Wilton lies in the place that it was seen to occupy within the evolution of gardening by the post-Restoration period; its line of descent is in fact much more complicated. I would place it at the end of a development which assimilates elements from Somerset House, Ham, the Hortus Palatinus and Moor Park. But the overriding concept is quite different from anything we have encountered so far and goes back surely to Inigo Jones. The bones of the garden as of the house are Venetian. That it was so was dictated by not only the Venetian architectural influence which shaped the Jonesian country house into a villa but also the actual terrain. Wilton, like the Palladian villas of the Brenta, was on a level site. Venetian gardens were different from those of either Rome or Tuscany; they were large rectangular, walled enclosures placed in front of the house, embracing its entire width, the dominating feature being a central road or vista leading from the main gate to the portico of the house. And this type of layout, described by Scamozzi, is the basic principle conditioning the garden at Wilton.[25] Into this overall concept de Caus has inset a sequence of gardens on the lines of Moor Park but without the terracing.

The visitor was meant to approach the garden via steps leading down from the *piano nobile*, from whose windows he was able to look on four *compartiments de broderie* in clipped box which centred on four fountains with statues by

Wilton

Nicholas Stone.[26] The corners of the beds and the edges were accentuated by cypress trees. Stone's statues form the first of a series of 'curious workes' which the sculptor's nephew records that his uncle executed and for which he was 'well paide'. They depicted Venus cradling Cupid, Diana, Susanna pulling a thorn from her foot, and Cleopatra with the serpent,[27] figures from classical mythology, Old Testament and ancient history respectively, symbolizing Love and Chastity.

Leaving the *compartiments* we continue our stroll along the broad centre path into the Wilderness. The River Nadder wended its irregular way right through the middle. This stream, the vital source for the waterworks, went clean against the concept of the garden and de Caus continues his symmetrical plan totally ignoring its existence, running a bridge to continue the broad walk and two further bridges so that the arbours either side would be uninterrupted.

149

92 Venus and Cupid   93 Diana

94 Susanna

Wilton

The four fountains in the parterres de broderie *had sculpture by Nicholas Stone. Some of these still survive at Wilton, unique evidence of the greatest of English Renaissance gardens.*

95 The Susanna Fountain

The rigidly balanced groves each side, focusing on statues of Flora and Bacchus, must have formed the least satisfactory part of the entire garden and the placing of the Wilderness at this point must surely have been dictated by an effort to conceal the river amidst a plantation of trees and boscage. At Moor Park the sequence had been parterres leading onto walks and fruit trees, with a third part of 'greens', the Wilderness, which, because of a roadway, had to be located elsewhere. The sequence was from extreme order to cultivated wilderness. At Wilton the last two seem to have been reversed in the interests of concealment.

Emerging from the groves the visitor was next confronted by two rectangular ponds from the middle of each of which arose a rusticated column with a ball on the top surmounted by a crown; 'by turning of Cockes that are close by, the water flyes spouting out, at the top of the Rockes; turning and whirling the Crownes'. In other words, here at Wilton de Caus made a

Wilton

96 The Wilderness centring on a statue of Bacchus. In the engraving de Caus has deliberately chosen to omit the River Nadder, which broke the symmetry.

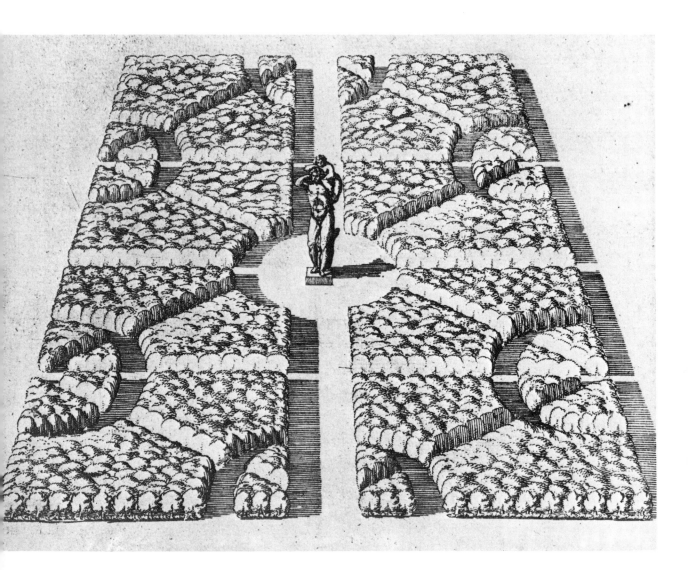

permanent feature of the effect that he had created fifteen years before in honour of Louis XIII's visit to Dieppe.

Beyond lay an oval circus in which stood a statue of a gladiator by Hubert le Sueur. The 8th Earl of Pembroke presented this statue to Sir Robert Walpole and it now stands indoors at the foot of the great staircase at Houghton. In *Le Jardin de Wilton* it is described as 'the most famous Statue of all that Antiquity hath left' and the Borghese Gladiator was one of those 'moulds and patterns of certain antiques' which le Sueur was paid for transporting from Italy in 1631.[28] That the great walk should culminate in a statue of an antique warrior must surely be meant to be read as a tribute to the Earl, whose prowess in the tilt-yard had been celebrated. The layout around the statue of oval walks planted with cherry trees recalls Ham House twenty years before and both stem from the garden tradition of Claude Mollet. And, as in the case of the Wilderness, there are huge arbours on either side.

97 One of the coronet fountains. The coronet was made to rise and fall on jets of water.

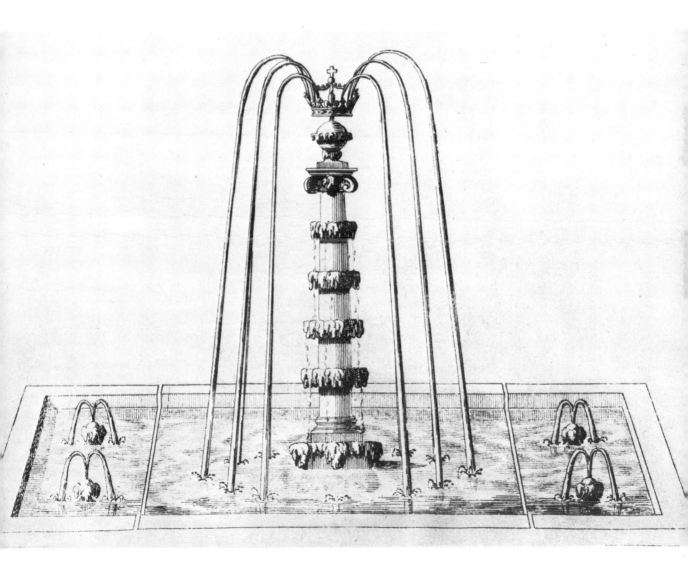

153

Wilton

The Grotto
and Water Parterre

facing page:
98 The immediate façade
of the grotto today

99 The façade as it
appeared *c.* 1700

this page:
100 Interior view of the
grotto looking into one of
the flanking rooms

101 The water parterre.
An important but
unlocated feature

102 Surviving figure by
Nicholas Stone from the
water parterre

The garden at its perimeter was bounded by a balustraded terrace stretching its entire width, upon which visitors could stroll and look down not only onto the garden but also out into the parkland beyond. In the centre of this by now familiar feature of the early Stuart garden stood the climax of Wilton's marvels, the grotto. This without doubt was its special distinction, still famous over half a century later when described at length by Celia Fiennes. Lieutenant Hammond saw it in the making, describing how 'the fat Dutch Keeper', as he unflatteringly refers to de Caus, took him straight to it:

> ... that rare Water-worke now making, and continuing by this outlandish Engineer, for the singing, and chirping of Birdes, and other strange rarities, onely by that Element, the finishing which rare peece of Skill, with satisfaction to the engenious Artist will cost (they say) a great Summe of Money.

Huygens describes it as 'the finest and most charming of grottos I remember ever hearing [sic] and seeing'. And here, for the last time before the disruption of war, we witness all the magic marvels of the Renaissance hydraulic engineer.

The outside façade of the grotto was a rusticated arcade through which, passing by sea-monsters which could spout water, the visitor was confronted by an inner façade which, reconstituted, still stands in the grounds. No engraving is supplied of this but only the walls of two sides of the first room in the grotto. Both are directly in the Woburn manner. In one, in the spandrels above, sea gods recline, while below to the left Venus and Cupid are borne through the water on a shell; to the right tritons float trumpeting a conch shell. Immediately on entering through the arch, the first room had a table of the sort seen in the grotto of the Hortus Palatinus and ultimately at Pratolino, from which jets of water could lift and toss into the air a crown, a branch or a gun. Figures in the corners wept water and the arches leading to the rooms on either side were also filled with surprise jets to wet the unwary. We only know the effect in one of the side rooms which was filled with the 'melody of Nightingerlls and all sorts of birds', something which de Caus describes at length in his *Waterworks*: 'To counterfeit the Voice of smal Birds by means of Water and Air'.[29] These engines were fed by fish-ponds in the roof of the grotto. There is no mention of automata but Lieutenant Hammond's reference to 'other rarities' in the making suggest that there were some initially.

The grotto by no means exhausts the wonders of Wilton. De Caus's *Le Jardin de Wilton* goes on to give two more engraved plates of garden characteristics; both are important. The first is of a water parterre, a feature best known in Italian gardens from the Villa Lante at Bagnaia, but in this case a descendant of that at St Germain-en-Laye via the Hortus Palatinus. The second is much more startling and severe, a planting resembling an amphitheatre cut out of a hillside, the terraces encircled by formal rows of cypress trees. Access from the first to the second upper terrace is by way of a staircase of a kind that appears in Serlio and which Inigo Jones had made use of for a pageant; Salomon de Caus also used such a staircase in the garden at Heidelberg. It is so purely Italianate in feeling that it reinforces one's overall conclusions as to Jones's influence. These monumental terraces, devoid of the fussy Mannerist trappings of de Caus, with their echo of the great amphitheatre in the Boboli Gardens, speak in the language of Inigo Jones.

103 The amphitheatre cut out of the hillside

104 Aerial view of the garden from the house looking towards the grotto

Where exactly were these terraces? They are elliptical and cut out of a hillside. The evidence of the perspective engraving by de Caus of the whole garden, the anonymous painting of *c.* 1700 and the actual terrain itself would point to it certainly being a continuation of the main garden schema up the hillside facing the south front. That it began to ascend we can gather from the steps visible in the engraving. But to what? In the painting the hillside is topped by what looks like a large triumphal arch with *allées* radiating from it. Even more remarkable is the fact that the arch appears to be surmounted by what must be an equestrian statue and is therefore presumably the cast of the Marcus Aurelius still at Wilton although long since resited. Tradition at Wilton has it that the statue was originally on a wooden arch on the hill before it was moved by Sir William Chambers to its present position. That all this was possible in the England of the 1630s seems to me to be highly likely. In 1633 le Sueur was commissioned by Lord Treasurer Weston to make an equestrian statue of Charles I for his garden at Roehampton. The statue still survives and is the one at Charing Cross. We know nothing of the Roehampton garden but it established that gardens were thought to be appropriate settings for this type of statue. In 1636 Inigo Jones was asked by the City Council to confer about a new Temple Bar and designs survive from the years 1636–8 which incorporate an equestrian likeness of the King on the top.[30] Across the Channel, Cardinal Richelieu's great garden at Rueil had a *pointe de vue* which was the arch of Constantine.[31] If this arrangement at Wilton did date from the thirties it must have formed a stunning climax to the whole *mise-en-scène*.

The picture records one other feature which may or may not have been part of the original complex, the cascade topped by the figure of Pegasus. This is also recorded in an engraving in William Stukeley's *Itinerarium curiosum* (1724).[32] The appearance of Pegasus has very definite links with the iconographic programme of the Double Cube Room, in which the ceiling panel of Perseus rescuing his mother from Pydectes is flanked by Perseus and Andromeda and Perseus and Pegasus.[33] But this programme relates to the south front as it was rebuilt after the disastrous fire of 1647–8, which had destroyed the de Caus building. The siting of Pegasus at the head of a cascade is natural, for it associated the cascade with the stream of Helicon which sprang forth when Pegasus stamped his foot on the Muses' mountain Parnassus. All this would point to the cascade – surely the earliest in an English garden – being post-1648 and not for consideration as part of the de Caus schema of the thirties.

The interpretation of the garden can, however, be taken a stage further. The theme of Love and Chastity in the embroidered parterres suggests a garden appropriate not to the Earl but to his Countess just as the Borghese warrior at the opposite end fuses antique virtue and knightly chivalry in a garden appropriate to him. The gardens either side of the groves are therefore concerned with civilizing influences and ideals of behaviour appropriate to the male and female domains of activity. The placing of the wild groves between, it could be argued, was not to conceal the irregularity of the Nadder but to emphasise the symbolic progression of the garden. Flora and Bacchus, gods of natural profusion, abundance and excess in nature, are posed as opposites. It is as though the central garden were the anti-masque of vices as in a Stuart court masque, and the flanking gardens the main masque, both utilizing recurring

Wilton

105 The cascade with Pegasus

themes in the imagery of the court in the thirties: the masques of ladies celebrate the virtues of neo-platonic, chaste love, those of lords the heroic virtues of the loyal knight. If the triumphal arch and equestrian Marcus Aurelius were also part of the overall scheme they would form a logical progression, for the imperial imagery of classical antiquity was evoked again and again by Charles I to sanctify Stuart rule over the Empire of Great Britain. The programme would also be wholly consistent with the masques, this being the equivalent of the pause in the revels – the dancing of the masquers and members of the court – to contemplate some new, amazing tableau by Inigo Jones celebrating the rule of Charles I.

The role of the Countess is an important one in any study of Wilton, but hitherto it has been totally overlooked. On 3 June 1630 the Earl married a second time, a great heiress and one of the most remarkable women of her age, Anne Clifford, Baroness Clifford in her right, widow of Richard Sackville, Earl of Dorset, and heiress to the mighty estates of George Clifford, 3rd Earl of Cumberland. The marriage was not a happy one and by 1637 she had already been living apart from Pembroke for at least two years because he had tried to marry off one of his younger sons to her daughter, Isabella. Much later she wrote of both the marriages: 'the marble pillars of Knolle in Kentt and Wilton in Wiltshire; were to me oftentimes but the gay Harbours of Anguish ... for I gave myselfe wholly to Retyredness, as much as I could, in both these great families, and made good Bookes and verteous thoughts my Companions'.[34] But all this lay in the future, during the period of the creation of the garden. The Countess was a highly educated lady. John Donne pays tribute to her knowledge and her tutor had been Samuel Daniel, the poet. She was also a passionate builder, restoring

159

or completely rebuilding her six northern castles, and her influence on the rebuilding of Wilton and its garden may have been immense. It could in the first instance account for the employment of de Caus, who was in the employ of her first cousins through her mother, the Earls of Bedford. If, looking at the Callot-style engraving with its elegant strolling cavaliers and their ladies, we are sometimes reminded of Rubens's *Garden of Love*, we might not be so far off part of its intent, as an expression of the short-lived marriage of Anne Clifford and Philip Herbert.

What are the influences that shaped Wilton? It is by far the most complex of all the gardens we have examined so far, the culmination of the *hortus conclusus* transmuted into the secular hieroglyphic garden of pleasure. The actual enclosure with its broad central avenue is pure Jones in the Venetian villa style, interlocking house façade and garden. But other influences are at work. On entering the garden from the house, there was no terrace from which to view the *parterres de broderie*, nor raised walks on either side as in the manner of Moor Park. This means that the parterres had always to be viewed from the rooms on the level of the *piano nobile*. The arrangement is indicative, however, of something else, the influence of the gardens of the Palais du Luxembourg.

The Earl of Pembroke must have known these gardens well for he had headed the embassy which had culminated in the marriage by proxy of Henrietta Maria and escorted her back to England. Pembroke, a noted Francophile, would not have missed the chance to study this magnificent new palace whose gardens had been laid out between 1611 and 1629.[35] In disposition they were modelled on those of the Queen Mother's youth, the Boboli Gardens of the Palazzo Pitti, thus introducing to France the transverse axis which Le Nôtre was to use to such overwhelming effect later at Versailles. In that Pembroke had no interest but the concentric walks may well have influenced the centre section of the Wilton garden and the position of the embroidered parterres directly adjoining the façade of the palace certainly did. In the case of the Luxembourg the great parterre was surrounded by terraces on the other three sides, an arrangement derived from the amphitheatre in the Boboli Gardens. The absence of the familiar feature of a terrace from which one descended into the garden at Wilton must have been derived from this peculiar arrangement at the Luxembourg. But there the similarity ends, for the great parterre was far more advanced than that at Wilton, the whole area being thrown into one large composition in parts as against the still tentative grouping in fours at Wilton.

Although it seems to me highly likely that Moor Park had embroidered parterres, these patterns recorded in the published *Hortus Pembrochianus* are the earliest for which we have evidence in England. Their nearest parallel, as one would expect, is the earlier French gardening tradition of Claude Mollet, who laid out Fontainebleau and St Germain-en-Laye. All these belong to an intermediate stage when although the parterre beds have not as yet become one sweeping bold Baroque composition they are beginning to be linked into groups of four with complementary designs centring on a fountain or statue. The patterns are of scrollwork interlaced with feathery motifs exactly in the manner of the designs of Mollet published by his son, André, in *Le Jardin de plaisir* (Stockholm, 1651). The arrangement of the walks at the far end of the garden is also a typical Mollet feature ever since St Germain-en-Laye.[36]

These resemblances have been pointed out by Sten Karling in his study of the Mollet family and raise the whole issue of the influence of André Mollet on Wilton. André states in the preface to *Le Jardin de plaisir* that he had been in the service of the King of England before he entered that of Prince Frederick Henry of Orange in 1633. He must, therefore, have served Charles I. Perhaps he came over with Henrietta Maria in 1625 but somehow it seems more likely that he arrived after the peace with France in 1629. As we shall see in the next chapter, he laid out *parterres de broderie* at St James's Palace during this period, which could have influenced Wilton.[37]

I would rather think that Wilton was solely the work of Inigo Jones and Isaac de Caus under the direction of Pembroke than evidence of Mollet. De Caus must have seen embroidered parterres as devised by the Mollet family before he came to England. André Mollet, however, must have seen Wilton or at least known the plans for it by May 1633. At that date, when he arrived in Holland, the laying out of Wilton was well advanced and it was doubtless with this garden spectacle in mind that he supervised the design of the gardens and parterres at Prince Frederick Henry's palace at Honselaersdijk. The broad arrangement of a garden axially aligned with the palace surrounded by canals is typically French but the division of the garden as a whole into three areas is strikingly reminiscent of Wilton. The embroidered parterres on either side of the palace re-echo Wilton in their positioning immediately below the windows and in the case of one even the design is of the same type. The centre portion of the garden, with its concentric circles of walks sparsely planted with trees, is again suggestive of a connection. Outside the palace garden proper the amphitheatre of trees recalls another Wilton feature.[38]

Wilton goes down as a unique synthesis of the Renaissance gardener's art. It combines in one experience the layout of villas of the Brenta with the grotto marvels of Pratolino, the disposition and details of the traditions of Henry IV's St Germain-en-Laye and Marie de Medici's Palais du Luxembourg with the museum garden of the Roman aristocracy. It was also to have an influence on the development of garden layout in the middle of the century. The broad central path crossing a series of rectangular gardens bounded within a wall and centralized on the façade of the house turns up several times in houses illustrated by Kip: at Haigh in Lancashire (now Greater Manchester), Staunton Harold in Leicestershire and above all at Dawley in the former county of Middlesex. None of them, however, manages to exceed either in size or originality the splendours of its prototype.

At this point we should pause and try to place the Wilton villa and its marvellous gardens in the context of Caroline civilization, as a symbol of the halcyon years of the King's Peace, those years between 1629 and 1640 when Charles ruled without Parliament. And there is no better document to do this than Thomas Carew's great masque *Coelum Britannicum*, with which the court ushered in the year 1634 and which is, therefore, exactly contemporary with the rebuilding of Wilton.[39] The masque celebrates the triumph of Charles I's personal rule by means of a purging of the vices from heaven and earth and the establishment of a new heaven and a new earth symbolized by the virtuous laws, behaviour and social ethics of the Caroline court. By extension the new age replaces the debauched Jacobean court by the refined preciosity of Charles and Henrietta Maria, and at the same time the new Empire of Great

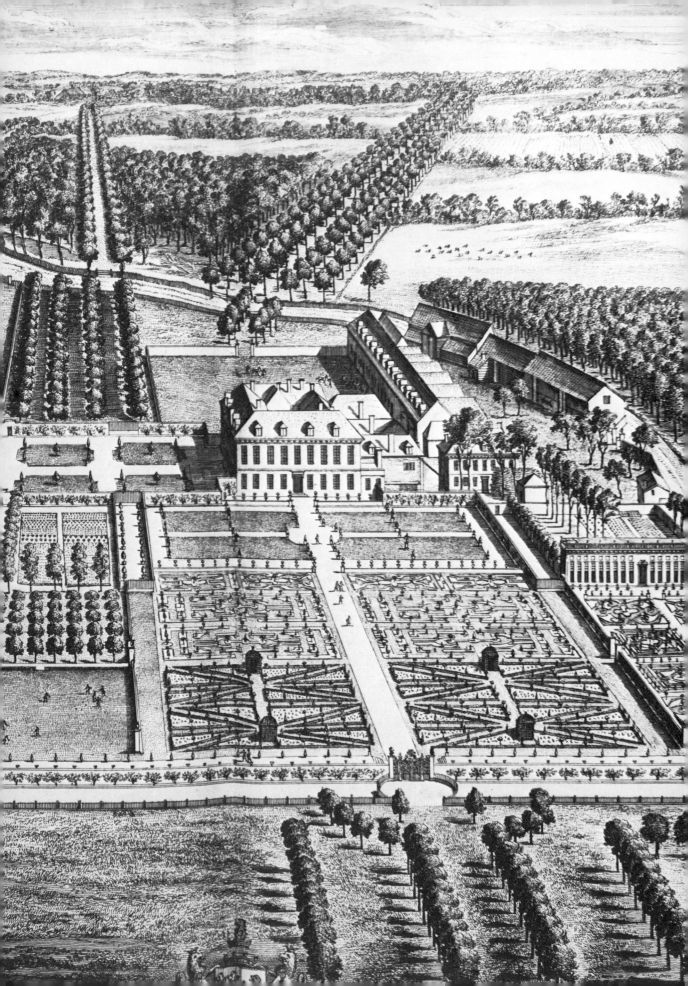

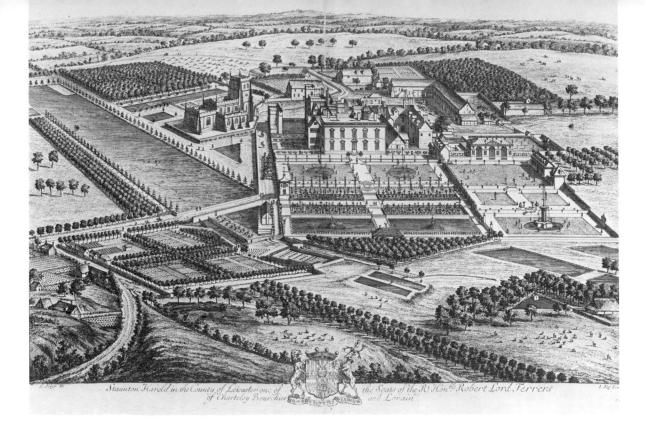

Staunton Harold in the County of Leicester one of of Chartley Bourchier the Seats of the R.t. Hon.ble Robert Lord Ferrers and Louain

106–8 The influence of Wilton. Three gardens recorded by Kip in his *Britannia illustrata* (1707) which owe their layout to Wilton: Dawley (*facing page*), Staunton Harold and Haigh

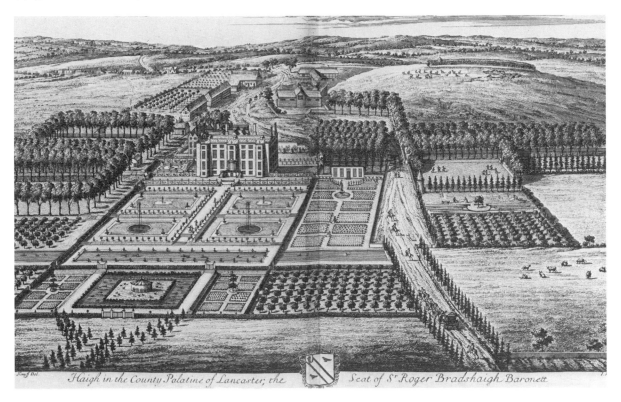

Haigh in the County Palatine of Lancaster; the Seat of S.r Roger Bradshaigh Baronett

Britain, that heroic re-creation by the Stuart kings of Ancient Britain, brings with it a new code of behaviour and new ideals of life. Inigo Jones's Vitruvian machine conjured up a huge mountain on which sat the kingdoms of England, Scotland and Ireland and from which issued Charles as the 'mighty British Hercules' and his band of heroes, who combine the virtues of the Romans with those of the knights of medieval chivalry (just as Pembroke did). The courtly audience in the Whitehall Banqueting House was looking at the birth of a new political dispensation, the prerogative rule of the King over his Empire of Great Britain. And this stupendous spectacle gave way to another which this time placed before the court the ideals that this age was to bring. The wild and rugged mountainside sank to disclose:

> . . . a new and pleasant prospect, clean differing from all the other, the nearest part showing a delicious garden with several walks and parterres set round with low trees, and on the sides against these walks were fountains and grots, and in the furthest part a palace, from whence went high walks upon arches, and above them open terraces planted with cypress trees, and all this together was composed of such ornaments as might express a princely villa.[40]

All this was visually bringing to fruition the scene which had opened the masque, one of ruined classical buildings, a 'great city of the ancient Romans or civilised Britons'. As in the case of the political rebirth, there is a complementary aesthetic one, epitomized in the restored classical architecture and nature tamed in the garden, the ideals of a villa by Inigo Jones with its fountains, walks, terraces, grottos, parterres and cypress trees. Jones's design for this scene is lifted from an engraving by Antonio Tempesta but he could as easily have put on stage the bird's eye view of the Wilton project as it was initially conceived. No wonder Charles I loved to visit Wilton every summer. Here he could stroll amidst the cultural expression of his political ideals. The garden at Wilton was indeed the King's Arcadia. In the masque the scene gives way to one final tableau of the virtues of Religion, Truth, Wisdom, Concord, Government and Reputation, the mainstays of prerogative rule as envisaged within the mind of the King, hovering above Windsor Castle. How ironic that when civil war finally broke out in 1642 Pembroke was to side with Parliament.

The end of de Caus

De Caus was not only active at Wilton in the thirties. In 1638 he designed a house for Richard Boyle, 1st Earl of Cork, Stalbridge Park in Dorset. This included a plan for part of the garden. Nothing, however, is known of this long-vanished house.[41] It may prove that he was considerably more active than we know. Could he, for instance, have been responsible for the 'pretty summer-house panell'd and ciel'd with looking-glass' at Wollaton which had beneath: 'a water house with grotesque work of shell, &c', as recorded by Stukeley?[42] His exact relationship with Inigo Jones still remains to be sorted out. In the main it seems that Jones may have brought in de Caus when a client wanted elaborate waterworks or when he was too busy himself to do anything more than supervise the design of a house and garden. And, as with Jones, everything must have come to a standstill when civil war broke out in 1642. De Caus at some unknown date returned to France and died in Paris on 22 February 1648; he was buried in the Protestant cemetery of Charenton.

During this period he produced two books: one was the uncertainly dated *Le Jardin de Wilton* (*c.* 1645) and the other *Nouvelle Invention de lever l'eau*,

164

which appeared in 1644 and was translated into English by John Leak as *New and Rare Inventions of Waterworks* in 1659 when the author was referred to as 'a late famous engenier'. *Nouvelle Invention* is illustrated with twenty-six copper plates for the most part derived from his brother's famous work *Les Raisons des forces mouvantes*.[43] The book is a selective translation of *Les Raisons* and was therefore to reinforce even more the enormous influence of the de Caus garden tradition into the post-Restoration period. There was even a new edition of the translation in 1704.

After 1660 these waterworks were to spread to the gentry and upper middle classes. John Woolridge in his *Systema Horti-Culturae, or the Art of Gardening* (1688) eulogizes fountains and waterworks including the familiar de Caus ball balanced on a single jet, or the hydraulic singing nightingales. He writes in praise of artificial streams and grottos:

> You may make secret Rooms and Passages within it, and in the outer Room may you have all those . . . Water-works, for your Own or your Friends divertisements.

And then he writes of the grotto at Wilton:

> The most famous in this kind that this Kingdom affords, is that *Wiltonian Grotto* near unto *Salisbury*, on which no cost was spared to make it compleat, and wherein you may view, or might have lately so done, the best of Water-works. . . .[44]

In this way Wilton was seen in retrospect fifty years on as a unique phenomenon of international standing, for Woolridge states that it excelled the devices at Richelieu's château at Rueil. Engravings of the *Hortus Pembrochianus* were known on the Continent and the fountains were included by Georg Andreas Böckler in his *Amoenitates hydragogicae*, published in 1664.[45] The influence of the de Caus family even passes into the eighteenth century in Stephen Switzer's *An Introduction to a General System of Hydrostatics and Hydraulics* (1729). Switzer lifts, with acknowledgment, from 'the famous de Caus' (Salomon) the speaking statue of Memnon recorded by Cornelius Tacitus and Pausanias, from Hero of Alexandria the birds who cease to chirp when an owl turns towards them, and two hydraulic organs.[46] In this way the world of late Renaissance mechanical marvels and magical science lived on into the Age of the Enlightenment.

CHAPTER VII

THE ECLECTIC GARDEN II
Inigo Jones, Sir John Danvers and André Mollet

During the reign of James I, relations with Italy became increasingly easier, something which was to continue right through the reign of Charles I, whose agents scoured the country acquiring Renaissance works of art for the royal collections. This change of atmosphere was apparent initially at the very close of Elizabeth's reign, when formal diplomatic relations were re-established with the Republic of Venice. Under James I this was extended to the courts of Savoy and Tuscany, with both of which matches were contemplated for Henry, Prince of Wales. Under Charles I there was even a papal agent at the Stuart court. All this meant that the routes to Italy were open and what was to be the precursor of the Grand Tour began; this, of course, was to have an incalculable effect on English civilization during the century. At last it was possible to assimilate at first hand the achievements of Renaissance and Baroque Italy.[1] And, although the advent of a French Queen in 1625 ensured the continuation of French influence on garden design, increasingly the English were actually experiencing the realities of the great gardens of Italy. The effects of this were already beginning to be felt during the 1620s and 1630s.

George Sandys, who undertook such a voyage at the opening of the second decade, was one of the earliest of these travellers to write an account of his journey. In fact, he eulogizes only one garden, that of the Duke of Toledo in southern Italy:

> A place of surpassing delight: in which are many excellent statues, recouered from the decayes of antiquity; and euery where fountaines of fresh water, adorned with Nymphes and Satyres: where the artificall rocks, shells, mosse and tophas, seeme euen to excell that which they imitate.[2]

In other words Sandys is seeing a museum garden full of real classical statuary besides fountains and grottos. More interesting is the guide by an anonymous traveller written during the same period: 'Of what is most worthy to be seen in all Italy orderly set down, And in sure manner, as that the Traveller may not oversee or neglect any thing that is memorable'.[3] In this, gardens figure surprisingly prominently and Pratolino, for example, gets a whole section to itself. The Pitti Palace has 'a great and brave garden', Caprarola has 'pleasant gardens, with curious and artificial waterworks', the villa of the Cardinal of Florence has

> ... in the garden, a cage wherein are all kinds of birds making sweet harmony, divers rare water-works, and plentifully planted with cypress-trees, yielding a savour so admirable sweet, as the body therewith may be ravished.[4]

109 Self-portrait of Inigo Jones (c. 1620)

The Cardinal Ferdinando de Medici, he relates

> . . . caused a hill to be made, and one hundred and fifty stairs to go up; on the top is
> built an excellent pleasant summer-house. . . . The hill is overgrown from the
> bottom to the top with cypress trees, which is as pleasant a prospect as a man can
> imagine. The garden is adorned with such and so many artificial and rare water-
> works, plants, and statues, as would drive a man to admire . . .[5]

As for the Villa d'Este at Tivoli, here the response to such marvels is a
crescendo of ecstasy. He enthuses over the water organ playing melodiously,
the dragon fountain with its four vast jets of black water, 'fearful to behold', the
grotto of Sibylla 'adorned with oriental coral and mother of pearl', the amazing
'artificial water-works' (which Montaigne described and which appears in de
Caus's *Les Raisons* being based on Hero of Alexandria) in which

> . . . the birds do sing, sitting upon twigs, so naturally, as one would verily think they
> were all quick and living birds . . . and, when they are in the midst of their best
> singing, then comes an owl flying, and the birds suddenly, all at once, are still.[6]

There was even an arch of water causing rainbows to be seen. If this account is
any indication of the impact of the magical marvels of the Italian Mannerist
garden on one Jacobean traveller, one can only speculate as to the effect all this
must have had on the highly receptive mind of the British Vitruvius, Inigo
Jones. And we must always remember that visitors saw these gardens as
accurate re-creations of what they had read about in Pliny and other classical
texts.

Up until now Inigo Jones seems to have played very much of a peripheral
role in the garden revolution which occurred in James I's reign. During his first
visit to Italy some time between the years 1597 and 1603, garden design does
not seem to have been an object of study. Jones was there solely as a young
painter to study the 'arts of design' so that it is hardly surprising that he
occupied a purely subordinate position in the grandiose schemes designed and
supervised by Salomon de Caus and Constantino dei Servi. Jones, in fact, was
never to become a hydraulic engineer but, as a result of his famous second
Italian visit, he was to have, it can be argued, a decisive impact on the
development of garden design during the decade and a half which prefaced the
outbreak of civil war in 1642.

Jones was already forty when he left England with the twenty-eight-year-old
Earl of Arundel and his Countess as part of the escorting entourage of the
Princess Elizabeth and the Elector Palatine. After completing the formal part
of this progress in Heidelberg they journeyed on to Italy where they stayed for
twenty-one months.[7] During these months Jones not only made an intensive
study of the remains of classical antiquity and of the art of the Renaissance, but
also advised the Earl on purchases for his collections. From the point of view of
the development of architecture in England, by far the most important of these
were the chests of architectural drawings by Palladio and Scamozzi. The
arrival of these in Jacobean England, together with all that Jones had studied
and noted during his travels, was to transform the Jacobean romantic, who up
until then had freely mingled Renaissance forms with Elizabethan neo-Gothic,
into the British Vitruvius. He and Arundel returned in January 1614. Eight
months later the death of the old Surveyor, Simon Basil, opened the way to a
domination of the visual arts by Jones which was to last until the Civil War.

It can be no coincidence, therefore, that the fundamental tenet of the Italian Renaissance garden theorist – that the garden was an extension of the architecture of the house and integral to it – appears in England in the years immediately after the return of Jones from Italy. Both directly and indirectly this must stem from Jones. The only garden, however, that we can definitely associate with him is that at Arundel House, which introduced to England that classical Renaissance type, the museum garden.

The museum garden: Thomas Howard, Earl of Arundel

Fynes Moryson in the 1590s describes that most familiar feature of the Italian Renaissance garden, antique sculpture, in the following way in his account of Pope Julius II's Belvedere. There were, he writes:

> many faire statuas, namely of the River Nilus, of the River Tyber, of Romulus and Remus playing with the papps of a shee-Wolfe, all being placed in the open Garden, and a most faire Statua of Apollo, another admirable statua of Lycaon with his children, another of the boy Antonous, whom the Emperor Adrian loved, another of Hercules, another of Cupid, another of Venus, another of Cleopatra sleeping with her arme over her face, and bearing a Serpent, being a faire Statua.[8]

In this manner an Elizabethan responds to some of the most famous and influential pieces of antique sculpture known to the Renaissance, examples whose influence on the development of the visual arts was profound: the Apollo Belvedere, the Laocoön or the recumbent Cleopatra. The garden of the Belvedere epitomized an ideal of the outdoors as a setting for the display of classical antiquities.

This tradition began earlier with Florentine Humanists, who were the first to make garden museums. About 1483 Poggio Bracciolini relates how he set up antique statues in the garden of his villa in Terra Nuova. Mantegna did the same, so did Cosimo and Lorenzo de Medici and Cardinal Bembo.[9] In spite of these forebears, however, the most famous configuration of all was in the gardens of the papal Belvedere palace, which established this combination as a fashion, to be copied by all the cardinals in the gardens of their villas surrounding Rome.

Although, of course, the Belvedere terracing was also revolutionary in its influence, here we shall confine ourselves to the garden purely in respect of its sculptural content. Bramante did much more than merely place the pieces in the open air: each was individually set within a niche or grotto or combined with a marble basin to become a fountain. Every effort was made to re-create the garden of an antique villa. The result of this was, of course, a new type of garden, one which belongs essentially to the high Renaissance. Ironically its arrival in England occurred later than the garden style which superseded it, that of the world of Mannerist marvels and automata. As far as England was concerned, it depended on personal contact of the type experienced by Moryson and even more on the importation of classical statuary. Inevitably it could never become a widespread fashion and its short-lived existence was confined to some of the royal gardens, as furnished with statuary from the collection of the Duke of Mantua and casts after the antique prototypes by Hubert le Sueur; above all to the gardens of Arundel House as replanned by Thomas Howard, Earl of Arundel, after his momentous visit to Italy in 1614.

Twenty years later, in 1634, Henry Peacham produced the enlarged edition of his *Compleat Gentleman*, in which it was stated that a knowledge of classical antiquities in the form of statues, inscriptions, coins and medals had become a desirable attribute of the Stuart gentleman.

> For next men and manners, there is nothing fairely more delightfull, nothing worthier observation, than these Copies, and memorials of men and matters of elder times; whose lively presence is able to perswade a man, that he now seeth two thousand yeeres agoe.[10]

Peacham refers to the collections formed by the Grand Dukes of Tuscany and by the popes in the gardens of the Belvedere and the Farnesina. He then goes on to give a very exact account of their arrival in England, opening the passage with a salute to the connoisseur and collector, Thomas Howard, Earl of Arundel:

> To whose liberall charges and magnificence this angle of the world oweth the first sight of Greeke and Romane Statues, with whose admired presence he began to honour the Gardens and Galleries of Arundel-House about twentie yeeres agoe and hath ever since continued to transplant old Greece into *England*. King *Charles* also ever since his coming to the Crowne, hath amply testified a Royall liking of ancient statues, by causing a whole army of old forraine Emperours, Captaines, and Senators all at once to land on his coasts, to come and do him homage; and attend upon him in his palace of Saint *Iames*, and Somerset-house.[11]

In this passage Peacham outlines succinctly the garden descent that we must follow, firstly that of Arundel, to whose son he was tutor, in the period after 1614, and secondly, Charles I in the years following his accession in 1625.

Thomas Howard, Earl of Arundel, was, of course, a member of the circle of Henry, Prince of Wales, and must have been very familiar with the work of Salomon de Caus but he was destined to import to England a quite different strand of Renaissance garden making, the formal garden as an outdoor sculpture gallery.[12] It was in Rome that the sculpture collection began, for there the Earl supervised excavations for antiquities, purchased the so-called Homerus and commissioned Egidio Moretti to carve four statues for him *à l'antique*. After his return to England in 1616 William Cecil, Lord Roos, 'gave the Earle of Arundell all the statues he brought out of Italie at one clap' and Sir Dudley Carleton presented him with a 'head of Jupiter' which he placed 'in his utmost garden, so opposite the Gallery dores, as being open so soon as you enter into the front Garden you have the head in your eie all the way'.[13] Arundel was an assiduous collector. He asked Sir Thomas Roe, ambassador to the Sublime Porte, to scour Greece and Asia for him and later sent his own agent, his chaplain, William Petty, who, after heroic journeys, sent to England, in 1627, the collection subsequently immortalized in the publication by Richard James, the *Marmora Arundeliana* (1628). So important and so exciting was the arrival of this consignment that John Selden, the lawyer and antiquarian, was woken up in the middle of the night in order to be present at the unpacking. The galleries and gardens of Arundel House at their height in the thirties contained some 32 statues, 128 busts, 250 inscriptions, sarcophagi, altars and other fragments. No wonder Francis Bacon, whose concept of a garden was so far removed from that of Arundel, 'coming into the . . . Garden, where there were a great number of Ancient Statues of naked Men and Women, made a stand, and as astonish'd cryed out: *The Resurrection*'.[14]

Joachim Sandrart visited the garden in 1627 and described it as follows:

> Foremost amongst the objects worthy to be seen stood the beautiful garden of that most famous lover of art, the Earl of Arundel; resplendent with the finest ancient statues in marble, of Greek and Roman workmanship. Here were to be seen, firstly, the portrait of a Roman Consul, in long and graceful drapery, through which the form and proportion of that body could be readily perceived. Then there was a statue of Paris; and many others, some full-length, some busts only; with an almost innumerable quantity of heads and reliefs, all in marble and very rare.[15]

By that date the collection was virtually complete so it must have been during the preceding decade that the gardens were laid out and composed to display them.

We in fact know very little in detail about Arundel House, the old Howard family town house which James I had given back to the Earl on his restoration to honours early in the reign.[16] Arundel's overall aim on his return from Italy was to remodel the house and its grounds to approximate as closely as possible to the villas he had seen in Italy. That the garden layout was regarded as something original is reflected in the series of drawings made by John Smythson on his visit to London in 1618–19. These include *The plateforme of the garden at Arundell house* and *The new Italyan gate . . . in the garden there*.[17] Jones's own design for the most important of the gates is extant,[18] as are three views of the garden: a glimpse in a view of the Thames by Cornelius Bol;[19] another in the background of Mytens's portrait of the Countess; and a bird's eye vista of a further section in the background of a full-length portrait of the Earl at Welbeck Abbey.[20] The last gives us the most spectacular impression and the view seems to commemorate the installation of the great 1627 consignment of antiquities.

We must, therefore, imagine the Arundel House garden evolving over a period of slightly more than a decade from the return of the Earl and Countess from Italy in 1614 to its heyday from *c.* 1630 onwards. The remodelling of the house and gardens belongs to Inigo Jones's transitional phase, *c.* 1615–19, when he was assimilating the consequences of his Italian journey and the great collections of architectural drawings by Palladio and Scamozzi.[20] It was a period typified by the overlaying of Italian features onto existing buildings, pergolas, gateways, porticoes, windows and chimney pieces. This also applied to gardens into which Jones introduced his most enduring and delightful innovation, the garden gate.[21] The earliest of these were the five which he designed for Anne of Denmark for her old Tudor palace of Oatlands immediately upon his return. Of these the most significant was the 'Greate gate' leading into the Vineyard, which figures prominently in Paul van Somer's full-length portrait of the Queen painted in 1617.[22] As a composition it was a Jonesian extemporization on Serlio. Over the years these gateways to courtyards and gardens were to be some of Jones's most pleasing architectural compositions. In relation to the history of garden design in England they were quite new, evoking by their mere presence and their assertive classicism the ideals of the new garden, conceived above all as emblematic expressions of the boundaries between ordered and disordered nature.

Inigo Jones,
Anne of Denmark
and the Earl of Arundel

Between 1614 and the early 1630s
Thomas Howard, Earl of Arundel,
employed Inigo Jones to remodel
his house and garden by the
Thames in the Italian manner as a
setting befitting his collections.

The: newe Italyan: gate at Arundell
houfe in the garden there:

facing page:
110 Inigo Jones's Great Gate at
Oatlands (1617). The garden
gate as the boundary between
tamed and untamed nature was
one of Jones's most distinctive
contributions to garden
architecture.

111 Inigo Jones's Italian gate for
the west garden of Arundel
House (1618)

this page:
112 Arundel: view from
the picture gallery into the
garden (1618)

113 Arundel: view of the
east garden with
balustraded terracing and
antique sculpture (*c.* 1627)

John Smythson records two garden gates at Arundel House. One is conveniently dated 1618, the other, which has three stone balls on the top of it, can be seen in the picture at Welbeck. Smythson provides a plan of one of the gardens on the same sheet as that of the 1618 gate, which gives a date also for this earliest garden essay. This is presumably the west garden, which can also be glimpsed in the Bol painting, a rectangular enclosure surrounded on three sides by buildings or walls, but with three flights of steps leading up to a terrace on the riverside. Arundel House was next to Somerset House, so that this riverside terrace would have repeated the arrangement in de Caus's garden for Anne of Denmark. Otherwise there was no terracing, the enclosed area being equally divided into four rectangles of grass planted with trees along the edges to form walks, the longest avenue presumably culminating in the Italian gate. There seems to be very little of startling originality about this garden apart from its gate and presumably, although it is difficult to establish, a deliberate effort to reconcile its plan in relation to the architecture of the house.

Nor is there much original in a second glimpse of the garden opening out from the picture gallery in the background of Mytens's 1618 portrait of the Countess. It focuses on a fountain, seemingly placed in the usual manner at the intersection of tree-lined paths and looks towards an architectural arbour of greenery with a central doorway and 'windows' looking onto the garden. In other words, it is a garden of the sort we are familiar with from the Hortus Palatinus. The most surprising of all the gardens must have been created later to receive the statuary and was on the east side. From the Welbeck painting we can see that this was a terraced garden with an approach up a flight of steps leading to a broad central walk parallel with the river. The wall surrounding has statues placed at the corners and at the staircase openings. Half-way along the wall, parallel with the river, there are two statues which presumably flank further steps leading down to a lower garden planted with trees.

This treatment must reflect Bramante's Belvedere and probably represents the earliest terracing in the Italian manner to be erected in a garden in England. But like so many of these early essays in Italianate gardening, the fulfilment of the basic principles was dogged by having somehow to marry a revamped Tudor building to a garden area on the banks of the Thames which certainly could never exactly duplicate the arrangements of a villa on the Brenta by Palladio. Nonetheless, the remodelling of Arundel House by Inigo Jones, with its broad monumental treatment of the garden walks, its efforts to link house and garden, its terracing and above all its astounding spectacle of antique statuary, must have been a remarkable novelty in late Jacobean London.

There is a footnote to add on the subject of Arundel and gardening. The Earl owned both Tart Hall on the outskirts of St James's Park and Albury Park in Surrey. Both had gardens. There is a curious engraving entitled *bey Albury* by Wenceslas Hollar, which shows a river with a view beyond to a low, rambling building in the classical style set amidst a series of terraced squares which ascend towards a hill in the distance. Figures promenade towards it along a riverside walk. What is it? There is an unmistakable Jonesian air about what seems to be a large ruined grotto or casino. Both Arundel and Jones had seen the grandest of Italian gardens which this type of building evokes. There is without doubt an element of abandonment about it as though it were some grandiose scheme for an elaborate terraced garden and casino which was

bey Albury

114 Arundel also created grottos in the hillsides around his country house at Albury Park, Surrey. Hollar's engraving *bey Albury* seems to record an unfinished casino in the classical style.

interrupted by the outbreak of civil war. It would seem to connect with a reference that we have to the grottos Arundel had cut out of the sandy sides of the hills around Albury, 'wherein he delighted to sit and discourse'.[23]

The garden of Tart Hall presents another kind of problem.[24] Bordering on St James's Park, the house had a large walled garden at the back, the appearance of which is recorded in Faithorne and Newcourt's map of the area surveyed in 1643–7, but not published until 1658. If this garden arrangement goes back to the thirties, it presents a coherent scheme of embroidered parterres below a broad terrace next to the house in the new bold French manner stemming from the great parterre at the Luxembourg as introduced into England by André Mollet.

Arundel remains an essentially unresolved figure in the history of gardening but the underlying principle on which he worked, in collaboration with Jones, is clear. It was chiefly and directly Italianate and the Earl probably exerted a great influence in this direction on John Evelyn, who refers to him as 'my noble friend whilst he lived' and who later redesigned the garden at Albury Park. By 1667, when he did this, the sculpture garden at Arundel House was a sad spectacle: 'these precious Monuments . . . miserably neglected, & scattred up & downe about the Gardens & other places of Arundell-house, & how exceedingly the corrosive air of *London* impaired them'.[25] Through Evelyn's intervention they were presented to the University of Oxford, where they remain to this day.

175

John Aubrey, however, relates that it was not Arundel but his relative Sir John
Danvers 'who first taught us the way of Italian gardens'.[26] Wilton was regarded
by Aubrey as the third garden in the Italian style to be created in pre-Civil War
England, but the first two had been made by Danvers: 'He had well travelled
France and Italy, and made good observations. He had in a fair body an
harmonicall mind. . . . He had a very fine fancy, which lay chiefly for gardens
and architecture'.[27] The gardens in question were firstly that at his house in
Chelsea begun in 1622–3 and secondly that at Lavington in Wiltshire, which he
came into by his second marriage in 1628.

Sir John Danvers (1588?–1655) was the third and youngest son of Sir John
Danvers of Dauntsey.[28] His eldest brother, Charles, was executed for his part
in Essex's uprising in 1601 and his second brother Henry, later Earl of Danby,

Danvers House, Chelsea

*Begun by Sir John Danvers
in 1622 and regarded by
Aubrey as the first garden
in the Italian style in
England. The influence of
Inigo Jones is likely.*

115 John Aubrey's plan
of the garden in 1691

facing page:
116 The garden as it
appears in Kip's *Britannia
illustrata* (1707)

had a distinguished career as a soldier and statesman and founded the Botanic Gardens in Oxford in 1621. John's first wife was Magdalen Herbert, a match which brought him Lord Herbert of Cherbury and George Herbert, the poet, as stepchildren. Lady Danvers herself was a close friend of John Donne. Aubrey wrote that Sir John 'was a great acquaintance and favorite of the Lord Chancellor Bacon, who took much delight in that elegant Garden at Chelsey'.[29] Bacon died in 1626, so that it must have been the garden and house in its initial stages with which he was familiar.

Aubrey regarded the garden at Chelsea as so important that he compiled a long description of it in 1691 together with a ground-plan.[30] The house was then in the possession of Danvers's second daughter. There is also a perspective view of it, little changed, in Kip's panorama of the Chelsea estate in

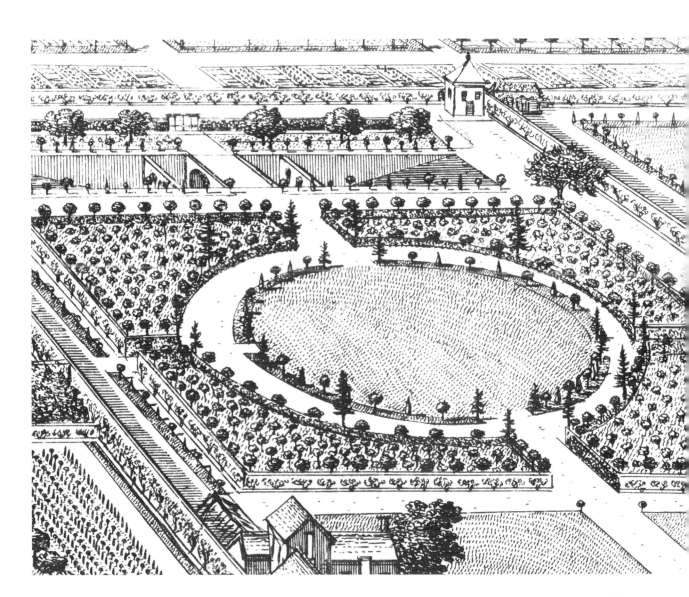

Britannia illustrata from a drawing of 1699 by Knyff. Why was it so novel? In the first place it seems to have been the earliest instance in which house and garden were conceived *ab initio* as a single unit. Salomon de Caus's gardens and that of Lord Arundel, for instance, were remodellings of existing ground in relation to old houses. Danvers's Chelsea House was remarkable for this new-found unity. 'As you sitt at Dinner in the Hall', Aubrey wrote, 'you are entertaind with two delightfull Visto's: one southward over the Thames & to Surrey: the other northward into that curious Garden.' Access to the latter was from the *piano nobile* by means of a double flight of steps from the hall with, in addition, a wall 'to hinder the imediate pleasure and totall view'. In this, Danvers fulfils Sir Henry Wotton's description of the ideal approach to a garden from a terrace 'whence might be taken a generall view of the whole *Plate* below, but rather in a delightfull confusion, than with any plaine distinction of the pieces'. Wotton describes the descent into the garden where 'every one of these diversities, was as if hee had beene *Magically* transported into a New Garden'.[31] Surprise and vista were two of the key features of Danvers House.

The garden as a whole was centralized axially on the house; it was divided into three sections carefully composed into alternate open and hidden areas. On arrival at the bottom of the flight of steps from the house the visitor found himself in a wilderness of sweet-briars, lilac, syringas, holly and juniper intermingled with apple and pear trees divided into walks. In the midst of these stood two polychrome statues of the gardener and his wife by Nicholas Stone, all of which had been swept away by Kip's day.[32] Emerging from this the east and west sides of the garden had two wide gravel walks, each terminated at the end nearest the house by statues, one of Hercules and Antaeus and the other of Cain and Abel. The walks were bordered with hyssop backed by more than twenty-four varieties of thyme:

> Sir John was wont in fine faire mornings in the summer to brush his Bever hatt on the Hysop and Thyme, which did perfume it with its naturall Essence: and would last a morning or longer.[33]

Between these walks there was a huge oval bowling green, an essentially English feature, with an oval walk encompassing it and to which access was gained by entrances on four sides, three being flanked by statues of shepherds and shepherdesses, the fourth, nearest the house, by sphinxes. The bowling green was surrounded by a wall of cypress trees and the spandrels were thick planted with evergreen shrubs and trees.

Aubrey explains that the problem of this garden lay in its flatness, which had led Sir John to have a very deep trench dug at the far end to form a terrace walk. In the centre of the dip was 'a round well or Basin' in a grotto of some sort with a brick banqueting house (gone by Kip's day) above it with stained glass windows and access to a roof from which to look down on the garden. The combination of watery grotto below and banqueting house above was exactly contemporary with the same arrangement being built by Inigo Jones and Isaac de Caus in the Whitehall Banqueting House.[34] The north terrace was terminated at each end by a summer house.

That this garden was regarded as in some way revolutionary and still so as late as 1691 calls for analysis. Aubrey's description makes it clear that vistas and prospects formed a central feature of its novelty. He praises the view from the hall and from the room over it. He admires the concealment of the view as the visitor descended from house to garden. He is 'entertained' by the 'stately pieces of Sculpture' which close the great walks. The banqueting house is both 'a gracefull Tower to your view' and the means 'whence you enjoy the prospect of the Garden'. From the north terrace 'you overlook the garden'. More even than this Aubrey suggests that the garden was designed to simulate psychological states of mind. Thus he writes when talking of the banqueting house and grotto below:

> . . . now, as you goe from this gay Paradise into the darksome, deep vault (*Grotto* written over) where the Well is, it affects one with a kind of Religious horrour.

Perhaps this psychological approach to the garden is understood even more easily by the six statues of shepherds and shepherdesses, figures which were to become clichés in garden decoration for the next two hundred years but which in the mid-1620s must have been startling novelties. The statues which were from the Stone workshop depicted an old shepherd and shepherdess, a second pair young and 'incumbent' and a third sitting and inclining to each other, the lids of their eyes almost closed. Aubrey speaks again here of mood and expression, praising the sculptor for 'expressing Love-passions in the very freestone: where you read rustick beauty mixt with antique innocent simplicitie: there you may behold the Faithful shepherd, and the Faithfull Shepherdesse: who have the honestest innocent countenances that can be imagined'.

This evocation of Arcadia in Chelsea in late Jacobean England is a realisation in gardening terms of the late Renaissance pastoral, a permanent evocation to the visitor of the world to which he was transported in the endless pastoral literature of the day. Danvers is doing something revolutionary for England. His garden *is* Arcady.[35] Our progression would perhaps be more easily made from the Jacobean and Caroline pastoral plays and masques. Samuel Daniel's *Queen's Arcadia* (1605) and *Hymen's Triumph* (1614) reflect Anne of Denmark's preoccupation with this dreamworld of idealized courtly dalliance, which was to take an even more forceful form under the impact of the Frenchified neo-platonic preciosity of Henrietta Maria and her ladies. *L'Artenice* (1626), *The Shepherd's Paradise* (1633) and *Florimène* (1635) were vehicles reflecting the love etiquette of the Caroline court. As we can see from Van Dyck's portrait of Lord Wharton, courtiers donned shepherds' weeds to gain admittance to this aristocratic circle. Here, under Danvers's supervision, the idealized nature of the garden is unequivocally presented as Arcady.

The two most important statues were of Hercules and Antaeus and Cain and Abel. The former was again from the Stone workshop, while the latter must have been a cast of the famous group by Giambologna recently set up in the garden of the Duke of Buckingham.[36] Both were obviously visually complementary but did they have any meaning beyond that? Perhaps our best initial clue is the sphinxes. They are always symbols of ancient wisdom, complementary to the allusions to Golden Age pastoral innocence in the shepherds.[37] In other words entrance into the garden is seen through the sphinxes to be an act of seeking lost ancient wisdom, a return to the Golden Age and to the Eden of man before the Fall. With this as a hypothesis we can approach the psychomachies which flank the two main garden walks, both of which, like the sphinxes, act as guardians to the garden. One group is from classical mythology, the other from biblical history. Cain slaying Abel marks the fall of man from innocence to crime, fraud and injustice. The entrance to the garden by means of this group is an act of seeking that lost innocence. In the same way, Hercules vanquishes Antaeus in a subjection of the carnal appetite by the rational soul, a defeat of earthly passions.[38] This, too, is an approach to lost innocence by means of a triumph of heroic virtue and a return to the Golden Age. Either as a comprehensive programme or as separate emblems Sir John Danvers's garden was designed for the contemplation of the virtues.

Did Inigo Jones have anything to do with this garden? Even though we know more about Jones after 1615 than before, apart from his work for the Crown, which is documented in the Works Accounts, we have very little evidence of his work for private clients other than Arundel. The drawing of the façade of Danvers House among the Smythson drawings could easily be Jones in his transitional manner.[39] At the very least he could have advised Danvers. The whole concept of house and garden linked, of terrace and grotto, and above all of the statuary suggest the hand of Jones. It is the type of arrangement Jones would have done at Arundel House if he had also been able to build the house instead of coming to terms with adapting an existing building. Although it is impossible to prove, Jones should have had a hand in the Chelsea garden.

Danvers's first wife died in 1628 and in the same year he married the heiress Elizabeth Dauntsey, who brought with her an estate in Wiltshire, at Lavington. Here Danvers laid out his second celebrated garden, which his relative Aubrey describes as follows:

> The garden at Lavington is full of irregularities, both naturall and artificiall, *sc.* elevations and depressions. Through the length of it there runneth a fine cleare trout stream; walled with brick on each side, to hinder the earth from mouldring down. In this stream are placed severall statues. At the west end is an admirable place for a grotto, where the great arch is, over which now is the market roade. Among severall others, there is a very pleasant elevation on the southside of the garden, which steales, arising almost insensibly, that is, before one is aware, and give you a view over the spatious corn-fields there, and so to East Lavington: where, being landed on a fine levell, letteth you descend again with the like easiness; each side is flanqued by laurells. It is almost impossible to describe this garden, it is so full of variety and unevenesse. . . .[40]

Aubrey considered this the second purely Italian garden in England but the description is so inadequate that it is impossible to get any impression of the layout of the garden's 'irregularities'. The central feature, the stream, is an old one but with an Italianate overlay of statues arising from the water. And, as at Chelsea, there was a grotto. The Lavington garden is probably an important one, a part of which was created before, but most simultaneously with, the more famous Hortus Pembrochianus, which lay only a few miles south east of it. Through his first wife, Danvers was related to the Herberts and like Lord Pembroke, when civil war broke out, fought for Parliament. Aubrey's description evokes little of what we know as the style of the de Caus brothers, although Isaac could easily have been consulted or have designed the grotto. In all, Lavington seems to be within the tradition of the naturalistic parts of the garden at Hatfield, the Island and the Dell, but with an overlay of imported accessories. If Danvers had an Italian prototype in mind for the 'variety and unevenesse', it would, of course, be Pratolino or the Villa d'Este.

The spread of the Italian style

Sir John Danvers's house at Chelsea itself seems to have been the prototype from which stemmed the Caroline Italian garden style down through the years of the Commonwealth to the Restoration. All these gardens share the same salient features first introduced in 1622–3, that is they are rectangular, walled enclosures related directly, in architectural terms, to the house. The approach to the garden was by means of a terrace from which steps led down to a strictly geometrical arrangement of beds in which fountains and statuary played a dominant role. The layout was always broad and simple, anticipating the rhythms of the Baroque style. At the end of the garden, opposite the house, there was always a terrace which could incorporate a grotto, banqueting houses, flights of steps, an arcade or other architectural features in the Italian classical manner. The terrace could in some instances also extend along one or both other sides of the garden.

Inigo Jones is always a touchstone for changes in fashion and the first glimpse that we have of this type of garden in his work is a back shutter that he designed for *The Shepherd's Paradise* in 1633.[41] Although this is based on Callot's famous engraving of *Le Grand Parterre de Nancy*, Jones always places on stage the ideals of the moment for the Caroline court. The drawing presents us with the view of the garden as it would have been seen from the terrace of a house, looking down on an elaborate *parterre de broderie* of the type propagated by the Mollet family or Isaac de Caus, with a fountain placed at the crossing. At the opposite end, balustrading encloses fountains and statuary and flights of steps lead to a terrace backed by cypress trees.

We need only turn to Cornelius Johnson's portrait of Arthur, 1st Baron Capel, and his family (*c.* 1639), to know that Jones in his customary manner was placing on stage what was already happening in the most advanced gardens of the period.[42] Hadham Hall in Hertfordshire was built between 1572 and 1578 by Henry Capel, whose great grandson inherited the house in 1632.[43] An ardent royalist, he was in the end executed for his part in the Second Civil War. Capel was therefore very much of the court, and Johnson's family group, which in formula emulates the famous portrait by Van Dyck of Charles I, Henrietta Maria and their children, celebrates also the creation of an Italianate garden. The view is from the terrace but that in another primitive painting of the house still at Hadham is usefully from the other way on. This is a purely Italianate garden in the manner of Danvers's Chelsea. It is in the first place architecturally as closely related to the house as it could be, a walled enclosure divided by broad walks into quarters and articulated by oval walks in the manner of Wilton. Each quarter is suitably adorned with fountains and statuary in the antique style and there is a gate to the park. The most impressive feature of all, however, is the terrace at the far end, with its noble flights of steps encompassing what may have included a grotto but certainly had a central door leading out into the country, an arrangement typically Italian and encountered before in Lucy Harington's Moor Park. The staircase reference can only be to Bramante's celebrated double staircase linking the terraces of the garden of the Belvedere.

117 The garden of Sir Arthur Capel at Little Hadham was laid out *c.* 1632–9. In this garden the direct influence of Jones seems highly likely.

118 View from outside the garden of Hadham Hall towards the house, late 17th century.

119 Design by Inigo Jones for a garden scene in the court play *The Shepherd's Paradise* (1633). Based on Callot's *Le Grand Parterre de Nancy*, it shows a garden with *parterres de broderie*, an elaborate grotto fountain with flights of steps and terracing and, beyond, rows of cypress trees.

Inigo Jones and the Italian style

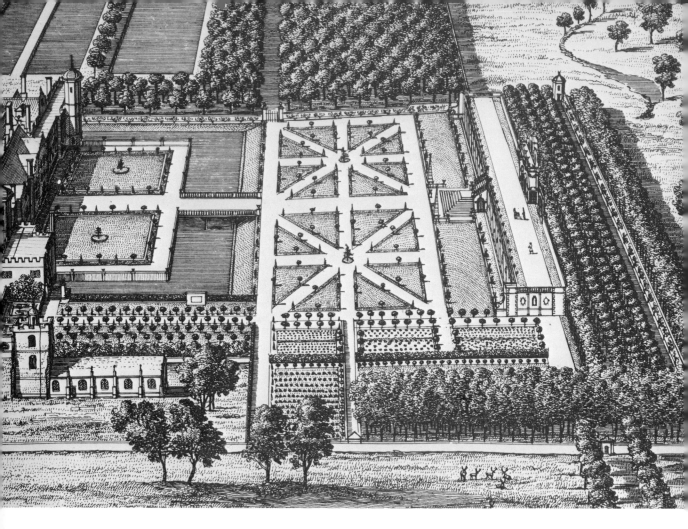

Two gardens in the Italian style

Who was it that designed this garden? Was it, as in the case of Wilton, a combination of de Caus and Jones? I think that the vital clue is the park gate to the right, which is a purely Jonesian concept. In addition, there is nowhere the fussiness of manner typical of de Caus. Capel as far as we know had never been to Italy so that all the evidence points to this garden being more directly inspired by Jones than any we know outside those of the royal residences. At Much Hadham the painted garden of the court masque came, as it were, solidly down to earth.

With Danvers's Chelsea and Capel's Much Hadham in mind we are able to look for other gardens of this type in country house views made at the close of the century, in particular by Knyff, which were used later for the various publications of Kip. One we know which is definitely pre-Civil War is the garden created by Sir Arthur Ingram at Temple Newsam in Leeds.[44] Ingram was Comptroller of the Port of London and knighted in 1613. In 1622 he purchased Temple Newsam, remodelling it in the vein of Blickling or Hatfield. The garden which he created in the thirties can be seen in Knyff's view of 1699. One side of the house opens out onto a broad terrace with a spectacular summer house in the classical style at one end of it. This we know was erected in 1635–6 and was extremely elaborate, with glazed windows, ornamental plasterwork and decorative painting. The chamber above included 'a pair of old leads for a water pipe', suggesting grotto effects below. Flights of steps lead down to a walled garden laid out in quarters with a fountain in the middle and a raised terrace at the far end, which has tiny pavilions flanking it reached by steps. Sir Arthur took an active interest in his garden, writing from the south about his rose trees, the planting of woodbine and honeysuckle, or ordering old-fashioned heraldic stone beasts in the manner of Henry VIII's Whitehall for the decoration of the parterres.

Kip's view of Rycote gives us another even more remarkable garden in this manner.[45] As in the case of Hadham it is grafted onto an Elizabethan house. The moat has been kept but a broad path has been made from one end of the garden to the other incorporating a bridge in the manner of Wilton. Its most spectacular feature, however, is the colonnade and terraces at the far end approached by way of obelisk-flanked flights of steps and culminating in a surprisingly large architectural object. This is unfortunately seen at too oblique an angle in the engraving ever to be certain as to what exactly it was: arch, grotto, fountain, or, perhaps, a combination of all three. Whatever it is, its debt to developments in fountains in Bernini's Rome is patently obvious. A drawing by Webb of such an object exists at Worcester College so that the arrangement cannot have been unique.[46]

What is the date of the Rycote garden? The extraordinary grotto can be seen in an early engraving of the house by Henry Winstanley, dedicated to Lord Norris. Lord Norris can only be James Bertie, who became Baron Norris in 1675 and was created 1st Earl of Abingdon in 1682, which dates the engraving. Prior to that he was a minor, which means that the garden layout must have been the work of either his mother, Bridget, Lady Norris (d. 1657), or grandmother, Elizabeth, also Lady Norris in her own right (d. 1645). The latter would seem to be the more likely candidate as she married Edward Wray, Groom of the Bedchamber to Charles I, who came to the house in 1625 when the chapel was refurnished in the latest Laudian manner. Rycote, if it does

120 Rycote, Oxfordshire, seat of the Norris family, probably laid out in the 1630s for Elizabeth, Lady Norris

121 Durdans House, Surrey, seat of the Coke family, probably laid out in the 1630s when the room in the style of Jones, to the right, was built

122 Design by André
Mollet for a *parterre de
broderie* of the type
planted at St James's
Palace and Wimbledon

123 Design by André
Mollet for a *compartiment
de gazon*, an arrangement
possibly used by him at St
James's for the display of
sculpture

belong to the 1630s, is by far the most elaborate of these Jonesian Italianate gardens.

Two other houses deserve mention. One is Skipton Moyne as recorded also in Kip; this is laid out in a simple manner, in quarters, but with a rudimentary terrace opposite the façade of the house suggesting how the new style could be adapted on a modest scale. The second is a house belonging to the Coke family, Durdans House at Epsom, Surrey.[47] Knyff's view dated 1673 records a spectacular great room added in the 1630s in the Jonesian manner and to the opposite side of the house a garden also in the new manner with a terrace. All this would seem to relate to the updating of the house in fashionable taste during the years leading up to the Civil War.

*The royal gardens:
André Mollet and
St James's*

Side by side with Arundel's museum garden and the Italianate gardens of Hadham, Temple Newsam and Rycote, there was a further, final influence, one of importance for the future, that of France. Charles I's queen, Henrietta Maria, inherited from her mother a taste for gardens.[48] John Parkinson dedicated to her his *Paradisi in Sole Paradisus Terrestris; or a garden of all sorts of pleasant flowers, which our English ayre will permitt to be noursed up* in 1629.

186

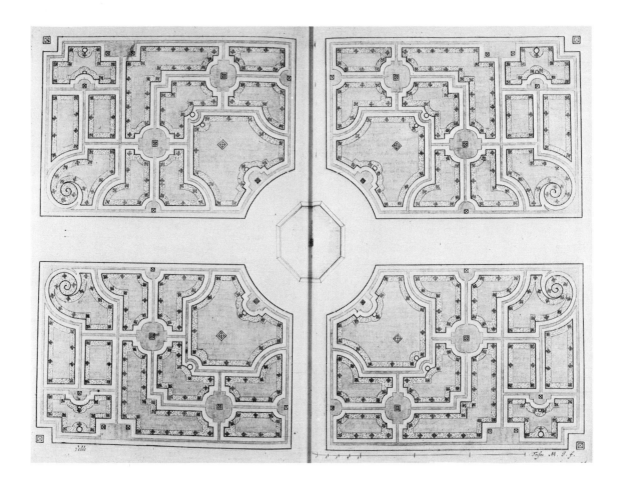

The Rose and Lily Queen wrote to her mother a letter seeking protection for a man who is going to France 'to get some fruit trees and some flowers'.[49] In the court masques she appears again and again in what might be described as almost horticultural terms, as a springtime goddess who brings peace after storms and with that the flowering of a garden. She not only created new gardens but also embellished and altered existing ones at Oatlands, Somerset House and Greenwich. Above all she was responsible for bringing over the man who was to form the bridge between the end of the Renaissance garden in England and the triumph of Baroque, André Mollet.

We have already mentioned the Mollet family more than once but who was this particular member of the family? André was a younger son of Claude Mollet the Elder, who had been trained as a gardener by his father, Jacques, at Anet in the second half of the sixteenth century.[50] Claude the Elder designed and supervised the gardens of Henry IV at St Germain-en-Laye, Fontaine-bleau and Monceaux-en-Brie, as well as the Tuileries. As a style these demonstrate the tendency towards a broader concept in design with an emphasis on large unified areas divided into geometrical fields by walks anticipating the Baroque. By 1614 these beds began to be laid out in box in embroidery-like scroll forms, replacing the earlier geometrical patterns.

Claude trained his four sons, Claude, André, Jacques and Noël, also to be gardeners. Claude the Younger remained at the Tuileries and was responsible for the parterre at Versailles in 1639. Jacques continued the family traditions at Fontainebleau. Without doubt, however, it was André who was to be the most famous, introducing by means of his travels and his book *Le Jardin de plaisir* the family style through virtually the whole of northern Europe. In his preface to the book he states that he had been in the service of the King of England before he entered that of Prince Frederick Henry of Orange in 1633.[51] Before the Civil War André Mollet was in fact in England twice, on both occasions at the instigation of Charles I's queen, Henrietta Maria.[52] On the first visit he laid out gardens at St James's Palace, *c.* 1629–33, and on the second in 1642 the gardens of Wimbledon House.

We know the least about the first. St James's Palace was built as a hunting lodge by Henry VIII between 1532 and 1540 and was a typical early Tudor building in the manner of Hampton Court and Whitehall.[53] Like both of them it had a majestic gateway but was built around only one large central court. It shared the same rambling red-brick appearance and was topped by a forest of chimneys. Under James I it was assigned to Henry, Prince of Wales (for whom Salomon de Caus built a picture gallery), and then to Charles I as Prince. It was also destined as the palace for a Catholic bride and work began on Inigo Jones's Catholic Chapel in 1623, in preparation for the arrival of the Infanta; this was completed in 1627 for Henrietta Maria.

Our knowledge of the St James's garden depends in the main on two sources. The first is the map by Faithorne and Newcourt mentioned earlier; this shows where the garden was. The approach to the palace lay along Pall Mall, through the great gateway and into the central courtyard which, on its south side, had a wall and a gateway leading out into the park. On the east and west sides there were suites of rooms, a king's and a queen's side as was the norm in all palace planning, and each had its garden. Both were walled and the map reveals little more than that they were laid out in a larger and smaller plot in relation to the palace building.

We have to wait until 1637 for a description of any consequence of these gardens. In that year the Queen's mother, Marie de Medici, was assigned St James's and the Sieur de la Serre includes an account of the gardens along with his detailed description of the state rooms. He writes of

> two grand gardens, one with parterres of different figures, bordered on every side by a hedge of box, carefully cultivated by the hands of a skilful gardener: and in order to render the walls on both sides which enclosed it appear the more agreeable, all sorts of fine flowers were there sowed. . . . The other garden . . . of the same extent, had divers walks, some sanded, and others of grass, but both bordered on both sides with an infinity of fruit trees, which rendered walking so agreeable that one could never be tired.[54]

One of these was he says 'bounded on one side by a long covered gallery, where one may see the rarest wonders of Italy in a great number of stone and bronze statues'.[55]

From the description, for we have no picture, the two gardens sound like the first and last sections of the Hortus Pembrochianus, one being an elaborate embroidered parterre in box, the other an orchard with walks. The parterre would have had a design on the same lines as those Mollet published in *Le*

Jardin de plaisir, with Baroque scrolling which would have been quite new at that date. To this was added the museum garden. Hubert le Sueur, the sculptor, was paid in 1631 for bringing from Italy 'moulds and patterns of certain antiques there'. Most of these, which included the Borghese Gladiator, are now on the terrace at Windsor Castle.[56] In addition, Charles I acquired, along with the collection of the Dukes of Mantua, a large number of antique statues and busts.[57] Although some of these were at Greenwich and Somerset House the vast majority were at St James's Palace. The inventories and valuations of the King's Goods in 1649 51 list no fewer than 95 'hole figures' (mostly small in size), 157 'single heads' and some 20 marble pedestals at St James's. Some, such as le Sueur's Gladiator and Spinario, are specifically listed as being 'in ye garden'.[58] The arrangement, therefore, must have been directly in imitation of Arundel House.

On the whole, the St James's garden does not seem to have been that spectacular and certainly nothing to compare with the vast works at Wilton which were proceeding simultaneously. The only completely new royal garden was to be that at Wimbledon House, laid out on the eve of civil war and for which the Queen brought over Mollet yet again. Otherwise royal gardening activity centred on slight alterations and embellishments to existing layouts, which we ought to consider briefly before examining Wimbledon.

Henrietta Maria's main palace was Somerset House, where building work went on continuously from 1627 to 1638.[59] The alterations included additions to the gardens, which took the form of two fountains, one by le Sueur of Mercury[60] and one by Francesco Fanelli of Arethusa, together with statuary, either antique or mock antique.[61] By far the most important addition was the Fanelli fountain which now, reassembled, stands as the culmination of the canal at Hampton Court; it is at Bushy Park and has been renamed the Diana Fountain.[62] In the Restoration period it stood in the Privy Garden where, in 1663, it was described as being

> composed of four syrens in bronze, seated astride on dolphins, between which was a shell, supported on the foot of a goat. Above the sirens on a second tier, were four little children, each seated, holding a fish, and surmounting all a large figure of a lady – all the figures being bronze and the basin of marble.[63]

This was the most elaborate fountain to be commissioned by the Caroline court. In the 1659 Commonwealth Inventory the 'lady' on the top of it is referred to as being 'called Arethusa'. The latter was one of the Nereids; Vergil reckons her among the Sicilian nymphs and as the divinity who inspired pastoral poetry. Numerous fountains bore her name.[64] In the context of the circle of Henrietta Maria, with its preoccupation with the pastoral *précieuse* literature epitomized by Honoré d'Urfé's *L'Astrée*, all this would seem to be right.

In 1636 the gardens of the Queen's House at Greenwich were altered under the auspices of Ury Babington, underkeeper of the house and gardens.[65] This must have included the introduction of the wall fountain dated 1637 for which the design by an anonymous French architect exists at Worcester College.[66] At Oatlands, never the Queen's favourite residence, John Tradescant was the gardener and was paid for alterations in 1636 that included an Orange Garden. The following year Inigo Jones designed cartouches 'for the painting in oyle on

124 The Arethusa
Fountain by Francesco
Fanelli, now at Bushy
Park. In an earlier
arrangement it adorned
the garden of Henrietta
Maria's Somerset House.

the open wale with landscips' and in 1638–9 the Works Accounts record a payment for painting 'vpon the walles in the open gallery in the privy garden' views of eight of the Queen's residences.[68] This was a typical Renaissance revival of a feature of antique gardens, executed in imitation of ancient *topia*.[69] All of this was, however, piecemeal compared to the one really grand project, that of Wimbledon.

André Mollet and
Wimbledon

Charles I purchased Wimbledon House from the Cecils for Henrietta Maria in 1639 and employed Inigo Jones to modernize the house, adding a new royal wing, new chimney pieces (of French design), new interior decoration and pictures.[70] The view from the south garden front made by Henry Winstanley in the 1670s shows, for instance, a typical Jonesian doorway. In addition to this the garden was remodelled by André Mollet, who in April 1642 was paid £50 for half a year's work.[71] In other words Henrietta Maria had recalled Mollet to lay out this her second garden in the latest manner. Ironically she was never to see this garden, for two months earlier she had fled to Holland not to return until the Restoration. The accounts of her treasurer, Sir Richard Wyn, in the National Library of Wales, record that the garden was maintained under a Frenchman, Laurence Coussin, until the house was formally handed over to the Parliamentarians in August 1649.

As in the case of Theobalds three months later, an itemized inventory was made of the actual garden, so particular that we are able to reconstruct it in the minutest detail and superimpose it on the plan of the garden as it was in 1609 by Robert Smythson.[72] The central purpose of the new planting was inevitably the sweeping away of Mannerist irregularity, of the series of enclosed gardens and banqueting house in favour of a completely balanced layout with a central vista from the south front hall door up to the gates set into the boundary wall. The Winstanley engraving gives us an impression of this reform, a path leading from the front porch to a flight of stairs which connected the upper and lower gardens with a glimpse to the right of the sunken Orange Garden. An impression only, because in the thirty years between the Survey and the engraving a new garden had to be created; this we can see in the new formal beds and enlarged Orange Garden.

With the aid of the Survey we can start our tour in the Orange Garden. This was divided into four knots 'fitted for the groweth of choyse flowers; bordered with box in the poynts, angles squares and roundles and handsomely turfed in the Intervalls or little walkes thereof'. At the corners of the knots there were stately cypress trees and at the cross point of the four walks 'one handsome fountaine of whyte marble'. The walk crossing from the side of the house terminated in a garden house, that crossing to the south wall in another, larger one in which to store the orange trees in winter. There were sixty of them, all in tubs, forty-eight laden with fruit. In addition there were six pomegranate trees and a lemon tree. We must imagine these in summer dotted around a large embroidered parterre of the Mollet type.

The approach to the main garden was over a bridge from the south porch and either side below on the basement level there were little grass squares with features that included a fountain and an aviary; from this level fig trees grew up the walls. Walking from the porch onto the south front, the visitor came to a terrace twenty-five feet wide with summer houses each end as at Moor Park.

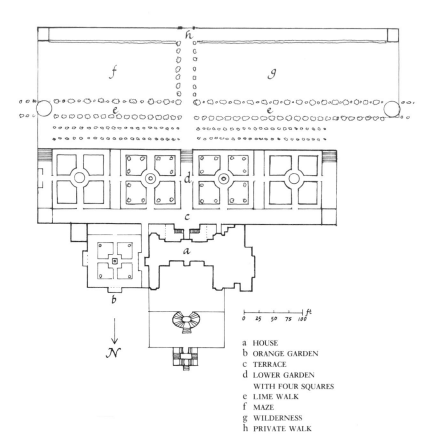

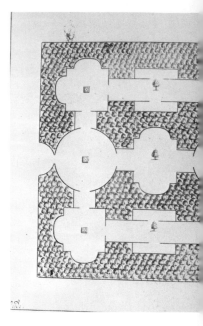

a HOUSE
b ORANGE GARDEN
c TERRACE
d LOWER GARDEN
  WITH FOUR SQUARES
e LIME WALK
f MAZE
g WILDERNESS
h PRIVATE WALK

125 Reconstruction of André
Mollet's reform of the gardens.
This should be read in relation
to pl. 29.

126 Design by André Mollet for
a wilderness of the type planted
at Wimbledon

top right:
127 Design by André Mollet for
a maze of the type planted at
Wimbledon

128 View of the south front of
the house in 1678. Elements of
the 1640s garden can still be
seen: the site of the sunken
Orange Garden to the right, the
path from the main entrance and
the flight of steps leading up
from the parterres to the lime
walk.

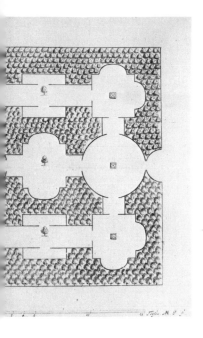

Wimbledon

Henrietta Maria's garden was designed and planted by André Mollet c. 1641–2 and maintained throughout the Civil War until handed over to Parliament in 1649.

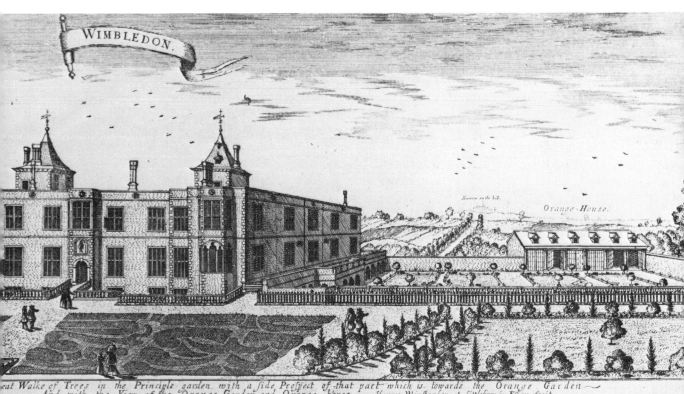

eat Walke of Trees in the Principle garden, with a side Prospect of that part which is towards the Orange Garden. And with the View of the Orange Garden and Orange house. *Henry Winstanley at Littlebury in Essex fecit.*

From the porch led the main broad walk, in the same way as Wilton, uniting all parts of the garden in one sweeping vista. In the first lower garden this was flanked on either side by two great squares, the innermost and outermost duplicating each other in total symmetry. The two inner ones centred on fountains, one of Diana, the other described as a mermaid; the two outer had at the centre 'one fayer cipress tree'. The fountain squares were knots with embroidered parterres exactly as in the Orange Garden but with the corners planted with flowering cherry trees. The flanking cypress knots were of grass with thorn hedges outlining them and again a planting of cherry trees. The whole of the lower garden was encompassed on the three sides 'with very hansome rayles piked with spired postes in every corner and angle all of wood varnished with white, which very much adornes and sett forth the garden'. Immediately within there was a row of cypress trees.

Passing up the flight of ten steps to the upper garden, the visitor came to an old feature, the great lime walk, twenty-five feet in width, the trees 'of a very high groweth, growing both topps and bodies and branches in a most uniforme and regular mannor, the height whereof being perspicuous to the country round about renders them a very spetiall ornament to the whole house'. In this way Mollet had incorporated a feature of the Jacobean planting. But he went on to improve it. It was elaborated by planting the south side with elms alternating with cypress trees and the north with elms alternating with 'borders of box'. At each end of this vast walk there was a circular wooden banqueting house painted green, each of which had two pairs of doors, one opening onto the walk, the other outside, one west to the church walk, the other east 'into a faire walke within the parke planted with elmes, and lyme trees, extending it self . . . in a direct lyne eastward, to the very parke pale'.

Progressing beyond this walk the garden divided itself into two different sections either side of the main broad walk. To the east there was a Maze 'of young trees wood and sprayes of a good growth and height cutt out into severall meanders circles semicircles wynding and Intricate turnings the walkes or intervalls whereof are all grass plotts'. To the west the same area was occupied by a Wilderness of the same type of planting but 'cut and formed into severall ovalls squares and angles very well ordered in mostt of the angular poynts whereof as allsoe in the center of every Oval stands one Lyme tree or elme'. This had gravelled walks.

The pleasure garden was rounded off by a second private walk running like the Lime Walk from east to west, also with summer houses at either end and hedged in with thorn. The main pathway from the south porch was bordered by lime, elm and cypress and terminated with a 'fair and large payre of rayled gates'.

To grasp the significance of these gardens by André Mollet we should turn to his book *Le Jardin de plaisir* (1651), which was published in Stockholm, in French, German and Swedish editions, when he was working for Queen Christina. Not only had Mollet worked in France, England, Holland and Sweden but also through this publication he was destined, as in the case of de Caus, to consolidate an influence which was to be European in its extent and which immediately prepared the way for the French dominance of garden art in the figure of Le Nôtre. The book is illustrated by thirty copperplates executed after his own drawings and showing his own compositions: those for

129 Plan of a house and garden from André Mollet's *Le Jardin de plaisir* (1651). In this, Mollet looks forward to the Baroque planning of Le Nôtre.

his celebrated *parterres de broderie* but much more besides. They open with a series of garden plans in which the basic principle is that the gardens must relate architecturally to the palace or château. There is an overall concern with the relationship of the parts to the whole, a concern with monumentality of concept in the use of the features of the pleasure garden: the parterre, bosquet, *allée*, canal, lake, fountain, cascade, temple and grotto.

Mollet enunciates the main principles of his theory of garden design as follows:

> Premierement nous disons que la Maison Royalle doit estre située en vn lieu avantageux, pour la pouvoir orner de toutes les choses requises a son embellissemens, vne grande aduenuë a double, ou triple rang soit d'ormes femelles, ou Teilleux (qui sont les deux especes d'arbres, que nous estimons plus propres a cet effect) laquelle doit estre tiree d'allignment perpendiculaire a la face du deuant de la Maison, au commencement de laquelle soit fait vn grand demy cercle, ou quarré . . .[73]

This was a statement of the Baroque approach to a house but there is no evidence that either at St James's or Wimbledon he applied this. He continues, however, on lines more evocative of the latter:

> Puis a la face de dérriere de la ditte Maison doiuent estre construits les parterres en Broderie prez d'icelle, afin d'estre regardez & considerez facilement par les fenestres sans auan obstacle d'arbres, palissades, ou autre chose haute qui puisse empescher l'oeil d'avoir son estenduë.[74]

With this we are contemplating the embroidered parterres below the south front. In the next passage he describes the component parts of the remainder of such a garden:

> En suitte des dits parterres en Broderie, se placeront les parterres, en compartimens de gazon, comme aussi bosquets, alleës, & palissades hautes, & basses, en leur lieux conuenables; faisant en sorte que la plus-part des dites alleës aboutissent & se terminent tousiours a quelque státuë, ou centre du fontaine, & aux extremitez d'icelles alleës y poser des belles perspectives peintes sur toile, afin de les pouuoir oster des injures du temps quand on voudra. Et pour perfectionner l'oeuure soit place les statuës sur leurs piedestaux, & les grottes bastiës en leurs lieux plus conuenables. Puis esleuer les alleës en terrasses suiuuant la commodité du lieu, sans y oublier les volieres, fontaines, iets d'eau, canaux, & autres bel ornamens, lesquels estans deüement pratiquez, chacun en lieu, forment le iardin de plaisir parfait.[75]

Alas for poor Henrietta Maria, her garden was far from being perfect. Beyond the formal garden the Lime Walk terminated at each end in a wooden summer house. The Wilderness and the Maze were sadly bereft of statuary, although perhaps that had been intended; the walks instead circled and intertwined but led to no Apollo or Diana. In gardening as in architecture Charles I never had the money to create on the scale he wished. As in everything else, it is piecemeal and scaled down, a reproduction in miniature and with little money of the grandiose schemes across the Channel or the pasteboard visions of the court masque.

Wimbledon is therefore the last Renaissance and the first Baroque garden in England. It is full of dying echoes of the past and pointers to the future. There was no extensive use of water, which within a generation was to be the central and essential feature of all major garden schemes. In France this had already happened in the spectacular cascades, fountains, lakes and huge jets of water deployed at Rueil and Liancourt. In this way Wimbledon is old-fashioned, with its tiny fountains as focal points for the new-fashioned parterres which must have been of the type in Mollet's book with intricate scroll patterns. The bold avenue that Mollet recommends is met only in the single avenue which stretched from the Lime Walk on one side to the boundary of the park. The Wilderness and the Maze must have been in the vein of the walks at the Luxembourg, which Henrietta Maria would have remembered from childhood. The central vista, like the whole, is a re-creation, on a vastly truncated scale, of the palace designs in *Le Jardin de plaisir*.

In other words we have reached an end and we shall have to wait until after the Restoration for the themes of Wimbledon to take on life and develop rapidly into the principles of the Baroque garden. Gardening is essentially one of the arts of peace. It was born in the aftermath of the Tudor pax and was destroyed by the Civil War. It is not until the 1650s that gardens once more become the subject of lively debate and of construction. This revival was prefaced, however, by a gigantic act of rejection. After the execution of Charles I in 1649 not only were the contents of the royal palaces dispersed and sold but also those of the gardens. In one gesture of stupendous barbarism the statuary and fountains were dismantled and auctioned off, the avenues of trees felled and disposed of as timber and the gardens abandoned. Nothing could have brought the curtain down with more appalling finality. The early Renaissance gardens of Whitehall, Hampton Court and Nonsuch vanished, so did Elizabethan Theobalds, Jacobean Somerset House, Richmond and Greenwich and Caroline St James's and Wimbledon. When Charles II returned in 1660, royal gardening had to begin again.

CHAPTER VIII

CONCLUSION
Renaissance into Baroque and magic into science

On 30 July 1634 William Cavendish, Earl of Newcastle, welcomed Charles I and his queen, Henrietta Maria, to Bolsover Castle on the triumphant return from their progress to Scotland. This was almost the apogee of the years of Personal Rule, those eleven years between 1629 and 1640 when Charles governed as king by Divine Right, without Parliament. Bolsover is a Jacobean fairy-tale castle built in the neo-Gothic style, but for the royal visit a gallery and garden had been added.[1] Within the gallery a banquet was staged after which the King and Queen 'retired into a garden'; from a walk around the walls of the garden the courtly spectators looked down to witness part of Ben Jonson's final royal entertainment *Love's Welcome to Bolsover*.[2] With bravura elegance, wit and grace, the poet presents in microcosm the assumptions of the Caroline court. There was a chorus sung during the banquet, a comic speech by Colonel Vitruvius and his men (a pointed tilt at Jonson's ex-colleague Inigo Jones), a dialogue between Eros and Anteros and a concluding speech by one Philalethes given after another banquet.

The theme of the entertainment, as D. J. Gordon has observed, is mutual love and its nature, finding its perfect exemplars in the King and Queen.[3] In the banquet sequence the theme of neo-platonic love, dear to the inner circle of the court, is expounded. Jonson elaborates it further in the action between Eros and Anteros, 'two Loves . . . one as the King's, the other as the Queen's' who set down a second banquet from the clouds. They tell the onlookers the mythological story of how Venus, her first son Eros failing to grow, had a second son, Anteros:

> *For Love, by Love, increaseth mutually.*[4]

The school they live and thrive in is the King's court and this is described allegorically in a final speech by Philalethes:

> The Place, I confesse, wherein (by the Providence of your Mother *Venus*) you are now planted, is the divine Schoole of Love . . . admire the Miracles you serve, this excellent *King*, and his unparalell'd *Queene*, who are the Canons, the Decretals, and whole Schoole-Divinitie of Love, Contemplate, and studie them. Here you shall read *Hymen*, having lighted two Torches, either of which enflame mutually, but waste not.[5]

The King and the Queen strolling in the newly created garden were walking in a Garden of Love, for the Earl's garden focuses on a statue of Eros and Anteros's mother, Venus, who presides over the central fountain. The image of the garden at Bolsover is that of Rubens's *Garden of Love*, in which cavaliers and their ladies engage in courtly dalliance in an eternal golden twilight. Jonson's entertainment, therefore, explains to us the precise significance of this the only

130 A Caroline Garden of Love. The Venus Fountain at Bolsover Castle, the setting for Ben Jonson's *Love's Welcome to Bolsover* (1634)

surviving Caroline garden, as a concrete expression of one of the fundamental myths of the court.

This intermingling of fact and fiction is an important clue guiding us to a wider understanding of the meaning of these Caroline gardens, that it is not in fact possible sharply to divide the real from the imaginary ones, that the ideas and aspirations they epitomize are often interchangeable. The association of the new gardening with the principles of Divine Right is one of the most potent of all the images. Gardening, with its central theme of taming wild nature by the exercise of art, becomes an assertion of the royal will. It is also no coincidence that the introduction and extensive application of the scientific principles of perspective to gardening happens during a period of absolutist rule. Both were to be shattered in the Civil War and to have only an uneasy revival as an 'attribute' of monarchy after 1660. The full Baroque palace garden was one of the supreme expressions of absolutism. The Civil War and the collapse of monarchical rule by Divine Right meant that England was never to adopt this style in its most assertive form. Everything, however, during the 1630s was pointing that way and there is no better guide to understanding this than the royal masques, where in pasteboard the aesthetic and political objectives of Charles I were unashamedly set forth.

The garden in the Caroline masques

The garden appears as a dominant image of royalist rule in two masques which span these years, the first is Jonson's *Chloridia* performed in 1631, which opened the sequence of royal masques during the thirties, and the other is Davenant's *Luminalia*, written in haste at the opening of 1638 to celebrate the victory of the court in the judges' decision in the Star Chamber over Ship Money. Both were Queen's masques.

The subject of *Chloridia* was the transformation of the nymph Chloris by the love of Zephyrus, the west wind, into Flora, goddess of flowers.[6] In it the raging passions of thwarted desire, expressed in a series of *ballet de cour* entries ranging from jealousy and disdain, human distortions of love, to thunder and tempests, perversions of the ordered cosmos, are overcome by the power of Juno, Queen of Heaven and patroness of marriage. The virtues of the absolute rule of Charles and the idealized love of the King for the Queen are presented to the court in a garden tableau in which Henrietta Maria as Chloris, attended by her ladies as stellified flowers, sits within an arbour of goldsmith's work encircled by a rainbow, the emblem of peace after storms:

> *Run out, all the floods in joys with your silver feet,*
> *And haste to meet*
> *The enamoured Spring,*
> *For whom the warbling fountains sing*
> *The story of the flowers*
> *Preservèd by the Hours*
> *At Juno's soft command, and Iris' showers,*
> *Sent to quench jealousy and all those powers*
> *Of Love's rebellious war;*
> *Whilst Chloris sits, a shining star*
> *To crown and grace our jolly song*
> *Made long*
> *So the notes that we bring*
> *To glad the spring.*[7]

200

131 Design by Inigo
Jones for Henrietta Maria
as Chloris in Ben Jonson's
masque *Chloridia* (1631)

And as in all the masques this spectacle of heaven transforming earth is taken to a final conclusion. Juno and Iris are revealed in the heavens while below, the arts which express the new ideals of Caroline absolutism – Poesy, History, Architecture and Sculpture – arise seated on a hill from which Fame slowly spirals her way into the empyrean. In this manner, in the first of the great Caroline masques, the garden is firmly established as epitomizing the ideals of the King's Arcadia.

Seven years later the association of the garden with the tenets of Charles I's Personal Rule and its interconnecting political and artistic policies was even more forcefully made. The masque *Luminalia* expressed the triumph of the royal will in the Ship Money case in the purest neo-platonic terms of light subjecting darkness.[8] Its association of this political victory with the royal patronage of the arts was even more overt, for the story unfolded how the Muses found refuge 'where this goddess of light' presided in 'the gardens of the Britanides'. Thus

> . . . the Britanides and their Prophetic Priests were to be re-established in this garden by the unanimous and magnificent virtues of the King and Queen's Majesties' making this island a pattern to all nations as Greece was amongst the ancients.[9]

The garden, which is eventually revealed after a journey through the phantasms of night, is of the new Italianate kind:

> . . . a delicious prospect, wherein were rows of trees, fountains, statues, arbours, grottos, walks, and all such things of delight as might express the beautiful garden of the Britanides.[10]

As in the case of Anne of Denmark thirty years before in 'Tethys' Festival', Henrietta Maria was revealed enthroned within an idealized vision of her own garden schemes but by 1638 the actual garden image within the royal repertory had travelled far beyond being harmless emblems of peace and order vanquishing war and chaos, into an outright statement of the infallibility of the royal will. When the Queen took her seat beside the King, they together contemplated the garden through a final transformation in which the heavens opened and the rule of Charles and Henrietta was overtly lauded as heaven come down momentarily to earth:

> *Be long expected in your thrones above!*
> *And stay on earth until our judgements know*
> *The noble use of that we so much love;*
> *Thus heaven still lends what we would ever owe.*[11]

No wonder that the Parliamentarians destroyed the royal gardens!

Inigo Jones once described the masques as nothing else but 'pictures with light and motion', that is they were moving emblems, much like the images in an emblem book dissolving one into another in succession. Up to the Civil War and beyond, the garden belonged decisively to that emblematic world. The Mannerist garden with its statuary, its ordered walks, fountains, grottos and automata was easily adapted into the old inherited schema of the *hortus conclusus*, but was now overlaid with the gloss of late Renaissance allegory, which for the court could be of royalist persuasion. We do not know what Lord

Treasurer Weston's garden at Roehampton was like but it was designed to be presided over by Hubert le Sueur's equestrian statue of Charles I, which now looks down from Charing Cross to Whitehall.

From this study of the royal masques and the garden arises the whole question of the optical relationship of the two. They are in fact parallel developments. Jones created his theatre of hermetic allegory as 'a machine for controlling the visual experience of the spectator', in which 'that experience is defined by the rules of perspective'.[12] Even in 1636 in Oxford a spectator recording his impression of *The Floating Island*, a play by William Strode with scenery by Inigo Jones, writes that what he actually *saw* was a series of 'partitions . . . resembling the desks or studies in a library'.[13] In other words, by then the broad mass of the population had not as yet learnt the new optical principles that dominated the culture of the Caroline court: scientific perspective, that converging lines meant distance, that objects became smaller the further away they were from the onlooker and that light and colour softened into a haze as they receded. This may seem to us a very elementary observation but the painting of the period provides ample corroboration that two ways of looking at things existed side by side. There was the courtly world of Van Dyck in which the picture frame had become a proscenium arch through which the spectator gazed into a separate world controlled by such optical principles. There was equally the provincial country world of a Gilbert Jackson, which remained Elizabethan; in this objects, whether near or far, were depicted with the same linear exactitude and evenness of tone and the canvas continued to be a series of separate areas recording attributes which, read separately or collectively, made up the personality of the sitter.

This is essential background for understanding the evolution of the garden. It, too, is deliberately developed into a machine for controlling the visual experience, this time of the visitor and it, too, is controlled by perspective. Instead of a seated, static spectator viewing successive platonic allegories miraculously changed on stage, it is a visitor strolling through a garden guided by means of hedges, walls, shrubs and trees, planted, pleached, pruned and cut, all manipulating the eye as it contemplates a perspective leading to an allegorical building or statue, or, indeed, a symbolic tree or flower-bed.

The symbolic garden: Packwood House and Andrew Marvell

The Bolsover entertainment, with Venus presiding over her Garden of Love, and the calculated visions of Henrietta Maria as a neo-platonic love goddess ruling over the flowers and seasons are important clues which have expanded our understanding of the way in which gardens were viewed during the Caroline period. Portraiture is another. What was to become a leitmotif in the portraits by Sir Peter Lely from the 1640s onwards was the lady with a *putto* and dolphin fountain in the background. This began with Van Dyck.[14] Eugenio Battisti has suggested that this motif of Renaissance fountain iconography has a connection with the statement of Hermes Trismegistus that the Just become dolphins among the fish, the dolphins being the neo-platonic symbol of the ascent of the soul.[15] Such a hypothesis should at least lead us to examine more seriously the introduction of gardens and fountains as backgrounds to portraits, for this is such a marked innovation of the Stuart period. Sitters move out from their airless, curtained niches with chair and

132 Unknown lady by Sir
Anthony Van Dyck
(*c.* 1635), with a dolphin
fountain

133 Mrs Watte by an unknown artist
(c. 1640), with a fountain topped by a
heraldic swan

134 Jane Shurley, Baroness Holles of
Ilfield, by an unknown artist (1630),
plucking a branch of symbolic laurel

Gardens and fountains in portraiture

*The development of gardens is reflected by their introduction into the background of late
Jacobean and Caroline portraits. Their primary function, however, remains symbolic.*

swagged drapery and, for the very first time, are placed in the open. As an iconographical theme these ladies recall the tradition of the Virgin in the *hortus conclusus*: they are at once symbolic and commemorative.

This extension of the attributes of the portrait is important for the future. One of the key themes of English portraiture is the relationship of the sitter to wild or tamed nature; these portraits are the first hesitant essays in that direction. They are celebrations of pride of possession but they also have an allegorical significance, one that is central to any interpretation of the contents of the Stuart garden. No other range of imagery could in fact be so ambiguously read as the natural phenomena of the garden. And up to the Civil War the emblematic tradition was without doubt the dominant one.

Stanley Stewart, in his important book on the *hortus conclusus* in Stuart poetry, gives us a vital clue to this approach when he writes: 'For certain individuals the garden performed a function strikingly similar to that of the Biblia pauperum and Speculum.'[16] Even that most defiant of Puritan voices of dissent against the claims of the court, William Prynne, insisted on the usefulness of gardens as aids to devotion. For him the natural contents of the garden replaced the graven images of Catholicism:

> *If Bibles faile, each Garden will descry*
> *Them* [the truths of Scripture] *to us, in a more sweete and lively wise,*
> *Then all the Pictures Papists can devise.*[17]

The garden is an image of Christ who himself was a gardener:

> *Christ, here on earth did* Gardens *highly grace*
> Resorting oft unto them, in which place
> He was betray'd, entomb'd, rais'd vp, and then
> First there appear'd *to Mary Magdalen.*
> *Each garden then we see, should still present*
> *Christ to our sight, mind, thoughts, with sweete content.*[18]

The Anglican divine Henry Vaughan could as equally share in this approach:

> *I walke the garden, and there see*
> *Ideas of his Agonie. . . .*[19]

In both cases these writers are referring to real gardens but the line between the gardens of reality and those of the mind was arbitrary. The mental hieroglyphics of the *hortus conclusus*, as expounded by George Wither in his *Emblemes* (1635), Henry Hawkins in *Partheneia Sacra* (1633) or Francis Quarles in his *Emblemes* (1635), could as easily be applied to real gardens. These three books indeed supply us with all that we really need to know about the meaning of the garden to the immediately pre-Civil War world.

We can begin by taking one emblem from the Puritan George Wither, depicting a hand watering plants, with a house and an enclosed garden in the distance:

> *When, thou shalt visit, in the Moneth of* May,
> *A costly* Garden, *in her best array;*
> *And, view the well-grown Trees, the wel-trimm'd Bowers,*
> *The Beds of Herbs, the knots of pleasant flowers,*

206

With all the deckings, and the fine devices,
Perteyning to those earthly Paradises,
Thou canst not well suppose, one day, or two,
Did finish all, which had beene, there, to doe.
. . . by this Emblem, *now perhaps, be brought,*
Perswade thee to consider, that, no actions,
Can come, but by degrees, *to their perfections. . . .*[20]

The moral of planning and patience is an obvious one. Wither, of course,
includes symbolic trees and flowers in the emblematic manner customary from
the previous century.

Things, to their best perfection come,
Not all at once; but, some and some.

95

ILLVSTR. XLV.   Book, 2

Hen, thou shalt visit, in the Moneth of *May*,
A costly *Garden*, in her best atray;   (Bowers,
And, view the well-grown Trees, the wel-trimm'd
The Beds of Herbs, the knots of pleasant flowers,

135 The garden as an emblem of patience, from George Wither's *Emblemes* (1635)

Vtriusq crepundia Merces
Will. Marshall sculpsit:

THE I. SYMBOL.

THE GARDEN.

THE DEVISE.

Quarles's search of the faithful soul for Christ also wends its way through elements of the garden. One of his emblems depicts a bowling green in which Cupid, Mammon and Satan contend with 'sinful thoughts' as the bowls,[26] another shows a labyrinth in which the Soul attired as pilgrim clutches the thread of faith[22] and the book's climax is enacted in the *hortus conclusus* itself, in which Christ and the Soul clasp hands, exchanging crowns while sheep safely graze and flowers and lilies flourish.[23] Quarles's *Emblemes* ran into edition after edition, an index to the immense vitality of what it presented, an

208

136 The bowling green as a setting for the dramas of the faithful soul, from Quarles's *Emblemes* (1635)

137 Garden emblem from Henry Hawkins's *Partheneia Sacra* (1633)

138 The medieval *hortus conclusus* of the Virgin Mary updated to a Renaissance garden. Frontispiece to *Partheneia Sacra*

allegorical drama of the psychological dilemma of the Soul, some of the settings for which were component parts of the garden.

But perhaps the most garden-obsessed of all is the Catholic Henry Hawkins's *Partheneia Sacra. Or the Mysterious and Delicious Garden of the Sacred Parthenes*, in which the author sets out to use '*Impresses*, and *Mottoes*, *Characters*, *Essayes*, *Emblemes* and *Poesies*' in honour not of 'feyned Deities' but the Virgin Mary.[24] The book opens with a general picture of the *hortus conclusus*; we are bidden to enter and climb its mount so that we may view the full range of its symbols. We need only take a couple of emblems to develop the layers of contemplative allegory that could be drawn from a Caroline garden. One figure shows an octagonal garden encircled by the serpent of eternity. It is walled and laid out within in formal walks punctuated with cypress trees. The motto attached to it is 'sacer principi'. Hawkins then proceeds gradually to unfold the layers of meaning which could be extracted from a garden by those brought up within the hieroglyphic tradition.

A garden, he writes, is 'a Monopolie of al the pleasure and delights that are on the earth, amassed togeather', 'a world of sweets'. This, 'The Character', as he categorizes it, is our garden of pleasure and delight, the moral of which is contained in the motto meaning that the garden is the sanctuary of princes. In the Essay which follows, Hawkins dismisses the topiary work beasts, the arbours and fountains, and concentrates on the emblematic features within it. This aspect he then expands, celebrating the fair, straight and therefore virtuous alleys, covered with the sand of humility, which articulate the garden, as also its virtuous flowers:

> the LILLIE of spotles and immaculate Chastitie, the ROSE of Shamfastnes and bashful Modestie, the VIOLET of Humilitie, the Gilloflower of Patience, the Marygold of Charitie, the HIACINTH of Hope, the SUN-FLOWER of Contemplation, the Tulip of Beautie and gracefulnes.[25]

He moves on to walk up the mounts, which are elevations of the mind and down into the valleys of depression, through the groves of solitude to espy the vines of spiritual gladness and the fountains of the graces. All these and yet more celebrate the Virgin:

> Heer lastly are statues of Her rare examples to be seene, Obelisks, Pyramids, Triumphal Arches, Aqua-ducts, Thermes, Pillars of Eternal Memorie, erected to Her Glorie, in contemplation of her Admirable, Angelical, and Divine life.[26]

In this passage the attributes of the new gardening are assimilated into the imagery of the medieval *hortus conclusus*. Another emblem evokes a list of symbolic trees:

> . . . *the Cedar of high* Contemplation, *the* Cypres *of odoriferous* fame *and* sanctitie *of life, the* Laurel *of* Constancie, *the* Palme *of glorious* Victorie, *the* Mulberie *of* Patience, *the* Myrtle *of* Mortification, *the* Olive *of* Mercie, *the* Almond *of* Fruitfulnes, *the* Figtree *of* Deliciousnes, *the* Plane-tree *of* Fayth. . . .[27]

Hawkins can read his garden in a Catholic way, which would suggest that this was perhaps what recusants actually did, forbidden as they were by law to express their beliefs overtly. One is reminded of Sir Thomas Tresham's use of numerical imagery based on the Apocalypse in his building projects as a method to express his Catholicism without infringing the law. Many of Hawkins's images of the virtuous flowers and trees would have been equally acceptable to an extreme Puritan such as Prynne. What links them is their mode of thought and their basic assumption that the garden is a place for contemplation. Counter-Reformation piety of the type of St John of the Cross or St Francis de Sales placed enormous emphasis on solitary meditation in a garden. Within the Anglican tradition we catch this as vividly with George Herbert as with Andrew Marvell, whose garden is a haven of 'Fair quiet' and 'Innocence':

> *Your sacred Plants, if here below,*
> *Only among the Plants will grow.*
> *Society is all but rude,*
> *To this delicious Solitude.*[28]

The vast development of gardens in the first forty years of the seventeenth century must connect with this desire for the contemplative life, perhaps a movement reinforced in England by the absence of monasteries. Thomas Bushell's weird hermitage grotto and gardens at Enstone become a kind of Protestant equivalent of Catholic Counter-Reformation piety. For the Protestant the summer house replaced the cloister in which one might seek solitude and dwell on *contemptus mundi* and in which the trees and plants became ladders of contemplative ascent. As one cleric wrote to Ralph Austen, who published in 1652 a book entitled *The Spiritual Use of a Garden*: 'I seldome come to your garden but what you made your trees *speak* something of Christ and the Gospel'.[29]

But what the garden spoke about most powerfully of all was time. And the object which precipitated these dark thoughts was that fundamental one, the sun-dial:

> *As Time and Howres paseth awaye*
> *So doeth the life of man decaye*
> *As Time can be redeemed with no cost*
> *Bestow it well and let no houre be lost.*[30]

Francis Quarles includes a sun-dial in his *Emblemes*. Cupid and the Faithful Soul standing within the *hortus conclusus* point to it: 'Are not my dayes few? Cease then, and let me alone that I may bewayle me a little'.[31] The garden, with its cycle of the seasons, of death, decay and resurrection, was a perpetual reminder of the transitoriness of life.

One garden which is full of this kind of sun-dial and which still survives is the celebrated Yew Garden representing the Sermon on the Mount at Packwood House, Warwickshire.[32] Long famous as a garden planted in the 1660s, it was, in fact, a mid-Victorian re-creation of a Mannerist garden from before the Civil War, whose symbolism is in terms of abstract moral geometry. Reginald Blomfield and F. Inigo Thomas describe it well in *The Formal Garden in England* (1892):

> At the entrance to the 'mount' at the end of the garden, stand four tall yews 20 feet high for the four evangelists, and six more on either side for the twelve apostles. At the top of the mount is an arbour formed in a great yew-tree called the 'pinnacle of the temple', which was also supposed to represent Christ on the Mount overlooking the evangelists, apostles, and the multitude below . . .'[33]

The account was given them 'by the old gardener, who was pleaching the pinnacle of the temple'. The walk to the mount is a gentle ascent, and was sometimes called the 'multitude walk' because here the trees made up the congregation gathered to hear the Sermon. I include it here because in the absence of any surviving instance this re-creation seems to capture the atmosphere of this type of religious emblematic horticulture. It is purely made up of topiary work in abstract shapes.

139 The 'Sermon on the Mount' at Packwood House, Warwickshire. A recreation of a Mannerist garden under the impact of Romanticism. Although planted in the mid-19th century, it seems to encapsulate the abstract moral geometry of pre-Civil War gardens.

At Packwood we move in the world of the early Stuart symbolic garden and are the closest that we shall ever get to the ovals, triangles, circles and orbs which made up the 'divine and moral remembrances' of the 3rd Earl of Pembroke's garden at Wilton in the 1620s.

Andrew Marvell has been mentioned more than once in this book and it is his poems on gardens and in particular 'Upon Appleton House, to my Lord Fairfax', written in the early 1650s, while he was tutor to the general's daughter, which capture the adjustments seventeenth-century man was having to make to the natural world around him as he moved away from magic and into science. As John Dixon Hunt writes, Marvell's gardens celebrate 'both an actual and a symbolic world'.[34] He is looking at gardens both in the old emblematic and hieroglyphic sense and, at the same time, as areas dedicated to the horticultural sciences. And Marvell was familiar with those of Italy which he had visited during the 1640s. In 'Upon Appleton House' his eye ranges over a provincial Mannerist garden and its setting and applies to it the same progression of thoughts and ideas that a visitor to the Villa d'Este or, for that matter, Caroline Wilton was meant to undergo. In a way parallel to Vieri on the symbolism of Pratolino the poet's eye ranges over the Fairfax estate, be it formal garden or meadow land, and provides an iconographic scenario celebrating national, local and familial history and its associations. By means of what Sir Henry Wotton would categorize as '*mountings* and *valings*' we are made to move through it and respond section by section.

The formal gardens were laid out in the form of a fort, emblematic of the five senses, its flowers marshalled in military manner in homage to the master of the house and his prowess in the art of war:

> *When in the* East *the morning Ray*
> *Hangs out the Colours of the Day,*
> *The Bee through these known Allies hums,*
> *Beating the* Dian *with its* Drumms.
> *Then Flow'rs their drowsie Eylids raise,*
> *Their Silken Ensigns each displayes,*
> *And dries its Pan yet dank with Dew,*
> *And fills its Flask with Odours new.*
>
> *These, as their* Governour *goes by,*
> *In fragrant Vollyes they let fly;*
> *And to Salute their* Governesse
> *Again as great a charge they press . . .*[35]

Like Danvers House the garden develops into a search for paradise and in particular the paradise of England before the terrible civil wars:

> *Oh Thou, that dear and happy Isle*
> *The Garden of the World ere while,*
> *Thou* Paradise *of four Seas,*
> *Which* Heaven *planted us to please,*
> *But, to exclude the World, did guard*
> *With watry if not flaming Sword;*
> *What luckless Apple did we tast,*
> *To make us Mortal, and the Wast?*[36]

That he sees the lost Edenic world of pre-Civil War England in garden terms is hardly surprising, so intertwined had gardens become with the ideals which had made up the King's Arcadia. No wonder that later in the poem his mind automatically moves on to that other vehicle for royalist hermetic allegory, the scenery of a court masque:

> *No Scene that turns with Engines strange*
> *Does oftener then these Meadows change.*[37]

And yet in the person of Marvell, with all his nostalgia for a world that was lost and which he reinstates within the confines of the Fairfax estate as a private closed domain, we stand on the brink of change and of the future. On the one hand his garden is still royalist and still emblematic, on the other it is scientific. More important it is a reflection of its owner's mind, stretching designedly out from the walls of the country house to embrace the estate around, whether formal gardens or parkland or meadow, all of which are to be read in the same manner as expressions of the ideals, aspirations and achievements of the owning family. With this we look forward to the ideas that were to create the revolutionary style of *le jardin anglais* in the eighteenth century.

Melancholy hours

There is another related element which was to have a profound effect on the development of the pleasure garden in England and that is melancholy. The late Elizabethan and early Stuart preoccupation with melancholy has already received considerable attention from literary historians but no one as far as I know has commented upon its influence on the development of landscape gardening.

Melancholy is one of the four humours.[38] The Renaissance inherited two traditions concerning it: the first, the Galenic, in which melancholy, because of its cold and dry qualities, is inimical to life; and the Aristotelian, in which melancholy of the right kind is favourable to the imaginative and intellectual powers. During the late fifteenth and early sixteenth centuries in Italy this latter concept was revived, principally by the Florentine Humanist and neo-platonist, Marsilio Ficino, whose book *De vita libri tres* sums up this revaluation. By following Aristotle's statement that all the intellectually brilliant were melancholic by temperament, he fused the *furor melancholicus* with the platonic *furor divinus*. In this way he transformed what in the Middle Ages had been regarded as the most inimical of all the humours into that which was a mark of genius. Gradually the attributes and attitudes of melancholy became an indispensable adjunct of any Renaissance man with artistic or intellectual pretensions.

All this arrived with force in late Elizabethan England when the generation of Elizabeth's favourite, Essex, adopted the pose. Portraits depict these fashionable young men negligently attired in black with their arms folded and wearing large floppy hats falling over their eyes. What was an affectation in its extreme form reflects an accepted truth, as enunciated above all by Burton in his *Anatomy of Melancholy* (1621):

> . . . melancholy men of others are most witty, causeth many times divine ravishment, and a kind of *enthiasmus* . . . which stirreth them up to be excellent Philosophers, Poets, Prophets, &c.[39]

Such men seek the shade of the greenwood tree and *not* the walks of a formal garden. The contrast is epitomized beautifully in a portrait by Isaac Oliver of an unknown gallant dressed in black with a large hat sitting in a 'dump' beneath a tree meditating, while in the distance can be seen an Elizabethan formal garden. In other words melancholy man requires a quite different setting, one at first glance totally naturalistic but which could and would eventually be simulated.

The melancholy man, Sir Thomas Overbury writes, will 'seldome be found without a shade of some grove, in whose bottome a river dwels'. Burton develops this:

> What is more pleasant than to walke alone in some solitary grove betwixt Wood and Water, by a Brook side, to meditate upon some delightsome and plesant subject. . . .[40]

Or, to take a final even more famous text, Milton's *Il Penseroso*:

> *There in close covert by som Brook,*
> *Where no profaner eye may look,*
> *Hide me from Day's garish eie,*
> *While the Bee with Honied thie,*
> *That at her flowry work doth sing.*
> *And the waters murmuring*
> *With such consort as they keep,*
> *Entice the dewy-feather'd Sleep;*
> *And let some strange mysterious dream,*
> *Wave at this Wings in Airy stream. . . .*[41]

We need only turn to Oliver's portrait of the black Lord Herbert of Cherbury reclining in a wood by a babbling brook to see its visual equivalent.

That this must have had a profound effect on the development of gardens is obvious. John Evelyn is a convenient starting-point because he specifically describes creating such a place of solace for melancholic meditation at his brother's house at Wotton in 1643:

> . . . I made . . . the stews & receptacles for Fish, and built a little study over a Cascade, to passe my Melencholy houres shaded there with Trees, & silent Enough. . . .[42]

This statement surely means that we must regard the whole development of the naturalistic garden outside the formal parterres – it being such a marked feature of the early Stuart period with its shady walks, islands and artificial streams – as, at least in one of its aspects, the deliberate creation of settings conducive to the melancholic mood. It is significant that Evelyn's creation follows a few months after his visit to Hatfield. Burton includes gardens as a whole as antidotes to melancholy:

> . . . to walke amongst orchyards, gardens, bowres, mounts, and arbours, artificiall wildernesses, green thickets, arches, groves, lawnes, rivulets, fountaines and such like pleasant places . . . brooks, pools, fish ponds, betwixt wood and water, in a faire meadow by a river side. . . .[43]

He goes on to cite the gardens of the court of Ferrara, the Belvedere and, significantly, 'many of our noblemens gardens at home'. Not only does the experience of gardens expel melancholy but also the practice of horticulture

itself. He cites the familiar examples, the Emperor Diocletian who laid down
his sceptre to become a gardener, the Emperor Constantine who wrote twenty
books on husbandry, Cincinnatus, Cato, Cicero and others whose delight it
was 'to prune, plant, inoculate, and graft'.

> If the theorick or speculation can so much affect, what shall the place and exercise it
> self, the practick part do? . . . If my testimony were ought worth, I could say as
> much of myself; I am *vere Saturninus*; no man ever took more delight in springs,
> woods, groves, gardens, walks, fishponds, rivers, &c.[44]

So both the practice of gardening in all its aspects and the experience of them
are conducive to abating the effects of melancholy. Gardening becomes an
attribute of the gentleman virtuoso[45] and it is in this capacity that an elaborate
garden appears in the background, for instance, of the portrait of William Style
(1636) along with his books and an emblematic globe.

217

141 The garden as an
attribute of the Stuart
gentleman virtuoso:
William Style of Langley,
1636

142 Democritus of
Abdera, from the title-
page of Burton's *Anatomy
of Melancholy* (1621). The
philosopher seeks the
shade of the greenwood
tree as opposed to the
formal garden behind the
balustrade.

All this is summed up in the vignette of Democritus of Abdera on the title-page of the *Anatomy*, in which the philosopher sits *outside* the walled *hortus conclusus*. No other image has such enormous potential for the whole future of landscape gardening in England.[46] On the one hand we can see the geometric, neatly ordered garden developing from the *hortus conclusus* which, through the achievements of French design, will by the close of the century subject whole tracts of the countryside to its principles. On the other there is the shade of the greenwood tree, the brook or stream and shadowed grove in natural or artificial disorder. And it was this second tradition which ultimately, fused with the tenets of Lockean philosophy, was to sweep away the formal gardens of Tudor and Stuart England. The important fact is that not only were the ideas there but that a garden tradition of this sort already existed.

Democritus : Abderites.

The Civil War meant that to all intents and purposes the art of gardening stood still for a decade. And then, in the 1650s, a new phase begins and this can briefly be summarized by one man, John Evelyn. In the year 1652 Evelyn helped to redesign his brother's garden at Wotton in Surrey. This project was largely undertaken while Evelyn himself was abroad by a cousin, Captain George Evelyn, 'who believed himselfe a better Architect than realy he was'.[47] On New Year's Day 1651 John wrote to his brother from Paris 'directing him concerning his Garden at *Wotton* & Fountaines'. On 22 February of the following year Evelyn went to Wotton to view the progress of the work. In order to create the garden the mount had been demolished by filling up the old moat. This was replaced by 'the Portico . . . with the fountaines in the Parterr, which were amenytys not frequent in the best Noble mens Gardens in England'. The construction by Captain George of the portico was much admired but the colonnade had 'great faultes'.[48]

143 View of the garden at Wotton, Surrey, designed by John Evelyn for his brother George in 1652. The view is from the top of the grotto and its plan directly derives from the Jonesian Italian-style gardens of the 1630s.

In 1653 Evelyn made two drawings of this, one 'in perspective from the top of the Grotto' and one from the opposite side. The arrangement twenty years on is directly in the Much Hadham manner. The garden is an enclosed rectangle with raised terraces around it, with a central fountain surrounded by a balustrade and large beds in a formal design. At the end, as in the case of Hadham and Wilton, there is a central portico in the classical style, which housed the grotto. At either side of the end terrace flights of steps lead up to gateways giving on to the terraced hillside which was excavated to create the

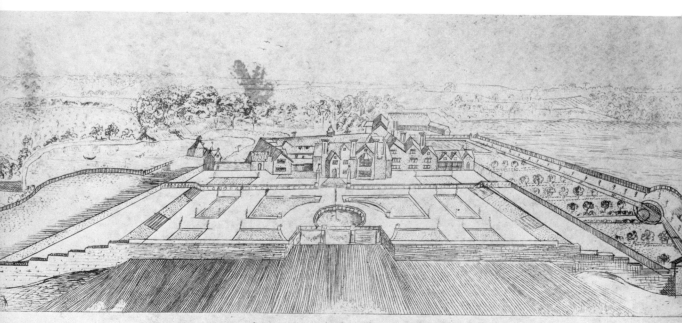

Wotton in Surrey
The house of Geo: Evelyn Esqr.
taken in perspective from
the top of the Grotto by
Jo: Evelyn 1653.

garden. A row of cypress trees has been planted along the top in the same manner as in Jones's garden for *The Shepherd's Paradise*. That this type of garden was still regarded as avant garde in 1653 is revealing. Fashion travelled slowly and progress was rudely interrupted by the Civil War. In the garden at Wotton we can see Evelyn taking up from the 1630s.

The same year that he did the drawings of Wotton he drew a ground-plan of a much more revolutionary garden, his own at Sayes Court, Deptford. This occupied a hundred acres and was immensely influenced by the gardens he had seen in Italy and France. There was a huge oval parterre, which in its shape owed much to the designs of the Mollet family, but whose scale recalls the vast parterre of the Luxembourg. There are axial avenues and geometric star-shaped walks and meanderings which look directly to the Boboli gardens, Pratolino and again to the Luxembourg. There was an island in a duck and carp pond with a summer house which could only be reached by a drawbridge. More to the point were the specifically horticultural and scientific features: the aviary, the vast orchard with its choice fruit trees, the transparent beehive, a private garden of rare specimen flowers and simples, and an 'elaboratorye' where he practised chemistry.[49]

John Evelyn here is taking us firmly on into the world of the Royal Society. We are witnessing the shedding of the old hieroglyphic and analogic reading of the garden in favour of empirical study. Magic and science part company and the garden becomes instead a living instance of man's understanding of the processes of nature. The garden as an expression of the royal will, of the King's Arcadia, vanishes, the garden of sacred emblems of Quarles or Hawkins declines and the garden of magical automata is transmuted. Horticulture and the myriad phenomena of nature are studied for themselves and no longer for their occult meaning.

In 1657 Evelyn wrote to his friend Sir Thomas Browne with the plans for a new garden revolution. He writes of his loathing for those 'which appeare like Gardens of paste board and March paine and smell more of paynt then of flowers and verdure'.

> ... our drift is a noble, princely and universall Elysium, capable of all the amoenities that can naturally be introduced into Gardens of pleasure. . . . We will endeavour to shew how the aire and genious of Gardens operat upon humane spirits towards virtue and sanctitie. I meane in a remote, preparatory and instrumental working. How Caves, Grotts, Mounts, and irregular ornaments of Gardens do contribute to contemplative and philosophical Enthusiasm; how *Elysium, Antrum, Nemus, Paradysus, Hortus, Lucus*, &c. signifie all of them *rem sacram et divinam*; for those expedients do influence the soule and spirits of man and prepare them for converse with good Angells; besides which, they contribute to the lesse abstracted pleasures. . . .'[50]

He urges the formation of 'a society of learned and ingenious' men to promote the cultivation of gardens, 'these innocent, pure, and usefull diversions', as an antidote to the 'ruines of our miserable yet dearest country'. Such an aim was to find its fulfilment in the gardens of the members of the Royal Society. Already in the 1650s he had begun compiling his *Elysium Britannicum or the Royal Gardens*, an outline of which was issued in 1699 and most of the first two books of which survive in manuscript.[51] A new chapter in the history of gardening in England is about to begin.

In garden design everything starts again with the Restoration in 1660 and the return of André Mollet to England. In 1661 he and another member of his family, Gabriel, are recorded as royal gardeners in charge of laying out St James's Park.[52] With this and Charles II's demand that André Le Nôtre come to England we are witnessing the triumph of the French style which was to be introduced to the re-created royal palace gardens. A glance at the views of country houses in Kip's *Britannia illustrata* (1707) will show a whole series of houses laid out along the lines dictated by Mollet in his *Le Jardin de plaisir*, with stately avenues approaching the façades, with embroidered parterres below the windows of the garden side of the house, with ordered *allées* terminating in statues and fountains, with bosquets, quincunxes, étoiles, wildernesses, cascades and grottos. And all were planned to relate and radiate from the great house, although never to the ruthless extreme of Versailles.

The Baroque garden like its predecessors in England, the Renaissance and the Mannerist garden, was to be a piecemeal affair. Parallel with the other arts it came in fits and starts and, true to the English tradition, was never altogether logical and doctrinaire. As it developed in the sixteenth century, gardening was fundamentally an imported art and that importation was always to be primarily via France. No other visual manifestation of the Renaissance in England has suffered such total obliteration as the garden. We still have the buildings of Hampton Court, Hatfield or Wilton, albeit changed, but the gardens that surrounded them, which were such an integral part of their initial conception, have vanished. A complete declaration of Renaissance ideals has disappeared and with it virtually any serious discussion of the subject by modern scholars of the period in England. And yet those gardens were a profound expression of the Renaissance mind. For those who saw and described them they were objects of wonder and admiration. They were tangible representations of Renaissance man's conquest of the physical universe by harnessing the magical powers of nature. John Aubrey realised just how extraordinary the garden development was: 'The pleasure and use of them were unknown to our grandfathers.'[53] In this simple statement he was recognizing that a gigantic revolution had taken place. I have tried to show in this book from the surviving, often inadequate and uneven evidence, precisely what that revolution was. I have attempted also to put the study of English Renaissance gardens back into the mainstream of serious historical enquiry. Not only are these gardens important in the history of art and architecture but they also provide abundant material in relation to the history of literature, theatre, science and ideas. To walk in a Renaissance garden is in fact to walk through the avenues of the Renaissance mind. Places of pleasure, as Francis Bacon once almost dismissively called them, is a term which belies the true significance of the great garden as one of the most transitory and miraculous achievements of the civilization of the Renaissance.

144 Plan of John Evelyn's garden at Sayes Court, Deptford, 1653.

Notes

The Renaissance garden

1 Ben Jonson, *Works,* ed. P. Simpson and C. H. Herford, Oxford, 1941, VII, pp. 136–44.
2 *Ibid.*, p. 139.
3 H. Inigo Triggs, *Formal Gardens in England and Scotland*, London, 1902, pp. 11–12.
4 Avray Tipping, *Gardens Old and New*, London, n.d., III, pp. 89–100.
5 See Mark Girouard, *Montacute House*, National Trust Guide, n.d., pp. 29–30. There is no study of this but on the cult of the 'old-fashioned' garden see Mark Girouard, *Sweetness and Light. The 'Queen Anne' Movement 1860–1900*, London, 1977, pp. 152–9.
6 Reginald Blomfield and F. Inigo Thomas, *The Formal Garden in England*, London, 1892 ed., Preface, p. xxi.
7 Ralph Dutton, *The English Garden*, London, 1937, chapter III. This approach is typical of virtually all histories of garden design in England until the present, e.g. Miles Hadfield, *Gardening in Britain*, London, 1960.
8 What follows is based on Eugenio Battisti, '*Natura Artificiosa* to *Natura Artificialis*' in *The Italian Garden*, First Dumbarton Oaks Colloquium on the History of Landscape Architecture, ed. David R. Coffin, 1972, pp. 1–36; Derek Clifford, *A History of Garden Design*, New York and Washington, 1967, pp. 17ff; L. Dami, *Giardini d'Italia*, Milan, 1924; A. Bartlett Giametti, *The Earthly Paradise and the Renaissance Epic*, Princeton U.P., 1966; M. L. Gothein, *A History of Garden Art*, London, 1928, I, pp. 207ff; R. W. Kennedy, *The Renaissance Painter's Garden*, New York, 1948; Harry Levin, *The Myth of the Golden Age in the Renaissance*, London, 1970; Elisabeth Macdougall, '*Ars Hortolorum*: Sixteenth Century Garden Iconography and Literary Theory in Italy' in

The Italian Garden, op. cit., pp. 39–54; Georgina Masson, *Italian Gardens*, London, 1966 ed.; M. Recchi, 'La Villa e il Giardino nel concetto della Rinascenza', *Critica d'arte*, II, 1937, pp. 131ff; J. C. Shepherd and G. A. Jellicoe, *Italian Gardens of the Renaissance*, London, 1925. Most of the above contains further extensive bibliographies.
9 As quoted in Clifford, *op. cit.*, p. 30.
10 *Ibid., loc. cit.*
11 Masson, *op. cit.*, pp. 60–63; Clifford, *op. cit.*, pp. 32ff; Gothein, *op. cit.*, I, pp. 207–8.
12 Quoted Battisti, *op. cit.*, p. 15.
13 *Ibid.*, p. 16.
14 Masson, *op. cit.*, pp. 66–9; Gothein, *op. cit.*, I, pp. 211–12.
15 James S. Ackermann, 'The Belvedere as a Classical Villa', *JWCI*, XIV, 1951, pp. 70–91; Hans Henrik Brummer, *The Statue Court in the Vatican Belvedere*, Stockholm, 1970.
16 L. Châtelet-Lange, 'The Grotto of the Unicorn and the Garden of the Villa di Castello', *Art Bulletin*, L., 1968, pp. 51–8; Masson, *op. cit.*, pp. 79–88.
17 David R. Coffin, *The Villa d'Este at Tivoli*, Princeton Monographs on Art and Archaeology, XXXIV, Princeton U.P., 1960.

The heraldic garden

1 The most extensive account together with the Wyngaerde drawings of Richmond Palace is in Gordon Kipling, *Triumph of Honour*, Leiden U.P., 1977, pp. 3–10. Kipling reproduces what he believes to be a view of one of the galleries in BM, Royal MS 19 C. VIII f.41 (see p. 43, n. 9 and fig. v).
2 For Wolsey's gardens see Ernest Law, *The History of Hampton Court*, London, 1885, I, pp. 89–91; Alicia Amherst, *A History of Gardening in*

England, London, 1896, p. 91; Mollie Sands, *The Gardens of Hampton Court*, London, 1950, pp. 13ff. For sources see *Letters and Papers of Henry VIII*, II, p. 2, p. 1427 includes payments for the moat, ponds and orchard; PRO S.P. 1/17, f. 213; E 36/235, pp. 685–836 includes payments for the creation of the garden, esp. pp. 690, 692 (including purchases of herbs, strawberries and primroses), 799, 811.
3 Samuel Wells Singer, *The Life of Cardinal Wolsey . . .*, Chiswick, 1825, II, pp. 10–11.
4 On Thornbury Castle see Amherst, *op. cit.*, p. 84; Miles Hadfield, *Gardening in Britain*, London, 1960, pp. 34–6; J. Gage, *Archaeologia*, XXV, 1834, pp. 311ff; *Letters and Papers of Henry VIII, 1519–23*, p. 506 (186).
5 Amherst, *loc. cit.*
6 *Ibid.*
7 The account of Henry VIII's garden is based on PRO E 36/237 (1530–34), E 36/238 (1534). Law, *op. cit.*, I, pp. 205–88, pp. 370–72 prints a haphazard selection from the accounts; Amherst, *op. cit.*, pp. 91–2.
8 PRO E 36/237: p. 374 (2 Jan 1531); p. 413 (April 1534), 'settyng up the bestes uppon the postes'; p. 419, large entry for painting with detailed description of beasts and colours; pp. 441 and 469, order for further beasts and painting.
9 *British Heraldry from its Origins to c. 1800*, Catalogue by R. Marks and A. Payne, 1978, pp. 30–31; H. Stanford London, *Royal Beasts*, The Heraldry Society, 1956; De Walden Library, *Banners, Standards and Badges from a Tudor Manuscript in the College of Arms*, London, 1904. For evidence of the continuity of this type of decoration in gardens see C. Gilbert, 'Newly-discovered Carving by Thomas Ventris of York', *Connoisseur*, CLXII, 1966, pp. 257–9.
10 Oliver Millar, *Catalogue of Tudor, Stuart and Early*

Georgian Pictures in the Collection of Her Majesty the Queen, London, 1963, I, pp. 55–6 (no. 25), pl. 11.
11 *British Heraldry*, p. 41 (no. 67).
12 PRO E 36/237, p. 301; E 36/238 (Dec. 1534), payment for painting 194 'postes with white and greene'; p. 164 (April–May 1534), long entry for painting. With each queen they had to be updated: p. 508 (March 1537), 'payntyng of the quenys beestes whiche were alteryd'.
13 PRO E 36/237, p. 306. The supporting rails were 'wrought wyth antyke a bothe sydes'. See also E 36/238, p. 36 (Dec. 1534).
14 PRO E 36/237, pp. 148, 169, 614, 728 (1 June 1534).
15 PRO E 36/237, p. 19.
16 PRO E 36/237: p. 193, 'for makyng of iij lyons, ij dragons, ij gray hondes, a lybert and a gryffyth in fre ston Sytting a bowght the mounte'; p. 195, 'for a greatt vayn with a crown standyng uppon the toppe of the Mount'.
17 Millar, *op. cit.*, I, p. 153 (no. 397).
18 PRO E 36/238, p. 521 (March 1537), 'for xiiij^th vanes servyng the stoon beestes that standyth a bowght the pondes'.
19 For mounts see R. Blomfield and F. Inigo Thomas, *The Formal Garden in England*, London, 1892, pp. 136ff; Amherst, *History*, pp. 76–8.
20 For early French Renaissance gardens see M. L. Gothein, *A History of Garden Art*, London, 1928, I, pp. 391ff; Ernest de Ganay, *Les Jardins de France et leur décor*, Paris, 1949, pp. 25ff; F. Hamilton Hazlehurst, *Jacques Boyceau and the French Formal Garden*, University of Georgia Press, 1966, pp. 12–14.
21 Gothein, *op. cit.*, I, p. 400; Ganay, *op. cit.*, pp. 36–8.
22 On Burgundian gardens see Marguerite Charageat, *L'Art des jardins*, Paris, 1962, pp. 93–6; C. A. J. Armstrong,

'The Golden Age of Burgundy' in *The Courts of Europe, Politics, Patronage and Power, 1400–1800*, London, 1977, p. 74.
23 BM Add. MS 8219 f.133^v.
24 Clare Williams, *Thomas Platter's Travels in England, 1599*, London, 1937, p. 200. Someone more conversant with sixteenth-century garden conventions would probably have translated this passage differently.
25 *Ibid.*, loc. cit.
26 *Ibid.*, loc. cit.
27 E.g. PRO E 36/237, p. 61.
28 On Whitehall and its gardens see *L.C.C. Survey of London*, ed. Montagu Cox and Philip Norman, The Parish of St. Margaret, Westminster, pt. ii, Neighbourhood of Whitehall, I, London, 1930, pp. 88–96; George S. Dugdale, *Whitehall Through the Centuries*, London, 1950, pp. 15–17.
29 On Wolsey's gardens see PRO 36/236, pp. 19–24, 42 (the last referring to 'the great garden at Yorke place').
30 Quoted in *L.C.C. Survey*, *op. cit.*, p. 61.
31 Some accounts, much damaged, survive in BM, Royal MS 14 B. IV A and B. These refer both to the Privy Garden and the new Great Garden and also to the Cockpit, which can only be Whitehall. They were building the banqueting house in the orchard in August 1541 (Bodleian MSS Eng. Hist. b.192/i.f.30).
32 By Leopold von Wedel, 1584, quoted in *L.C.C. Survey*, *op. cit.*, p. 90.
33 Johann Wilhelm Neumayr von Ramssla, *Des Durchlauchtigen hochgebornen Fürsten . . . Johann Ernsten des Jüngern, Hertzogen zu Sachsen . . . Reise in Frankreich, Engelland und Neiderland*, Leipzig, 1620, p. 180. I am deeply indebted to Miss P. Sigl for providing translations of the relevant passages. These are only partially abstracted in W. B. Rye, *England as seen by Foreigners in the Days of Queen*

Elizabeth and James I, London, 1865.
34 Millar, *Catalogue*, I, pp. 63–4 (no. 43).
35 The Whitehall fountain is also recorded in Ralph Agas's map of London, *c.* 1570, *L.C.C. Survey*, *op. cit.*, p. 23. See Naomi Miller, *French Renaissance Fountains*, Garland Dissertation, 1977, pp. 64ff, pl. 47. On the Italian background see P. H. Wiles, *The Fountains of Florentine Sculptors from Donatello to Bernini*, Harvard U.P., 1933, pp. 22ff.
36 Millar, *op. cit.*, pp. 99ff.
37 Martin Biddle, 'Nicholas Bellin of Modena', *Journal of the Archaeological Association*, XXIX, 1966, pp. 106–21.
38 On Whitehall and its sun-dial see *L.C.C. Survey*, *op. cit.*, p. 91; Dugdale, *op. cit.*, p. 51.
39 On Kratzer see Mrs Alfred Gatty, *The Book of Sun-Dials*, London, 1900 ed., p. 21.
40 John Dent, *The Quest for Nonsuch*, London, 1962, p. 51. Dent gives no reference for this statement.
41 For Nonsuch see A. W. Clapham and W. H. Godfrey, *Some Famous Buildings and their Story*, London, 1913, pp. 3–12. The fullest account, including a long chapter on the garden, is Dent, *op. cit.*, pp. 113ff.
42 The Parliamentary Survey is printed in W. H. Hart, *Surrey Archaeological Collections*, v, 1871, pp. 142–4. The arbours are referred to in the Jacobean Works Accounts: PRO E 351/3244, 1609–10: 'the seate in the greate Arbor'; E 351/3256, 1622–3: 'for taking doune vij Arbors in the garden, newe making parte of them and mending and repairing thother parte'.
43 Quoted in Dent, *Quest for Nonsuch*, p. 113.
44 Williams, *The Travels of Thomas Platter*, p. 197.
45 Quoted in Dent, *loc. cit.*
46 Williams, *Thomas Platter's Travels*, p. 197.
47 See the description in *Surrey Archaeological*

Collections, *op. cit.*, p. 146; and Dent, *op. cit.*, pp. 113ff.
48 For knots see Sir Frank Crisp, *Medieval Gardens*, London, 1924, I, pp. 58–64, figs. CLXXXI–CLXXXIX; Eleanour Sinclair Rohde, *The Old English Gardening Books*, Minerva Press, 1972 ed., esp. pp. 63–4, 102–9; Amherst, *History*, pp. 87–8.
49 Gervase Markham, *The English Husbandman*, London, 1613, pp. 120ff. For lesser gardens these were clearly still a total novelty in the 1560s. Thomas Hill includes two designs for labyrinths 'as proper adournementes upon pleasure to a Garden, that who that listeth . . . may place the one of them . . . in that voyde place of the garden, that may best be spared' (Thomas Hill, *The Proffitable Arte of Gardening . . .*, London, 1568, f.10^v).
50 Francis Bacon, 'Of Gardens' in *The Works of Francis Bacon*, ed. Spedding, Ellis and Heath, London, 1890, VI, pp. 488–9.
51 J. L. Nevinson, *The Embroidery Patterns of Thomas Trevelyon*, Walpole Society, XLI, 1966–8, pp. 1–38.
52 John Summerson, *Architecture in Britain 1530–1830*, London, 1963 ed., p. 6.
53 Stephen Hawes, *The Pastime of Pleasure*, Percy Society, 1845, p. 79.

The emblematic garden

1 *The Works of George Peele*, ed. A. H. Bullen, London, 1888, II, pp. 303–20.
2 The most comprehensive collection of literary material on the mythology of Elizabeth I is E. C. Wilson, *England's Eliza*, Harvard Studies in English, XX, Cass Reprint, 1966, pp. 133ff on the rose.
3 Roy Strong, *The Cult of Elizabeth*, London, 1977, pp. 68–71.

4 ll. 56–64, 136–44.
5 See Frances A. Yates, *Astraea. The Imperial Theme in the Sixteenth Century*, London, 1975, pp. 29–87, esp. pp. 59ff.
6 *The Works in Verse and Prose of Sir John Davies*, ed. A. B. Grosart, The Fuller Worthies Library, 1869, Hymnes to Astraea, no. iii.
7 *Ibid.*, no. ix.
8 See *inter alia* Strong, *op. cit.*, pp. 50–52 and note 64.
9 John Nichols, *The Progresses of Queen Elizabeth I*, London, 1823, III, pp. 108–9.
10 Roy Strong, *The Portraits of Queen Elizabeth I*, Oxford, 1963, portraits with olive: pp. 80 (no. 85), 82 (no. 86), 111 (no. 17); with roses, e.g. pp. 60 (no. 24), 89 (no. 3), 109 (no. 15), 114 (no. 29).
11 *Ibid.*, p. 62 (no. 29).
12 For surveys of Elizabethan gardening see M. L. Gothein, *A History of Garden Art*, London, 1928, I, pp. 435ff; Eleanour Sinclair Rohde, *The Old English Gardening Books*, Minerva Press, 1972 ed.; Reginald Blomfield and F. Inigo Thomas, *The Formal Garden in England*, 1892 ed., pp. 35–41; Alicia Amherst, *A History of Gardening in England*, London, 1896, pp. 105ff, 160–73; Henry N. Ellacombe, *The Plant-Lore and Garden-Craft of Shakespeare*, Exeter, 1878; R. E. Prothero, 'Agriculture and Gardening' in *Shakespeare's England*, Oxford, 1916, I, pp. 368–80.
13 On Kenilworth Castle see M. W. Thompson, *Kenilworth Castle, Warwickshire*, London, 1977. *Victoria County History, Warwickshire*, ed. L. F. Salzman, London, 1904–, VI, pp. 134–9.
14 Nichols, *Progresses*, I, pp. 427, 472–7.
15 John Summerson, 'The Building of Theobalds 1564–1585', *Archaeologia*, XCVII, 1959, pp. 107–26.
16 Francis Peck, *Desiderata curiosa*, London, 1732, p. 34; B. W. Beckingsale, *Burghley, Tudor Statesman*, London, 1967, pp. 262–4.
17 The Parliamentary Survey is printed in Amherst, *Gardening in England*, pp. 327–30. Visitors' accounts: 1598: *Travels in England during the Reign of Queen Elizabeth by Paul Hentzner . . .*, London, 1889, ed. pp. 52–3; 1613: J. W. Neumayr, *Des Durchlauchtigen . . .*, *op. cit.*, Leipzig, 1620, pp. 190–91; 1640: *Les Voyages du*

Sieur Albert de Mandelslo, Leiden, 1719, pp. 737–8.
18 The dating of the creation of the Privy Garden as described in the Parliamentary Survey is open to question. In 1607–9 there are payments for works in 'the newe privy garden' (PRO E 351/3243). Perhaps it was relaid out for Anne of Denmark.
19 PRO E 351/3245: 1610–11: 'painting carnacion cullor in oyle the wilde menes heades handes & feete in the garden'. The armorial knot had carved embellishments: E. 351/3243: 1607–9: 'for cutting and carving twoe great heades fower handes and fower feete for supporters of the Queenes Armes being made in a knott in the garden'.
20 Hentzner, *loc. cit.*
21 Neumayr, *op. cit.*, p. 191. This is also described by Mandelslo.
22 On Elizabeth as Venus-Virgo see Strong, *Cult of Elizabeth*, pp. 47ff; Strong, *Portraits of Queen Elizabeth*, pp. 63–4 (nos. 35–8).
23 Gothein, *History of Garden Art*, II, p. 44.
24 On Wollaton see Mark Girouard, *Robert Smythson and the Architecture of the Elizabethan Era*, London, 1966, pp. 77–95; Mark Girouard, *Architectural History*, V, 1962, p. 38 (1/25); *Country Life*, XLI, 1917, pp. 544–50, 568–75, 592–7; *H.M.C. Middleton MSS.*, pp. 565–6.
25 Girouard, *Robert Smythson*, p. 79.
26 John Summerson, *The Book of Architecture of John Thorpe*, Walpole Society, XL, 1966, p. 50 (T 49 and 29), pl. 12.
27 See Gothein, *A History of Garden Art*, I, pp. 409–10; Ernest de Ganay, *Les Jardins de France et leur décor*, Paris, 1949, pp. 40–46; F. Hamilton Hazlehurst, *Jacques Boyceau and the Formal French Garden*, University of Georgia Press, pp. 17–19.
28 John Summerson, *Architecture in Britain 1530 to 1830*, London, 1963 ed., p. 23.
29 C. S. Higham, *Wimbledon Manor House under the Cecils*, London, 1962, pp. 21ff.
30 Girouard, *Architectural History*, V, 1962, p. 37 (1/24).
31 E. K. Chambers, *The Elizabethan Stage*, Oxford, 1923, IV, Appendix A. Court Calendar: 1592 April 14–17; 1594 June 3; 1599 July 27–30; 1602 April 9 or 10.

32 For the pillar see E. K. Chambers, *Sir Henry Lee*, Oxford, 1936, pp. 139–40, 290; Yates, *Astraea*, pp. 116–17; Wilson, *England's Eliza*, opp. p. 216; Strong, *Portraits of Queen Elizabeth*, pp. 68–9 (nos. 45–6), 84 (no. 99), 100 (no. 5), 113 (no. 23).
33 On Lumley see Roy Strong, *The English Icon. Elizabethan and Jacobean Portraiture*, London, 1969, pp. 45–7 and note 3.
34 For Nonsuch sources see above chapter II note 41. Visitors' accounts: 1598: Hentzner, *Travels*, p. 78; 1599: Clare Williams, *Thomas Platter's Travels in England, 1599*, London, 1937, pp. 195–7; 1613: J. W. Neumayr, *Des Durchlauchtigen . . .*, *op. cit.*, pp. 199–200.
35 See A. M. Hind, *Engraving in England in the Sixteenth & Seventeenth Centuries*, Cambridge, 1952–64, I, p. 72 (8), pl. 35. The engraving is dated 1582 but is from a drawing of 1568.
36 Dent, *Quest for Nonsuch*, p. 113.
37 Williams, *op. cit.*, p. 197.
38 Hentzner, *Travels, loc. cit.*
39 *Surrey Archaeological Collections*, V, 1871, p. 145.
40 The fountain was repainted in 1616–17 (PRO E 351/3251).
41 Strong, *Portraits of Queen Elizabeth*, pp. 22, 60 (no. 23), 113 (no. 23), 114 (no. 30).
42 *Ibid.*, e.g. pp. 94–5 (nos. 13, 14, 16, 17).
43 Williams, *op. cit.*, pp. 195–6.
44 PRO E 351/3243: 1607–9: 'mending the pipes where they were broken in Dianes Maze'; E 351/3244: 1609–10: 'For newe painting Diana and her Nymphes with Acteon and his houndes in the woodes'; E 351/3249: 1614–15: 'repayring Diana and her Nymphes', including repainting and the mention that there were three dogs; E 351/3252: 1617–18: 'For couloring the rayles about Diana . . . for paynting Diana her Nymphes Acteon and the dogges'.
45 G. P. V. Bolzani, *Les Hieroglyphes*, trans. I. de Montyard, Lyons, 1615, Garland Reprint, pp. 81, 86–7; Filippo Picinelli, *Mundus symbolicus*, Cologne, 1694, Garland Reprint, I, p. 147.
46 PRO E 351/3244: 1609–10: 'rearinge and makinge vpp the Banquettinge House in the walkes belowe the

Fountayne of Diana'; E 351/3255: 1621–2: 'takeinge doune a little square banquettinge house by Dianes fountayne which was decayed; newe framinge and settinge vpp an other in the same place'.
47 Dent, *op. cit.*, p. 122.
48 *Ibid., loc. cit.*
49 J. W. Neumayr, *Des Durchlauchtigen . . ., op. cit.*, p. 200. The Works Accounts refer to this: PRO E 351/3243: 1607–9: 'taking doune and setting vp a Tymber peramides in the walkes that the plombers might mend the pipes'.
50 Neumayr, *op. cit.*, p. 200. Hentzner, *op. cit*, p. 33 records this poem but wrongly attaches it to Whitehall.
51 Dent, *op. cit.*, p. 122.
52 Ovid, *Metamorphoses*, trans. Mary M. Innes, Harmondsworth, 1955, pp. 84–5. This is noted by Eugenio Battisti, '*Natura Artificiosa* to *Natura Artificialis*' in *The Italian Garden*, First Dumbarton Oaks Colloquium on the History of Landscape Architecture, ed. David R. Coffin, 1972, p. 19 note 38.
53 Strong, *Portraits of Queen Elizabeth*, p. 113 (no. 23).
54 David N. Durant, *Bess of Hardwick*, London, 1977, pp. 198–9.
55 On the Elvetham lake see below, pp. 125–6.
56 On Zouche see *DNB*; L. Pearsall Smith, *The Life of Sir Henry Wotton*, Oxford, 1907, II, pp. 482–3; Miles Hadfield, *Gardening in Britain*, London, 1960, pp. 59–60.
57 Francis Thynne's continuation of Holinshed's *Chronicles*, London, 1587, p. 1512; *Country Life*, XV, 1904, pp. 906–13; Mea Allan, *The Tradescants*, London, 1964, p. 30.
58 John Parkinson, *Paradisus in Sole, Paradisium Terrestris*, London, 1629, p. 610.
59 Strong, *Portraits of Queen Elizabeth*, p. 80 (no. 85), pl. XI.
60 E. Auerbach, *Nicholas Hilliard*, London, 1961, pp. 258–61, pls 227, 331 (no. 262). It is now in the Victoria and Albert Museum.
61 *Ibid.*, pp. 240–42, pls 202, 328 (no. 237).
62 *Ibid.*, pp. 119–20, pls 94, 303 (no. 44).
63 See George Wingfield Digby, *Elizabethan Embroidery*, London, 1963, esp. pp. 36ff.
64 Strong, *The English Icon*, esp. pp. 14–15.
65 Summerson, *The Book of*

Architecture of John Thorpe, op. cit., p. 89 (T 167 and 68), pl. 77.

The Mannerist garden I

1 See in particular C. S. Maks, *Salomon de Caus*, Paris, 1935; also Eugène and Emile Haag, *La France Protestante*, Paris, 1852, III; *Dictionnaire de biographie française*, ed. M. Prévost and Roman d'Arnat, VII, 1956; Théodore Lebreton, *Biographie normande*, Rouen, 1857, I; Jacques Pannier, *L'Eglise Reformée de Paris sous Louis XIII*, Paris, 1922, pp. 350–56; Horace Walpole, *Anecdotes of Painting in England*, ed. R. N. Wornum, London, 1862, I, pp. 233–4; E. Frère, *Manuel du bibliographie normand*, Rouen, 1858; *DNB*; *Bulletin de la Commission des Antiquités de la Seine-Inférieure*, Rouen, 1890, VIII, p. 87.
2 De Caus's only surviving letter written while in England is undated but from Richmond Palace (PRO S.P. 14/69 no. 13).
3 The various payments to de Caus while in England are as follows: payment of £998 11s for work done to the gardens at Greenwich and Somerset House, BM Lansdowne MS 164, f. 447; for work for Henry, Prince of Wales, PRO E 101/433/15 and E 351/2793 (1610–11); *Extracts from the Accounts of the Revels at the Court of Queen Elizabeth and King James I*, ed. Peter Cunningham, London, 1842, p. xv. Final payment (PRO S.P. 39/3 no. 56): warrant of 27 July 1613 to pay de Caus 'being entertained for some services by our late deare sonne Henry, Prince of Wales, hath, since his death, attended here by our comaundement' but who now sues 'to returne into his owne Countrey, for some speciall occasions concerning his owne particular'.
4 On which see Bertrand Gille, *The Renaissance Engineer*, London, 1966; Giovanni Canestrini, 'Il quattrocento e le macchine', *Civiltà delle macchine*, May, 1954, pp. 16–18; Paolo Portoghesi, 'I designi tecnici di Leonardo', *Civiltà delle macchine*, Jan., 1955, pp. 30–48; Paolo Rossi, *Philosophy, Technology and the Arts in the Early Modern Era*, New York, 1970.
5 Alfred Chapuis and Edouard Gélis, *Le Monde des*

automates, Paris, 1928, pp. 31ff; Alfred Chapuis and Edmond Droz, *Les Automates*, Neuchâtel, 1949, pp. 33ff, 77ff; Eugenio Battisti, *L'Antirinascimento*, Milan, 1962, pp. 220ff. There was also a northern tradition of courtly hydraulic automata epitomized by those at the Burgundian castle of Hesdin; see Richard Vaughan, *Philip the Good*, London, 1970, pp. 137–9.
6 See G. E. R. Lloyd, *Greek Science after Aristotle*, London, 1973, pp. 95ff; A. G. Drachmann, *The Mechanical Technology of Greek and Roman Antiquity*, Copenhagen, Munksgaard, 1963, pp. 18ff and 197–8 on his mechanical art.
7 Fynes Moryson, *An Itinerary*, Glasgow, 1907, I, pp. 327–8.
8 On the Renaissance grotto see L. Châtelet-Lange, 'The Grotto of the Unicorn and the Garden of the Villa di Castello', *Art Bulletin*, L, i, 1968, pp. 51–62; Detlef Heikamp, 'La Grotta Grande del Giardino di Boboli', *Antichità viva*, anno IV, no. 4, 1965, pp. 27–48; Francisco Guarrieri and Judith Chatfield, *Boboli Gardens*, Florence, 1972, pp. 26ff; Naomi Miller, *French Renaissance Fountains*, Garland Dissertation, 1977, pp. 299ff; B. H. Wiles, *The Fountains of Florentine Sculptors and Their Followers from Donatello to Bernini*, Harvard U.P., 1933, pp. 74–9.
9 Moryson, *op. cit.*, pp. 328–30.
10 On the villa and gardens of Pratolino see C. da Prato, *Firenze ai Demidoff. Pratolino e S. Donato*, Florence, 1886, pp. 242–74; Christian Hülsen, 'Ein deutscher Architekt in Florenz (1600)', *Mitteilungen des Kunsthistorischen Instituts in Florenz*, II, 1919, pp. 152–75; Vera Giovannozzi, 'La vita di Bernardo Buontalenti scritta da Gherardo Silvani', *Rivista d'arte*, XIV, 1932, pp. 304–24; Vera Giovannozzi, 'Ricerche su Bernardo Buontalenti', *Rivista d'arte*, XV, 1933, pp. 299–327; Giulio Lenzi Orlandi, *Le ville di Firenze di qua d'Arno*, Florence, 1954, pp. 119–21; Webster Smith, 'Pratolino', *Journal of the Society of Architectural Historians*, XX, no. 4, 1961, pp. 155–68; Detlef Heikamp, 'Pratolino nei suoi Giorni Splendidi', *Antichità viva*, anno VIII, 1969, argomenti 2, pp.

14–34; Battisti, *L'Antirinascimento*, pp. 235ff; *Mostra di Disegni di Bernardo Buontalenti* (catalogue by I. M. Botto), Uffizi, Florence, nos. 1–2.
11 Webster Smith, *op. cit.*, pp. 166–8.
12 Francesco de' Vieri, *Delle maravigliose opere di Pratolino & d'Amore*, Florence, 1586.
13 David Coffin, *The Villa d'Este at Tivoli*, Princeton Monographs on Art and Archaeology, XXXIV, Princeton U.P., 1960.
14 Jacqueline Theurillat, *Les Mystères de Bomarzo et des jardins symboliques de la Renaissance*, Geneva, 1973; Maurizio Calvesi, 'Il sacro bosco di Bomarzo', *Scritti di storia dell'arte in onore di Lionello Venturi*, I, Rome, 1956, pp. 369–402.
15 Moryson, *op. cit.*, p. 419.
16 On Fontainebleau see Gothein, *A History of Garden Art*, I, p. 427; Ernest de Ganay, *Les Jardins de France et leur décor*, Paris, 1949, pp. 55–8; Sten Karling, 'The Importance of André Mollet and his Family for the Development of the French Formal Garden' in *The French Formal Garden*, Dumbarton Oaks Colloquium on the History of Landscape Architecture, III, ed. Elisabeth B. Macdougall and F. Hamilton Hazlehurst, 1974, pp. 10–11.
17 On St Germain-en-Laye see Gothein, *op. cit.*, pp. 424–7; Ganay, *op. cit.*, pp. 52–5; Karling, *op. cit.*, p. 11.
18 Albert Mousset, *Les Francine*, Paris, 1930, pp. 31ff; Chapuis and Gélis, *Le monde des automates*, pp. 75ff.
19 R. N. Needham and A. Webster, *Somerset House*, London, 1905; Nikolaus Pevsner, 'Old Somerset House', *Architectural Review*, 116, no. 693, Sept. 1954, pp. 163–7; John Summerson, *Architecture in Britain 1530 to 1830*, London, 1963 ed., pp. 16–17; John Summerson, *The Book of Architecture of John Thorpe*, Walpole Society, XL, 1964–6, p. 70.
20 Mark Girouard, *Architectural History*, V, 1962, p. 53 (no. 1/13).
21 Roy Strong, *The English Icon*, London, 1969, pp. 283 (275), 299 (305).
22 Works Accounts: 1611–12 (PRO E 351/3246), 'Richarde Barnwell for makeinge and settinge vppe an Engine to

force vpp water from a well at the end of the Terrasse in the garden to the great Cesterne over the Strand lane which serveth the new Fontaine with water the said Engine consistinge of diverse wheles pipes of Tymber and Iron woorkes . . .'; 1623–4 (E 351/3257), 'mending the greate Cesterne that holdeth water about the rocke in the garden'; S.P. 14/45 no. 5 includes for 1 May 1609 'making of the new Terrass in the garden with the railes and ballesters of stone'.
23 *CSP Domestic, 1603–10*, p. 490.
24 See Frances A. Yates, *Astraea. The Imperial Theme in the Sixteenth Century*, London, 1975, pls 36–7.
25 Works Accounts 1611–12 (PRO E 351/3246).
26 Works Accounts 1611–12 (PRO E 351/3246): 'bringing vpp the foundacones of the twoe Terras walls to the banqueting house'; 'the framing and setting vp of a house for orange trees in the garden'.
27 *Les Voyages du Sieur Albert de Mandelslo*, Leiden, 1719, p. 750.
28 J. W. Neumayr, *Des Durchlauchtigen . . ., op. cit.*, p. 184.
29 *Ibid.*, pp. 184–5.
30 Repro. in Battisti, *L'Antirinascimento*, p. 246.
31 Vieri, *Delle maravigliose*, p. 47.
32 Stephen Orgel and Roy Strong, *Inigo Jones. The Theatre of the Stuart Court*, University of California Press, 1973, p. 198 (55).
33 *Ibid.*, p. 194.
34 Frances A. Yates, *The Valois Tapestries*, London, 1959, pp. 67–9, pls 24, IV, X(b); Roy Strong, *Splendour at Court. Renaissance Spectacle and Illusion*, London, 1973, pp. 151–3.
35 Strong, *Splendour at Court*, pp. 188–9, pl. 136.
36 *Ibid.*, p. 202, pl. 195.
37 E. K. Chambers, *The Elizabethan Stage*, Oxford, 1951 ed., I, pp. 168–9.
38 On Greenwich see George Chettle, *The Queen's House, Greenwich*, London Survey Committee, 1937.
39 In the Works Accounts for 1613–14 (PRO E 351/3248) there are payments for 'rayling about the walke and knottes in the garden'; eleven seats in the privy garden were marbled and eleven more in the 'little garden'.

40 Neumayr, *op. cit.*, p. 211.
41 *Les Voyages du Sieur Albert de Mandelslo*, pp. 755–6.
42 The Works Accounts are for 1611–12 (PRO E 351/3246). The Accounts for 1614–15 record either a new fountain or a reworking of this one (E 351/3249): payment to William Cure for 'viij maskeheades for the fountayne at iiijˢ the pece xxxijˢ For new making the vpper parte of the Piramides of the same fountayne of white marble with a ball and Pike to the same xxvjˢ vjᵈ'; 'taking downe the Fountaine of Marble in the privie garden polishing newe woorking and setting it vp againe'; 'laying diverse small pypes for the Fountaine of white Marble'; to John de Critz 'for often oyling and pryming viiij maskeheads guilded with fine gould standing aboute the fountaine'.
43 Neumayr, *op. cit.*, pp. 211–12.
44 The Works Accounts 1611–12 (PRO E 351/3246) refer to payments 'for raiseing the roofe of the birdhouse makinge the gutters rounde about bourdinge the roofe of the same Birdhouse'; 'five arches xᵉⁿ foot broade' with ribs, freize, architrave and cornice. In 1614–15 (E 351/3249) there is reference to 'making the square pypes for the Birdehouse in the garden with Cesternes to them'.
45 The best guide is E. C. Wilson, *Prince Henry and English Literature*, Cornell U.P., 1946; Frances A. Yates, *Shakespeare's Last Plays; A New Approach*, London, 1975, chapter I; *CSP Venetian, 1610–13*, introduction.
46 Sir Charles Cornwallis, *An Account of the Baptism, Life, Death and Funeral of . . . Frederick Henry, Prince of Wales*, London, 1751, p. 53.
47 *CSP Venetian, 1610–13*, p. 162 (no. 159); J. Nichols, *The Progresses of James I*, London, 1826, II, p. 489, n.
48 I. M(axwell), *The Laudable Life And Deplorable Death of our late peerlesse Prince Henry*, London, 1612, sig B2ᵛ–B3ᵛ.
49 Summerson, *Architecture in Britain, ed. cit.*, p. I.
50 PRO E 101/433/15: 'Mountayne Jennynges . . . for his charges attending the Prince about his workes at Richmond, and for drawing sundry plots of

the orchardhouse, friers(?), and the three islands'.
51 *The King's Arcadia. Inigo Jones and the Stuart Court* (exhibition catalogue by John Harris, Stephen Orgel and Roy Strong), 1972, p. 43. The first payment to de' Servi is from 1 Aug. 1611 (PRO E 351/2793, 1610–11). The whole problem of de' Servi and the prince's various projects is complex and needs fuller treatment than can be given here.
52 *The Works of Dr. Thomas Campion*, ed. A. H. Bullen, London, 1889, p. 213.
53 *The King's Arcadia, loc. cit.*
54 PRO S.P. 14/63: 'An Estimate of the charge of the pyling plancking and Brickworks for the three Islands at Richmont'.
55 PRO 101/433/15.
56 Strong, *The English Icon*, p. 248 (226).
57 Salomon de Caus, *La Perspective, avec la raison des ombres et miroirs*, London, 1612, pl. 28. Richmond seems to have been virtually 'abandoned' after 1612. There is no seeming trace of Prince Henry's works in the 1649 Parliamentary Survey: *Surrey Archaeological Collections*, v, 1871, pp. 82ff.
58 See Orgel and Strong, *Inigo Jones*, I, pp. 204–28; Stephen Orgel, *The Jonsonian Masque*, Harvard U.P., 1965, pp. 82–91.
59 Orgel and Strong, *Inigo Jones*, I, p. 285.
60 Yates, *Shakespeare's Last Plays*, pp. 92ff.
61 See *H. M. C. Hatfield*, XI, pp. 206, 292, 316–17, 318–19, 380–81, 407–8. See particularly the letter of Houghton to Cecil, 24 Aug. 1602: 'Jennings is in hand with a plott of your park & river, which will be finished as he says on Thursday next . . .'. For a brief period Cecil had enlarged and altered, c. 1595–7, Sir Thomas More's house at Chelsea. A plan shows the garden, which is divided into enclosed areas on the lines of Wimbledon, but this may reflect an inherited arrangement. See A. W. Clapham and W. H. Godfrey, *Some Famous Buildings and Their Story*, London, 1913, p. 90.
62 All the accounts relevant to the building of Hatfield House and the laying out of its gardens and park are transcribed and bound into one volume in the Hatfield Archives

and I am deeply indebted to Mr Robin Harcourt Williams for enabling me to study these and for providing xeroxes. For the building of the house, see H. Avray Tipping, 'Hatfield House', *Country Life*, LXI, 1927, pp. 416–34 and especially Lawrence Stone, 'The Building of Hatfield House', *Archaeological Journal*, CXII, 1955, pp. 100–128. The only account of the garden apart from that of Stone which makes use of the manuscripts is Alicia Amherst, *A History of Gardening in England*, London, 1895, p. 127.
63 *The Diary of John Evelyn*, ed. E. S. de Beer, Oxford, 1955: 11 May 1643.
64 Robert Bell to Wilson, 26 Sept. 1609, Cecil Papers Box U 72, BHH/24.
65 Cecil Papers Bills 35/6, BHH/34, Wilson to Houghton 6 Jan. 1610 on the payment to Chaundler who 'hath made plotts thereofe' although 'the worke hath ben disposed to others'. This is puzzling as he continues to be paid for work on the East Garden: Jan. 1611 (BHH/128), June (BHH/133), July (BHH/133), and Aug. (BHH/152).
66 Notes of works 17 May 1611 (Cecil Papers Dom 63/88, BHH/79ff): 'In the East garden the terras is levelled and perfitted, and the little river is indented, and stones and shelles laide in the bottom, and this daye the water runneth in yt'.
67 Cecil Papers BHH/267, Nov. 1611: Buckett was paid 'for coulloringe the rocks in the greate cesterne in the East garden and coulloringe the picture of Neptune'.
68 Cecil Papers BHH/155, 30 Sept. 1611: 'To Mountaine Jenings upon his bill for altering of a rocke twice in the east garden . . . against his Majesties come to Hatfield in July 1611'.
69 Cecil Papers BHH/164, 9 Nov. 1611: 'To a Frence Mann vpon his bill for makinge a Fountaine in the garden'; further payments on 31 Jan. 1612, 7 March 1612 and 25 April (BHH/4): 'To Monsr de Cause in parte of his agrement of £110 to make a fountaine in the easte garden there'.
70 PRO S.P. 14/67 no. 62: 'He (de caus) meanes to make in the est garden 4 fountaynes, first that which is already begone, second (and) third two in the quarters of the upper

part of the garden and one in the midst of the lower part, receyuing ther water aboue it. What they will cost he hath not estimated.
Att the river he meaneth to make a force all the going out of the water from the Iland which by the consent of the water should dryue up water to the topp of the banke aboue the dell and soe descend into two fountaynes. Of all thes things he will make your lordship modells by the next Saturday . . .'.
71 Notes on the Works, Jan. 1612 (Cecil Papers 142/122, BHH/88ff): Jennings 'hath drawne a plott for all the garden which he hath or will shew his lordship. The little river that cometh from the rocke is made in the manner of a chenerne very shallow, just like that which we saw at the Earl of Exeters, yet it is not pleasing to the eye, but to be altered unto another forme according to Mountayne Jennings his plott which I thinke will doe better'.
72 Cecil Papers Bundle 69, BHH/221, 298 payments to 'the princes Inginer'.
73 Cecil Papers Bills 77, BHH/300, May 1612: 'Item for workinge the figgure like copper which standeth one the fontaine in the east garden'.
74 Cecil Papers Bills 58, BHH/282, 24 Dec. 1611.
75 Cecil Papers Bills 58, BHH/286. De Caus also arranged for shells to be brought from France, de Caus to Wilson (PRO S.P. 14/69 no. 13) sending Wilson 'les coquilles et desseings'.
76 Cecil Papers Dom 61/37, BHH/78, 30 Jan. 1611; PRO S.P. 14/61, 30 Jan. 1611.
77 PRO S.P. 14/61, 30 Jan. 1611.
78 Cecil Papers 142/122, BHH/91.
79 R. A. Skelton and John Summerson, *A Description of Maps and Architectural Drawings . . . at Hatfield House*, Oxford, 1971, p. 86 (no. 183).
80 Cecil Papers BHH/128, 28 Feb. 1609: payment to Colonel Cecil for four hundred sycamore trees from the Low Countries. There are many bills for purchasing stock and visits by John Tradescant to Flanders and France (BHH/136, 137, 140, 284).
81 Wilson to Cecil, 25 Nov. 1611, PRO S.P. 14/67.
82 Wilson to Cecil, 5 Feb. 1610, Cecil Papers Dom 61/50.

83 Cecil Papers Dom 48/136, 27 Oct. 1609.

84 S. Sorbière, *A Voyage to England*, London, 1709, pp. 64–5.

85 John Steegman, 'The Artist and the Country House', *Country Life*, (1949), p. 35.

86 Frances A. Yates, *The Rosicrucian Enlightenment*, London, 1972, p. 11ff.

87 Salomon de Caus, *Hortus Palatinus*, Frankfurt, 1620. See Gothein, *A History of Garden Art*, II, pp. 37–43; Ludwig Schmieder, 'Probleme der Gestaltung des Heidelberger Schlossgartens', *Deutschekunst und Denkmalpflege*, 1939–40, pp. 2–17.

88 Summerson, *Architecture in Britain*, ed. cit., p. 65.

89 On whom see Frances A. Yates, *The Theatre of the World*, London, 1969, pp. 42ff.

90 See *DNB*; R. J. W. Evans, *Rudolf II and his World*, Oxford, 1973, pp. 189–90.

91 For the ideological background see Evans, *op. cit.*

The Mannerist garden II

1 See *English Masques*, ed. H. A. Evans, London, n.d., pp. 100–113; *A Book of Masques*, in honour of Allardyce Nicoll, Cambridge, 1967, pp. 151–71.

2 *Book of Masques*, p. 167.

3 *Ibid.*, p. 171.

4 Report on England, 21 September 1618, *CSP Venetian, 1617–19*, p. 320.

5 Wadham College, Oxford, was laid out during the Civil War and the mount was topped by a figure of Atlas, 'holding a world curiously gilded'; see Eleanour Sinclair Rohde, *Oxford's College Gardens*, London, 1932, pp. 122–3. For Sidney Sussex College, Cambridge, see *Royal Commission on Historical Monuments, City of Cambridge*, pt ii, 1959, pp. 203ff.

6 Rohde, *op. cit.*, pp. 41–4.

7 Mark Girouard, *Architectural History*, V, 1962, p. 34 (no. 1/17); Mark Girouard, *Robert Smythson and the Architecture of the Elizabethan Era*, London, 1966, p. 136; C. S. Willis, *A Short History of Ewell and Nonsuch*, Epsom, 1948, p. 73; *Surrey Archaeological Collections*, V, 1871, pp. 150–51.

8 On Worcester see Roy Strong, *The Cult of Elizabeth*, London, 1977, pp. 27–8, 40–41.

9 Girouard, *Architectural History*, p. 31 (no. 1/7).

10 There is very little on the original Ham House. The date 1610 is over the door: see C. Roundell, *Ham House, its History and Art Treasures*, London, 1904, p. 23; J. Britton and E. W. Brayley, *The Beauties of England and Wales*, London, 1813, XIV, Surrey, pp. 191–2; O. Hill and J. Cornforth, *English Country Houses, Caroline, 1625–1685*, London, 1966, pp. 65–74; *Ham House*, Victoria and Albert Museum, 1973, pp. 7, 53. On Sir Thomas Vavasour see E. K. Chambers, *Sir Henry Lee*, Oxford, 1936, pp. 158–9, 242.

11 Girouard, *Architectural History*, V, p. 32 (1/12). On Northumberland House, as it became, see *Survey of London*, XVIII, chapter 2, pls 2–6; A. W. Clapham and W. H. Godfrey, *Some Famous Buildings and Their Story*, London 1913, pp. 184ff; John Summerson, *Architecture in Britain 1530 to 1830*, London, 1963 ed., p. 43. On Northampton see *DNB*.

12 John Summerson, *The Book of Architecture of John Thorpe*, Walpole Society, XL, 1964–6, pp. 49–50 (no. T.28).

13 Girouard, *Architectural History*, p. 58 (no. 111/16). For Wollaton see chapter III, n. 24.

14 Roy Strong, *The English Icon. Elizabethan and Jacobean Portraiture*, London, 1969, p. 55; Stephen Orgel and Roy Strong, *Inigo Jones. The Theatre of the Stuart Court*, University of California Press, 1973, I, pp. 7–8, 11–12.

15 On Lucy Harington see J. H. Whiffen, *Historical Memoirs of the House of Russell*, London, 1833, II, pp. 63–120. A study of the long list of dedications to her gives an insight into the wide range of her patronage and interests: Franklin B. Williams, Jr, *Index of Dedications and Commendatory Verses in English Books before 1641*, London, 1962 (Bibliographical Society).

16 *John Donne. The Complete English Poems*, ed. J. A. Smith, London, 1971, p. 82.

17 Sir Thomas Roe, *Negotiations in his Embassy to the Ottoman Porte*, London, 1740, V, p. 583.

18 Quoted in Gladys Scott Thompson, *Life in a Noble Household 1641–1700*, London, 1937, pp. 285–6.

19 On Twickenham Park see Girouard, *Architectural History*, p. 30 (no. II/2(1)) and references. The house was demolished in the nineteenth

century. See also *Victoria County History, Hertfordshire*, ed. W. Page, London, 1908, I, p. 378.

20 Fynes Moryson, *An Itinerary*, Glasgow, 1907, I, p. 30. See also R. J. W. Evans, *Rudolf II and His World*, Oxford, 1973, p. 121.

21 The sphere could be variously interpreted: see Filippo Piccinelli, *Mundus symbolicus*, Cologne, 1694, II, pp. 178–82.

22 On Chastleton see Margaret Dickins, *A History of Chastleton*, Banbury, 1938; H. Inigo Triggs, *Formal Gardens in England and Scotland*, London, 1902, p. 17; P. Mainwaring Johnston, *Country Life*, XLV, 1919, pp. 90. 116; *Gardens Old and New*, ed. John Leyland, London, n.d., II, pp. 131–4; Alan Clutton-Brock, *A Short Guide to Chastleton House*, n.d.; I. Whitmore Jones, *Chastleton House*, n.d.; Girouard, *Robert Smythson*, pp. 147–9.

23 John Taylor, *A New Discovery by Sea, with a Wherry from London to Salisbury*, London, 1623, see Avray Tipping, *Gardens Old and New*, London n.d., I, pp. 41–2.

24 Summerson, *Architecture in Britain*, ed. cit., pp. 38–9.

25 Frances A. Yates, *The French Academies of the Sixteenth Century*, London, 1947, pp. 248–9, n.3; John C. Meagher, 'The Dance and the Masques of Ben Jonson', *JWCI*, XXV, 1962, pp. 269–70.

26 On Sir Henry Fanshawe see *DNB*; *Memoirs of Lady Fanshawe . . .*, London, 1829.

27 *The Letters of John Chamberlain*, ed. N. E. McClure, Philadelphia, 1939, I, p. 235.

28 Andrew Marvell, *Upon Appleton House, to my Lord Fairfax* in *The Poems and Letters of Andrew Marvell*, ed. H. M. Margoliouth, Oxford, 1971 ed., I, p. 67.

29 See J. R. Hale, *Renaissance Fortification. Art or Engineering?*, London, 1977, p. 44.

30 *The Letters of John Chamberlain*, I, p. 468. Further mentions in respect of plants and seeds occur on pp. 247, 557.

31 Sir Henry Wotton, *The Elements of Architecture*, London, 1624, p. 110.

32 Quoted in *Memoirs of Lady Fanshawe*, p. 13.

33 John Nichols, *The Progresses of Queen Elizabeth*, London, 1823, I, pp. 457–9, 498–501.

34 *Ibid.*, III, pp. 101ff; Harry

H. Boyle, 'Elizabeth's Entertainment at Elvetham: War Policy in Pageantry', *Studies in Philology*, 68, 1971, pp. 146–66.

35 Yates, *French Academies*, p. 252; Frances A. Yates, *The Valois Tapestries*, London, 1959, pp. 53–4.

36 Yates, *Valois Tapestries*, pp. 56–8.

37 *Ibid.*, pls I, IX(a).

38 M. L. Gothein, *A History of Garden Art*, London, 1928, I, pp. 417–18; Ernest de Ganay, *Les Jardins de France et leur décor*, Paris, 1949, p. 35; Naomi Miller, *French Renaissance Fountains*, Garland Dissertation, 1977, pp. 227–8, 261. On the Tuileries island and grotto see Derek Clifford, *A History of Garden Design*, New York and Washington, 1967, pp. 78–9.

39 BM Add. MS 27278 f.24ᵛ–25ᵛ. I am indebted to my colleague Mr Michael Archer for signalling this to me.

40 *Aubrey's Brief Lives*, ed. Oliver Lawson Dick, London, 1949, pp. 13–15. See also Charlotte Grimston, *The History of Gorhambury*, c. 1821, where she describes the ponds and finding traces of the foundations of the banqueting house in 1802, p. 56.

41 I am grateful to Sir John Summerson for information on this. There was already a 'great pond' of which there was a Keeper (F. Devon, *Issues*, London, 1836, p. 273). The following Works entries tell of the creation of the new waterworks: 1625–6 (PRO E 351/3259): 'makeing of twoe newe pondes and frameing of a mount, and a new stand about a tree at the head of the lower pond, laying of a floore within the standing, and making a paire of stayres with Postes, railes, and Ballesters making of five Seates within the said Mounte, and a dooreacase with a paire of doores to the same and makeing and setting of gates, and Sluces with the Piramides and Arches belonging to them at Northall brooke, making of diuerse brydges . . . and laying the sides of the said pondes round aboute with greene turfes . . . and setting of Quicksettes, planteing of Cherry Trees, Plombe Trees and diuerse other kindes of fruit Trees set about the Island in the great Ponde and also on the Mounte at the heade of the lower ponde of Strawberries, Primroses and

Violett round about the border of the Pallisadoe at the greate Island ponde . . .'; further work was done in 1626–7 (E 351/3260) and 1627–8 (E 351/3261), the latter including 'A Boatehouse in the great Island ponde'; 'new bankeing and turffinge aboute the Peare trees and cherry trees in the twoe longe walkes, at the great Islande pondes and about thother pondes, and layinge newe Turffes vppon the Banckes, round aboute, and within the Pallizadoe . . .' and 'laying downe fower Tymber bridges over the River in the newe garden'.

42　On Thomas Bushell see Anthony à Wood, *Athenae Oxoniensis*, London, 1817, III, pp. 1007–10; *DNB*; Abraham de la Pryme, 'Memoirs of Thomas Bushell', *Manx Society*, XXX, 1878.

43　On the Enstone Marvels see Robert Plot, *Natural History of Oxfordshire*, Oxford, 1677, pp. 236–9; William Stukeley, *Itinerarium curiosum*, London, 1724, p. 45; *A Relation of a Short Survey of the Western Counties*, ed. L. G. Wickham Legg, Camden Miscellany, XVI, 1936, pp. 81–2. For the royal entertainment see Thomas Bushell, *The Severall Speeches and Songs at the Presentment of Mr. Bushell's Rock. Aug. 23. 1636*, Oxford, 1636; Miles Hadfield, *Gardening in Britain*, London, 1960, pp. 86–8.

44　*The Works of Francis Bacon*, ed. Spedding, Ellis and Heath, London, 1857, III, p. 158.

45　John Bate, *The Mysteryes of Nature and Art*, London, 1634.

46　For which see Christopher Hill, *The Intellectual Origins of English Revolution*, London, 1972, ed.

47　For Babington see *DNB*.

48　On which and Wotton see F. A. Yates, 'Paolo Sarpi's "History of the Council of Trent"', *JWCI*, VII, 1944, pp. 123–4.

49　Wotton, *The Elements of Architecture*, p. 108.

50　*Ibid.*, pp. 108–9.

51　*The Works of Francis Bacon, ed. cit.*, VI, pp. 485–92.

The eclectic garden I

1　On Isaac de Caus see *Dictionnaire de biographie française*, ed. M. Prévost and Roman d'Arnat, VII, 1956, p. 1467; E. Frère, *Manuel du bibliographie normand*, Rouen, 1858. Isaac is referred to in most of the literature about his brother; see chapter IV, n.1.

2　David Asseline, *La Antiquitez et chroniques de la ville de Dieppe*, Bibliothèque Dieppoise, Paris and Rouen, 1874, II, pp. 193, 196.

3　On the grotto and its documentation see Per Palme, *Triumph of Peace*, London, 1957, p. 66, quoting PRO E 351/3258 and A.O. 1/2424/56.

4　Ben Jonson, *Works*, ed. C. H. Herford and P. Simpson, Oxford, 1925–6, VIII, pp. 220ff.

5　*Ibid.*, *loc. cit.*

6　Stephen Orgel and Roy Strong, *Inigo Jones. The Theatre of the Stuart Court*, University of California Press, I, p. 376 (no. 129).

7　John Summerson, *Architecture in Britain 1530 to 1830*, London, 1963 ed., pp. 77 and 351, in which he refers to the Bedford Archives.

8　We have no evidence for de Caus having laid out the gardens of Woburn Abbey but it must be taken as a serious possibility. The information on the Woburn gardens is unfortunately virtually all post-1660; Gladys Scott Thomson, *Life in a Noble Household, 1641–1700*, London, 1937, pp. 246ff.

9　*Country Life*, XXXI, 1912, pp. 18–27.

10　*The Works of Sir William Temple*, London, 1814 ed., III, pp. 235–7.

11　Pepys records a visit to a Mr Povey in Lincoln's Inn Fields whose house had a grotto in the basement on the lines of Whitehall and Woburn and therefore likely to be by Isaac de Caus: 'after dinner up and down to see his house . . . his grotto and vault, with his bottles of wine, and a well therein to keep them cool . . . do surpass all that I did ever see of one man in all my life', *Diary of Samuel Pepys*, ed. H. B. Wheatley, IV, 1904, p. 135.

12　On Bedford House and garden see Scott Thomson, *op. cit.*, pp. 239ff; *Survey of London*, XXXVI, The Parish of St Paul Covent Garden, London, 1970, pp. 205–7.

13　On Pembroke see *DNB*; G.E.C., *The Complete Peerage*, ed. Vycary Gibbs, X, pp. 415ff.

14　This is a result of an examination of the works dedicated to him as listed in Franklin B. Williams, Jr., *Index of Dedications and Commendatory Verses . . .*, London, 1962 (Bibliographical Society). The quotes are from Anthony Nixon, *The Wars of Swethland*, London, 1609; Thomas Herbert, *A Relation of Some Yeares Travaile . . .*, London, 1634, and Thomas Palmer, *Bristolls Military Garden*, 1635.

15　A. A. Tait, 'Isaac de Caus and the South Front of Wilton House', *Burlington Magazine*, CVI, 1964, p. 74 from PRO L.C. 5/133 f.53. See also H. M. Colvin, 'The South Front of Wilton House', *Archaeological Journal*, CXI, 1954, pp. 181–90, quoting the Receiver General's accounts of the Earl at Wilton for 1632–3.

16　John Aubrey, *The Natural History of Wiltshire*, ed. John Britton, Wiltshire Topographical Society, 1847, p. 83.

17　Previous accounts of the Wilton garden are in Gothein, *A History of Garden Art*, I, pp. 453–6; J. Lees-Milne, *The Age of Inigo Jones*, London, 1953, pp. 96–103; Christopher Hussey, 'Gardens of Wilton House, Wiltshire', *Country Life*, CXXXIV, 1963, pp. 206–9.

18　Isaac de Caus, *Le Jardin de Wilton* (c. 1645), reissued London, n.d.

19　*A Relation of a Short Survey of the Western Counties*, ed. L. G. Wickham Legg, Camden Miscellany, XVI, 1936, pp. 66–7.

20　Journal of Lodewijk Huygens in the Koninklijke Nedelandsche Akademie van Wetenschappen, The Hague. Entry of 11 May 1652. Communicated and translated by Professor A. G. H. Bachrach.

21　*The Journeys of Celia Fiennes*, ed. G. C. Morris, n.p., 1947, pp. 9–10.

22　Colin Campbell, *Vitruvius Britannicus*, London, 1717–25, II, pp. 62ff.

23　Sidney, 16th Earl of Pembroke, *A Catalogue of the Paintings and Drawings in the Collection at Wilton House, Wiltshire*, London, 1968, p. 44 (no. 114). The painting in the lower half is full of *pentimenti* which include a ground-plan of the garden.

24　Aubrey, *Wiltshire*, *op. cit.*, p. 93.

25　On Venetian garden layout see Georgina Masson, *Italian Gardens*, London, 1966 ed., pp. 221ff; Lionello Puppi, 'The Villa Garden of the Veneto from the Fifteenth to the Eighteenth Century' in *The Italian Garden*, First Dumbarton Oaks Colloquium on the History of Landscape Architecture, ed. David R. Coffin, 1972, pp. 83–114.

26　W. L. Spiers, *The Notebook and Account Book of Nicholas Stone*, Walpole Society, VII, 1919, pp. 115–16. On p. 137 his nephew notes 'Hee desined & built many curious workes for the Earle of Pembroke at his Hon.s House at Wilton, near Salsbury & well paide'. See also George Vertue, *Notebooks*, I, p. 91 (Walpole Society, XVIII, 1929–30).

27　We owe the identifications to Hammond's account, *op. cit.*, p. 67.

28　See chapter VII note 56.

29　Isaac de Caus, *New and Rare Inventions of Water-Works . . .*, trans. John Leak, London, 1659, pp. 20ff. Aubrey writes: 'The grotto is paved with black and white marble; the roofe is vaulted. The figures of the tritons, &c. are in bas-relieve, of white marble, excellently well wrought. Monsieur de Caus had here a contrivance, by the turning of a cock, to shew three rainbowes [cf. Thomas Bushell above, pp. 130–33], the secret whereof he did keep to himself; he would not let the gardener who shewes it to strangers, know how to doe it; and so, upon his death, it is lost. The grott and pipes did cost ten thousand pounds. The garden is twelve acres within the terrace of the grott'. The bas-reliefs, which are of considerable quality, far superior to Stone's work, are now set into the garden loggia. It is interesting that Vertue (*Notebooks*, v, p. 24 (Walpole Society, XXXVI, 1937–8)) noted a copy of Salomon de Caus's *Les Raisons* at Wilton.

30　Margaret Whinney, *Sculpture in Britain 1530 to 1830*, London, 1964, p. 36; Roy Strong, *Van Dyck. Charles I on Horseback*, London, 1972, pp. 56–7.

31　Marcel Fouquier, *De l'art des jardins*, Paris, 1911, p. 23 (repro.); Gothein, *A History of Garden Art*, I, p. 430; Ganay, *Les Jardins de France*, pp. 72–4.

32　William Stukeley, *Itinerarium curiosum*, London, 1724, p. 50.

33　Edward Croft-Murray, *Decorative Painting in England,*

1537–1837, London, 1962, I, pp. 41–2.

34 On the Countess during this period see *DNB*; G. C. Williamson, *Lady Anne Clifford, Countess of Dorset, Pembroke and Montgomery . . .*, Kendal, 1922, pp. 160ff.

35 On which see F. H. Hazlehurst, *Jacques Boyceau and the French Formal Garden*, University of Georgia Press, 1966, pp. 49ff; Ganay, *op. cit.*, pp. 68–70.

36 Sten Karling, 'The Importance of André Mollet and His Family for the Development of the French Formal Garden' in *The French Formal Garden*, Dumbarton Oaks Colloquium on the History of Landscape Architecture, III, ed. Elisabeth B. Macdougall and F. Hamilton Hazlehurst, 1974, pp. 3–25, e.g. figs 10–12.

37 See below, pp. 188–9.

38 Karling, *op. cit.*, pp. 19–21.

39 Orgel and Strong, *Inigo Jones*, II, pp. 566ff.

40 *Ibid.*, pp. 579, 586–8.

41 Colvin, *Archaeological Journal, op. cit.*, p. 183.

42 Stukeley, *op. cit.*, p. 50.

43 C. S. Maks, *Salomon de Caus 1576–1620*, Leiden, 1935, pp. 53–4.

44 J. Woolridge, *Systema Horti-Culturae or The Art of Gardening*, London, 1688, pp. 51ff.

45 G. A. Boecleri [Böckler], *Amoenitates hydragogicae*, Nuremberg, 1664, pls 36–40 are from Wilton. The book also includes plates lifted from Salomon de Caus's *Les Raisons* and from Fanelli's *Varie architetture*, Paris, 1661.

46 Stephen Switzer, *An Introduction to a General System of Hydrostaticks and Hydraulicks . . .*, London, 1729, II, pp. 345ff; and notes to chapter XXXV for his eulogy of 'the famous de Caus'.

The eclectic garden II

1 On Italian travel see A. Lytton Sells, *The Paradise of Travellers*, London, 1914, pt II; Carlo Segré, *Itinerari di Stranieri in Italia*, Milan, 1928; George B. Parks, 'Travel as Education' in R. F. Jones *et al.*, *The Seventeenth Century*, Stanford U.P., 1951.

2 George Sandys, *A Relation of a Journey begun An. Dom. 1610*, London, 1615, p. 272.

3 *The Harleian Miscellany*, London, 1811, XII, p. 73.

4 *Ibid.*, p. 93.

5 *Ibid.*, pp. 109–110.

6 *Ibid.*, pp. 115–16.

7 See *The King's Arcadia. Inigo Jones and the Stuart Court* (catalogue by John Harris, Stephen Orgel and Roy Strong), 1972, pp. 55–6.

8 Fynes Moryson, *An Itinerary*, Glasgow, 1907, I, pp. 280–81.

9 On the museum garden see Gothein, *A History of Garden Art*, I, pp. 222ff.

10 *Peacham's Compleat Gentleman, 1634*, ed. G. S. Gordon, Oxford, 1906, pp. 104ff.

11 *Ibid.*, pp. 107–8.

12 On the Arundel Marbles see D. E. L. Haynes, *The Arundel Marbles*, Oxford, 1975; Mary S. Hervey, *The Life, Correspondence and Collections of Thomas Howard, Earl of Arundel*, Cambridge, 1921, pp. 84, 94–5, 97, 100ff, 102–3, 107; W. N. Sainsbury, *Original Unpublished Papers . . .*, London, 1859, pp. 275–8.

13 Hervey, *op. cit.*, pp. 101–2.

14 Thomas Tenison, *Baconiana*, London, 1679, p. 57.

15 Hervey, *op. cit.*, p. 255.

16 *Ibid.*, p. 41.

17 Mark Girouard, *Architectural History*, V, 1962, p. 53, nos. 111/7 (i–ii), 111/7(2)(i).

18 RIBA 1/7(i).

19 *The King's Arcadia, op. cit.*, p. 101 (no. 179) (repro.).

20 Richard W. Goulding and C. K. Adams, *Catalogue of the Pictures Belonging to His Grace the Duke of Portland . . .*, Cambridge, 1936, p. 208 (no. 520), attributed to Mytens.

21 On Jones's gateways see *The King's Arcadia, op. cit.*, pp. 197–200.

22 *Ibid.*, p. 97 (nos. 173–5).

23 Hervey, *op. cit.*, p. 346.

24 For the Tart Hall garden see the map by Faithorne and Newcourt in *Survey of London*, ed. F. H. W. Shepherd, XXX, *The Parish of St. James Westminster*, pt i, pl. 1.

25 Evelyn, *Diary*, ed. E. S. de Beer, Oxford, 1955: 19 September 1667.

26 John Aubrey, *The Natural History of Wiltshire*, ed. J. Britton, Wiltshire Topographical Society, 1847, p. 93.

27 *Ibid., loc. cit.*

28 See *DNB*.

29 Bodleian Library Aubrey MS 2 f.53.

30 On Danvers House, Chelsea, see Bodleian Aubrey MS 2 f. 59, 'Plan of Sir John Danvers Garden at Chelsea'; f. 53–56ʳ, a description. The latter has been reprinted in A. M. Charles, *A Life of George Herbert*, Cornell U.P., 1977, pp. 61–5, although the author assumes the garden and house were in existence in 1617. Miles Hadfield, *Gardening in Britain*, London, 1960, pp. 74–5. A plan of the house and a drawing of the garden façade is in John Summerson, *The Book of Architecture of John Thorpe*, Walpole Society, XL, 1964–6, p. 48 (T 21 and 22), pl. 8; *The Survey of London*, IV (*Parish of Chelsea*), pt 2, 1913, pp. 9–14. A. W. Clapham and W. H. Godfrey, *Some Famous Buildings and Their Story*, London, 1913, pp. 92–103.

31 Sir Henry Wotton, *The Elements of Architecture*, London, 1624, p. 110.

32 On Stone's work for Danvers see W. L. Spiers, *The Notebook and Account Book of Nicholas Stone*, Walpole Society, VII, 1919, p. 50.

33 Bodleian Aubrey MS 2, f.56.

34 See above, pp. 138–9.

35 On the pastoral cult in which the garden becomes a vehicle for returns to the lost innocence of the Garden Eden see Renato Poggioli, 'The Pastoral of the Self', *Daedalus*, LXXXVIII, 1959, pp. 686–99; Harry Levin, *The Myth of the Golden Age in the Renaissance*, London, 1970, chapter 2.

36 Margaret Whinney, *Sculpture in Britain 1530 to 1830*, London, 1964, p. 28; Sainsbury, *Original Papers*, pp. 65, 70, 71; John Pope-Hennessy, *Samson and a Philistine*, V & A Monographs, VIII, 1949. The siting of the statue in the grounds of York House would indicate that Buckingham's garden in the 1620s was also Italianate. Likewise the drawing by Esselens: see P. M. Hulton in Walpole Society, XXXV, 1954–6, pt i, pp. 32–3, pl. 28(b).

37 See, for example, G. P. V. Bolzani, *Les Hieroglyphes*, trans. I. de Montlyard, Garland Reprint, 1976, p. 75.

38 See Bolzani, *op. cit.*, p. 441.

39 *The Book of Architecture of John Thorpe, op. cit.*, pl. 8.

40 Aubrey, *Natural History of Wiltshire*, p. 93.

41 Stephen Orgel and Roy Strong, *Inigo Jones. The Theatre of the Stuart Court*, University of California Press, 1973, II, pp. 518–19 (no. 252).

42 See Oliver Millar, *The Age of Charles I. Painting in England, 1620–49* (exhibition catalogue), 1972, p. 34 (no. 38).

43 *Victoria County History: Hertfordshire*, IV, pp. 52–3.

44 I am much indebted to Christopher Gilbert for communicating information on the garden at Temple Newsam on which see C. Gilbert, 'The Park and Gardens at Temple Newsam', *Leeds Art Calendar*, no. 53, 1964, pp. 4–9; D. G. Wild and C. G. Gilbert, 'Excavation of the Garden Banqueting House', *Leeds Art Calendar*, no. 60, 1967, pp. 4–7; N. Pevsner, *Yorkshire. The West Riding*, London, 1959, p. 348; *Country Life*, LII, 1922, pp. 428–9.

45 On Rycote see C. Hussey, 'Rycote', *Country Life*, LXIII, 1928, pp. 16ff; N. Pevsner and J. Sherwood, *Oxfordshire*, London, 1974, pp. 748–9.

46 John Harris and A. Tait, *Catalogue of the Drawings by Inigo Jones, John Webb and Isaac de Caus in the Collection of Worcester College, Oxford* (forthcoming).

47 J. Britton and E. W. Brayley, *The Beauties of England and Wales*, London, 1813, XIV, Surrey, p. 171; *The Journeys of Celia Fiennes*, ed. G. C. Morris, n.p., 1947, pp. 342–3.

48 Carola Oman, *Henrietta Maria*, London, 1936, pp. 82–3.

49 M. A. Everett, *Letters of Queen Henrietta Maria*, London, 1857, p. 19.

50 By far the most important study of the Mollet family is Sten Karling, 'The Importance of André Mollet and His Family for the Development of the French Formal Garden' in *The French Formal Garden*, III, Dumbarton Oaks Colloquium on the History of Landscape Architecture, ed. Elisabeth B. Macdougall and F. Hamilton Hazlehurst, 1974, pp. 3–25. See also Ernest de Ganay, *Les Jardins de France et leur décor*, Paris, 1949, pp. 50–63. Gothein, *A History of Garden Art*, I, pp. 420–21.

51 André Mollet, *Le Jardin de plaisir*, Stockholm, 1651, sig A 2. Later in the book he recalls England when he writes of *allées*: 'On se sert du mesme Rouleau comme nous avons dict cy deuant le gazon apres y avoir passé premierement vn

Rouleau de bois pour oster les crottes des vers de dessus iceluy gazon, c'est la facon & maniere que l'on tient en Angleterre pour la contruction des allées & gazonage, laquelle donne vne tresbelle decoration dans les jardins.'

52 The lack of documentation for his first visit means that he was personally employed by the Queen, not all of whose Privy Purse accounts survive. This is paralleled by other French designers who worked for her: see *The King's Arcadia, op. cit.*, p. 156 (nos. 288–9).

53 On St James's Palace see Ernest Sheppard, *Memorials of St. James's Palace*, London, 1894, chapters 1 and 2. The Works Accounts begin recording alterations to the garden from 1629–30 onwards (PRO E 351/3263): 'John Marre Mathematition for working and squareinge a Dyall of Portland Stone . . . sett vpp in the Privy Garden . . .'; 'Zachary Taylor for Cutting and Carving iiij^er. greate Cartoches . . . to stand vnder a Pergola in the Privy Garden . . .'; 'And to Andrew Durdaunte for his paines Travell and care in lookeing to the safe landing and carriage of divers statues and marbles and for takeing severall Notes of them in A Booke by way Inventory'. 1637–8 (PRO E 351/3271): 'for mending and repainting three Marble Statues viz: Apollo Bacchus and Cupid'. For the disposition of the gardens see Faithorne and Newcourt's map, surveyed 1643–7 and published in 1658: *Survey of London*, ed. F. H. W. Sheppard, xxx, *The Parish of St. James Westminster*, pt i, pl. 1.

54 Sieur de la Serre, *Histoire de l'Entrée de la Royne Mere . . . dans la Grande Bretagne*, London, 1639, sig K. The description by Mandelslo in 1640 is of the orchard only: 'Le jardin du palais de S^t. James n'est pas fort grand, & n'a rien de remarquable, si ce n'est qu'au milieu on void dans une grande pierle carrée & creuse au milieu cent dix-sept quadrans. Il est accompagné d'un verger d'arbres fruitiers, plantez en échiquier, ayant au milieu un gros pilier de bois, qui jette d'eau, & d'un petit bois, qui forme quelques allées assès agreables . . .' (*Les Voyages du Sieur Albert de Mandelslo*, Leiden, 1719, p. 749).

55 The Works Accounts for 1633–4 mention this (PRO E 351/3267): 'in woorking vppon a greate quantitie of Stuffe cutt into Ledges for Letticing to inclose the side of the wall next the parke Orchard where the Marble Statues are placed'.

56 Whinney, *Sculpture in Britain*, p. 36; C. C. Stopes, 'Gleanings from the Records of the Reigns of James I and Charles I', *Burlington Magazine*, XXII, 1922, p. 282.

57 A. H. Scott-Elliot, 'The Statues from Mantua in the Collection of King Charles I', *Burlington Magazine*, CI, 1959, pp. 218–27.

58 *The Inventories and Valuations of the King's Goods 1649–51*, Walpole Society, XLIII, 1970–72, pp. 143ff. For payments for garden statuary see *CSP Domestic, 1636–37*, p. 325 nos. 96 and 97.

59 R. Needham and A. Webster, *Somerset House Past and Present*, London, 1905, pp. 89ff; *The King's Arcadia, op. cit.*, pp. 149–54.

60 1631–2 (PRO E 351/3265): payments for the 'intended' fountain; 1633–4 (E 351/3267): for the fountain; 1637–8 (E 351/3271): 'making a new fountaine in the Queen's privy Garden'. In May 1636 Nicholas Stone was paid to produce a cistern of black marble for the fountain and to 'mak it agreey with the work of Hubert le sur': Spiers, 'Notebook', *op. cit.*, pp. 105–6.

61 These are listed in *Inventories and Valuations, op. cit.*, pp. 135–6. Statues began to be introduced in 1628–9 (PRO E 351/3262): 'for working twoe pedistalls for figures to stand on in the garden'; for 'goeing downe diverse tymes to twoe shippes that lay in the Poole viewing of diverse figures and statues in them taking them oute . . . for his Majesty . . .'; 1631–2 (PRO E 351/3265): 'mending and peecing the Armes hed or feete and other partes of divers white Marble Statues dismembered and broken in their Carryadge'. There seems also to have been a Jonesian park gateway for 'workeing vpon [a] great Cornish for the Garden gate towardes the parke', as well as an elaborate water-gate (E 351/3265 and 3269).

62 Whinney, *Sculpture in Britain*, pp. 37–8; John Harris, 'The Diana Fountain at Hampton Court', *Burlington Magazine*, CXI, 1969, pp. 444–7.

Neither spots that this must have been the Somerset House fountain which was moved to Hampton Court while Cromwell was Protector.

63 Quoted in Harris, *op. cit., loc. cit.*

64 Ernest Law, *The History of Hampton Court Palace*, London, 1888, II, p. 244 and p. 302 quoting the Inventory of Cromwell's goods, 1659; Mollie Sands, *The Gardens of Hampton Court*, London, 1950, pp. 109ff. For Arethusa see Ovid, *Metamorphoses*, trans. Mary M. Innes, Harmondsworth, 1955, pp. 142–4.

65 All the alterations under the direction of Ury Babington were carried out in 1636: see National Library of Wales, Wynnstay MS 181 (1636). Information kindly communicated by Mr G. C. Thomas.

66 *The King's Arcadia, op. cit.*, p. 157 (nos. 293–4).

67 This was created in 1634–5 (PRO E 351/3268): 'for bringing vpp with brickes a new wall in the Parke . . . with Buttresses to enclose an Orenge Garden there . . . making and setting vpp a dore case and doore in the wall betweene the privy Garden and Orrenge Garden'. John Tradescant was paid £60 for alterations to the garden in December 1636: Wynnstay MS 181 (1636). See Mea Allan, *The Tradescants*, London, 1964, pp. 141ff. In 1637 Nicholas Stone provided a fountain: Spiers, 'Notebook', *op. cit.*, 111.

68 *The King's Arcadia, op. cit.*, p. 158 (no. 296). Under 1638–9 (PRO E 351/3272): 'to George Portman Painter for paintinge vppon the walles in the open gallery in the privy Garden being iiij^xx foote longe xij foote broade and x^en fo di highe viij of the Queenes Ma^te housses in Landskipp in oyle and vnderneath a leaninge place aboute three foote high painted with devisions of marble and the deelinge [?ceiling] wth Cloudes and sky coulor and for puttinge out and alteringe of diverse thinges by his Ma^te Command lxxiij^li viij^s vj^d'.

69 See Georgina Masson, *Italian Gardens*, London, 1966 ed., p. 149. There are two surviving damaged examples, possibly of this date, at Ham House.

70 On Wimbledon House see *The King's Arcadia, op. cit.*, pp. 158–9 (nos. 297–8); C. S. Higham, *Wimbledon Manor*

House under the Cecils, London, 1962, pp. 30ff.

71 Warrant given at The Hague, 10 April 1642, Wynnstay MS.

72 The Parliamentary Survey is printed in *Surrey Archaeological Collections*, v, 1871, pp. 112ff.

73 Mollet, *Le Jardin de plaisir*, chapter XI.

74 *Ibid.*, *loc. cit.*

75 *Ibid.*, *loc. cit.*

Conclusion

1 On Bolsover Castle see Hayman Rooke, *Sketch of the History of Bolsover and Peak Castles* in Bibliotheca Topographica Britannica, no. XXXII, 1790; R. W. Goulding, *Bolsover Castle*, Oxford, 1928; F. W. C. Gregory, 'Bolsover Castle', *Thoroton Society*, LI, 1947, pp. 4–49; Mark Girouard, *Robert Smythson and the Architecture of the Elizabethan Era*, London, 1966, pp. 159ff.

2 Jonson, *Works*, ed. Herford and Simpson, Oxford, 1941, pp. 807–14.

3 D. J. Gordon, *The Renaissance Imagination*, University of California Press, 1975, pp. 96–101.

4 Jonson, *Works*, ed. cit., p. 812.

5 *Ibid.*, pp. 812–13.

6 This discussion of *Chloridia* is based on Stephen Orgel and Roy Strong, *Inigo Jones. The Theatre of the Stuart Court*, University of California Press, 1972, I, pp. 56–7.

7 *Ibid.*, II, p. 411.

8 *Ibid.*, I, p. 72.

9 *Ibid.*, II, p. 706.

10 *Ibid.*, p. 708.

11 *Ibid.*, p. 709.

12 *Ibid.*, I, p. 7.

13 *Ibid.*, II, p. 827. The subject of perspective in the masques is discussed in detail in chapters I and II.

14 R. B. Beckett, *Lely*, London, 1951, pls 9 (*c.* 1644), 14 (*c.* 1647), 29 (*c.* 1651) and later examples pls 51, 52, 76 and 109.

15 Eugenio Battisti, '*Natura Artificiosa* to *Natura Artificialis*' in *The Italian Garden*, First Dumbarton Oaks Colloquium on the History of Landscape Architecture, ed. David R. Coffin, 1972, pp. 19–20 and n. 40.

16 Stanley Stewart, *The Enclosed Garden. The Tradition and the Image in Seventeenth*

Century Poetry, Wisconsin U.P., 1966, p. 116; John Dixon Hunt, *The Figure in the Landscape. Poetry, Painting, and Gardening during the Eighteenth Century*, Johns Hopkins U.P., pp. 9–12; see also Brendan O'Hehir, *Expans'd Hieroglyphicks. A Critical Edition of Sir John Denham's Cooper's Hill*, University of California Press, 1969; Leonard Foster, 'Meditation in a Garden', *German Life and Letters*, Special number for William Witta, 1977, pp. 23–35.
17 Quoted in Stewart, *op. cit.*, p. 116.
18 Quoted *ibid.*, *loc. cit.*
19 Dixon Hunt, *op. cit.*, pp. 9–10.
20 George Wither, *A Collection of Emblemes 1635*, English Emblem Books, no. 12, ed. John Horden, Scolar Press, 1968, p. 107. The collection made use of the engravings from Gabriel Rollenhagen's *Nucleus Emblematum Selectissimum* (1611–13). Other garden, tree and flower emblems are on pp. 35, 46, 102, 140, 159 and 209.
21 Francis Quarles, *Emblems, Divine and Moral*, London,

1839 ed., Bk I, emblem X. See Rosemary Freeman, *English Emblem Books*, London, 1948, pp. 114ff.
22 Quarles, *op. cit.*, Bk IV, emblem II.
23 *Ibid.*, Bk V, emblem III.
24 H. A., *Partheneia sacra*, ed. Iain Fletcher, 1950.
25 *Ibid.*, p. 11.
26 *Ibid.*, p. 12.
27 *Ibid.*, p. 14.
28 *The Poems and Letters of Andrew Marvell*, ed. H. M. Margoliouth, Oxford, 1963 ed., I, p. 48.
29 Stewart, *The Enclosed Garden*, pp. 120–21.
30 *Ibid.*, p. 105.
31 Quarles, *op. cit.*, Bk III, emblem 13.
32 On Packwood House see *Packwood House, Warwickshire*, guide, n.d.; *Gardens Old and New*, ed. John Leyland, n.d., pp. 58–62; *Country Life*, LVI, 1924, pp. 218–24 and 250–57.
33 Reginald Blomfield and F. Inigo Thomas, *The Formal Garden in England*, London, 1892, pp. 72–4.
34 John Dixon Hunt, *Andrew Marvell. His Life and Writings*, London, 1978, pp. 90–109. D. C. Allen, *Image and Meaning. Metamorphoric*

Traditions in Renaissance Poetry, Johns Hopkins U.P., 1960, pp. 115–53, esp. p. 124 f.
35 *The Poems and Letters of Andrew Marvell*, ed. cit., p. 68.
36 *Ibid.*, p. 69.
37 *Ibid.*, p. 71.
38 On melancholy see Lawrence Babb, *The Elizabethan Malady*, East Lansing, Michigan, 1951 and bibliography, pp. 196–7; Bridget Gellert Lyons, *Voices of Melancholy*, London, 1971 and bibliography, pp. 180–86; Roy Strong, 'The Elizabethan Malady. Melancholy in Elizabethan and Jacobean Portraiture', *Apollo*, LXXIX, 1964, pp. 164–9.
39 Quoted in Strong, 'Elizabethan Malady', p. 265.
40 Quoted *ibid.*, p. 266.
41 Milton, *Il Penseroso*, ll. 139–48.
42 Evelyn, *Diary*, ed. E. S. de Beer, Oxford, 1955: 15–17 May 1643 and *De vita propria, ibid.*, I, p. 54.
43 Robert Burton, *The Anatomy of Melancholy*, London, 1806 ed., I, p. 407.
44 *Ibid.*, p. 411.
45 On which see W. E. Houghton, 'The English Virtuoso in the 17th Century',

Journal of the History of Ideas, III, 1942, pp. 51–73, 190–219.
46 Dixon Hunt, *Figure in the Landscape*, pp. 47ff.
47 Evelyn, *Diary*, ed. cit., 15–17 May 1643, 16 Feb. 1649, 1 Jan. 1651 and 22 Feb. 1652, and *De vita propria, ibid.*, I, p. 55.
48 *De vita propria, loc. cit.*
49 Dixon Hunt, *Figure in the Landscape*, pp. 25–6; W. G. Hiscock, *John Evelyn and his Circle*, London, 1955, pp. 28–33; John Evelyn, *Directions to the Gardiner at Sayes Court*, ed. Geoffrey Keynes, 1931. Alicia Amherst, *A History of Gardening in England*, London, 1896, pp. 190–95.
50 Quoted in *The Genius of the Place. The English Landscape Garden 1620–1820*, ed. John Dixon Hunt and Peter Willis, London, 1975, pp. 57–8.
51 *Ibid.*, pp. 67–9.
52 Karling (see chapter VII, n. 50); Amherst, *op. cit.*, pp. 196ff.
53 John Aubrey, *The Natural History of Wiltshire*, ed. J. Britton, Wiltshire Topographical Society, 1847, p. 92.

List of Illustrations

1 Medieval garden. Miniature from the *Roman de la rose*, late fifteenth century. British Library, London, Harl. MS 4425 f. 12ᵛ

2 Humanist garden. Wood engraving from Francesco Colonna, *Hypnerotomachia Poliphili*, Venice, 1499

3, 4 Topiary work. Wood engraving from Francesco Colonna, *Hypnerotomachia Poliphili*, Venice, 1499

5 Plan for a knot garden. Wood engraving from Francesco Colonna, *Hypnerotomachia Poliphili*, Venice, 1499

6 The *Vatican and Belvedere*. Painting by an unknown artist, second half of sixteenth century. Formerly Kunsthistorisches Museum, Vienna

7 *The Garden of the Villa d'Este*. Painting by an unknown artist, seventeenth century. Collection of Sir Harold Acton.

8 *Panorama of Hampton Court and its Gardens as seen from the Thames*. Drawing by Anthonis van Wyngaerde, c. 1555. Ashmolean Museum, Oxford

9 The gardens of Blois. Engraving from J. A. Du Cerceau, *Les Plus Excellents Bastiments de France*, Paris, 1576

10 The gardens of Gaillon. Engraving from J. A. Du Cerceau, *Les Plus Excellents Bastiments de France*, Paris, 1576

11 The gardens of Fontainebleau. Engraving from J. A. Du Cerceau, *Les Plus Excellents Bastiments de France*, Paris, 1576

12 *Guillebert de Lannoy presenting his book, 'L'Instruction d'un jeune prince', to Charles the Bold, Duke of Burgundy*. Flemish miniature, fifteenth century. Bibliothèque de l'Arsenal, Paris, MS 5104, f. 14ʳ

13 *The Family of Henry VIII*, details showing the Great Garden at Whitehall Palace. Painting by an unknown artist, c. 1545. Royal Collection, reproduced by gracious permission of Her Majesty Queen Elizabeth II

14 *View of Whitehall Palace with the Great Garden and its Fountain*. Drawing by Anthonis van Wyngaerde, c. 1555. Ashmolean Museum, Oxford

15 Design for a pavilion adorned with the king's beasts, c. 1520. British Library, London, Cotton MS Augustus iii f. 18

16 Design for a knot garden. From Didymus Mountain, *The Gardeners Labyrinth*, 1571

17 Design for a rectangular maze. Wood engraving from Thomas Hill, *The Profitable Art of Gardening*, 1568

18 Design for knot gardens. Drawing by Thomas Trevelyon for his *Miscellany*, 1618. Boies Penrose MS, Barbados Hill, Devon, Penn.

19 *Elizabeth I as 'Rosa Electa' flanked by Tudor Roses and Eglantine*. Engraving by William Rogers, c. 1590–1600. British Museum, London

20 Plan of Kenilworth Castle. Engraving from William Dugdale, *Antiquities of Warwickshire*, 1656

21 *Melancholy Young Man*. Miniature by Isaac Oliver, c. 1590–95. Royal Collection, reproduced by gracious permission of Her Majesty Queen Elizabeth II

22 Design for a garden in the Ionic style. From J. Vredeman de Vries, *Hortorum viridariorumque elegantes et multiplicis formae*, 1583

23 Diagram of the Privy and Great Gardens at Theobalds, second half of sixteenth century. Drawing by Ian Mackenzie-Kerr

24 The gardens of the Duke of Brunswick at Hesse. Engraving, 1630s. Victoria and Albert Museum, London

25 *Wollaton Hall and Park, Nottinghamshire*. Painting by Jan Siberechts, 1697. Yale Center for British Art, Paul Mellon Collection

26 Plan of house and gardens at Wollaton. Drawing by Robert Smythson, *c*. 1580. British Architectural Library – RIBA Drawings Collection

27 Château d'Anet. Engraving from J. A. Du Cerceau, *Les Plus Excellents Bastiments de France*, Paris, 1576

28 Wimbledon House, Surrey (now Greater London). Engraving by Henry Winstanley, 1678. British Museum, London.

29 Wimbledon House and gardens. Drawing by Robert Smythson, 1609. British Architectural Library – RIBA Drawings Collection.

30 The Obelisk at Nonsuch Palace, Surrey (now Greater London). Drawing from the *Lumley Inventory*, 1590. Collection the Earl of Scarbrough. Photo National Portrait Gallery, London

31 The Privy Garden of Nonsuch Palace. Detail from engraving by Jodocus Hondius, *Map of Surrey*, in John Speed, *Theatre of the Empire of Great Britaine*, 1611–12

32 One of the Falcon Perches at Nonsuch. Drawing from the *Lumley Inventory*, 1590. Collection the Earl of Scarbrough. Photo National Portrait Gallery, London

33 Diana Fountain in the Privy Garden of Nonsuch Palace, *c*. 1590. Drawing from the *Lumley Inventory*, 1590. Collection the Earl of Scarbrough. Photo National Portrait Gallery, London

34 Fountain in honour of Elizabeth I as Diana at Nonsuch Palace, *c*. 1590. Watercolour from the *Lumley Inventory*, 1590. Collection the Earl of

Scarbrough. Photo National Portrait Gallery, London

35 Portrait of Salomon de Caus. Painting by an unknown artist, 1619. Kurpfälzisches Museum, Heidelberg

36 Automaton. Theorem XXXVII from Aleotti's translation of the *Pneumatics* of Hero of Alexandria, 1589

37 Automaton. Theorum XL from Aleotti's translation of the *Pneumatics* of Hero of Alexandria, 1589

38 *The Gardens of Pratolino*. Painting by Giusto Utens, 1599. Museo Topografico, Florence. Photo Soprintendenza alle Gallerie, Uffizi, Florence

39 Grotto with automata at Pratolino. Engraving by Stefano della Bella, 1653. British Museum, London

40 View of the palace and gardens at Fontainebleau. Engraving after Alessandro Francini, 1614. Bibliothèque Nationale, Paris

41 View of the palace and gardens at St Germain-en-Laye. Engraving, 1614. Bibliothèque Nationale, Paris

42 The Grotto of Orpheus at St Germain-en-Laye. Engraving by A. Bosse after Francini. Bibliothèque Nationale, Paris

43 *Anne of Denmark*, showing the garden of Somerset House. Painting by Marcus Gheeraerts, *c*. 1605–10. From the Woburn Abbey Collection, reproduced by kind permission of the Marquess of Tavistock and Trustees of the Bedford Estates

44 Plan of the gardens of Somerset House. Drawing by Robert Smythson, *c*. 1609. British Architectural Library – RIBA Drawings Collection

45 Somerset House. Engraving from W. Kip, *Britannia illustrata*, 1707

46 The Parnassus in the garden at Pratolino. Drawing by H. Schickhardt. Württembergische Landesbibliothek, Stuttgart, Cod. Histo. Q. 148, fasc. B C

47 Design for a Parnassus, probably for Somerset House. Engraving from Salomon de Caus, *Les Raisons des forces mouvantes*, 1624

48 *Ballet of the Provinces of France*. Drawing by Antoine Caron, 1573. Collection Mr and

Mrs Winslow Ames, Saunderstown, Rhode Island

49 *View of Greenwich Palace*. Drawing by Anthonis van Wyngaerde, *c*. 1555. Ashmolean Museum, Oxford

50 Design for an aviary with elements of that at Greenwich. Engraving from Salomon de Caus, *Les Raisons des forces mouvantes*, 1624

51 Design for a fountain similar to that for Greenwich. Engraving from Salomon de Caus, *Les Raisons des forces mouvantes*, 1624

52 The Tiber fountain at Fontainebleau. Engraving by M. Lasne after Tommaso Francini. Bibliothèque Nationale, Paris

53 Design for a reclining giant as an island, probably for Richmond Palace. Engraving from Salomon de Caus, *Les Raisons des forces mouvantes*, 1624

54 Giant, Mount Apennine, by Giambologna at Pratolino, near Florence, *c*. 1580. Photo Alinari

55 Project for a giant, probably for Henry, Prince of Wales, at Richmond Palace, *c*. 1610. Engraving from Salomon de Caus, *Les Raisons des forces mouvantes*, 1624

56 *Henry, Prince of Wales*, detail showing view of lakes and islands, probably at Richmond Palace. Painting by Robert Peake, *c*. 1610. National Portrait Gallery, London

57 An artificial mountain with an aviary within it, probably for Richmond Palace. Engraving from Salomon de Caus, *Les Raisons des forces mouvantes*, 1624

58 *Oberon's Palace in Ben Jonson's 'Oberon, the Fairy Prince'*. Drawing by Inigo Jones, 1611. Devonshire Collection, Chatsworth. Reproduced by permission of the Trustees of the Chatsworth Settlement. Photo Courtauld Institute of Art, University of London

59 The Dell at Hatfield. Drawing attributed to Mountain Jennings, Public Record Office, London, S.P. 14/67, no. 63 (Crown copyright)

60 Design for a knot garden surrounded by terraces, possibly for Hatfield. Courtesy of the Marquess of Salisbury

61 Design for a fountain of the type Salomon de Caus made for

Hatfield. Engraving from Salomon de Caus, *Les Raisons des forces mouvantes*, 1624

62 Aerial view of Hatfield House and gardens. Photo Aerofilms Ltd

63 Massey's Court, Llanerch, Clwyd. Painting by an unknown artist, 1662. Yale Center for British Art, Paul Mellon Collection

64 *The Hortus Palatinus*. Painting by an unknown artist, showing the garden created by Salomon de Caus. Kurpfälzisches Museum, Heidelberg

65 *Portrait of a Lady of the Hampden Family*. Painting by an unknown artist, *c.* 1610-15. Museum of Art, Rhode Island School of Design, Providence, Rhode Island. Gift of Miss Lucy T. Aldrich

66 Wadham College, Oxford. Engraving from David Loggan, *Oxonia illustrata*, 1677

67 New College, Oxford. Engraving from David Loggan, *Oxonia illustrata*, 1677

68 Plan of the house and garden of Worcester Lodge, Nonsuch. Drawing by Robert Smythson, *c.* 1609. British Architectural Library – RIBA Drawings Collection

69 Plan of the house and garden at Ham, Petersham. Drawing by Robert Smythson, *c.* 1609. British Architectural Library – RIBA Drawings Collection

70 Plan of the house and garden for Dowsby Hall, Lincolnshire. Drawing by John Thorpe, *c.* 1603-10. Trustees of Sir John Soane's Museum, London. Photo Courtauld Institute of Art, University of London

71 Plan of Northampton House and gardens, London. Drawing by Robert Smythson, *c.* 1609. British Architectural Library – RIBA Drawings Collection

72 Plan of the garden of Lucy Harington, Countess of Bedford, at Twickenham Park. Drawing by Robert Smythson, *c.* 1609. British Architectural Library – RIBA Drawings Collection

73 The pre-Copernican universe. Woodcut from *Practica compendiosa artis Raymond Lull*, 1523

74 The garden at Chastleton House, Oxfordshire, originally created *c.* 1602-14. Photo Charles Latham, from H. Inigo Triggs, *Formal Gardens in England and Scotland*, 1902

75 Emblematic lake dug for the entertainment at Elvetham, Hampshire, 1591. Wood engraving from John Nichols, *Progresses of Queen Elizabeth*, 1823. Photo Warburg Institute, University of London

76 Water festival at Bayonne, 1565. One of the Valois tapestries. Uffizi, Florence. Photo Alinari

77 *Fête on the Lake at Fontainebleau*. Drawing by Antoine Caron, *c.* 1570. National Gallery of Scotland, Edinburgh

78 The water garden at Gaillon *c.* 1550. Engraving from J. A. Du Cerceau, *Les Plus Excellents Bastiments de France*, 1576

79 Diagram based on Francis Bacon's description of a pond with islands and a house at Gorhambury, 1608. Drawing by Ian Mackenzie-Kerr

80 Decoy for hunting duck at Haughton House, Nottinghamshire. Engraving from W. Kip, *Britannia illustrata*, 1707

81 The hermitage and grotto built by Thomas Bushell at Enstone, Oxfordshire, 1628-35. Engraving from Robert Plot, *Natural History of Oxfordshire*, 1677

82 The approach and exterior of Thomas Bushell's hermitage at Enstone. Engraving from Robert Plot, *Natural History of Oxfordshire*, 1677

83 Automaton. Wood engraving from John Bate, *The Mysteryes of Nature and Art*, 1634

84 Hydraulic automaton. Wood engraving from John Bate, *The Mysteryes of Nature and Art*, 1634

85 *The House of Oceanus in 'The Fortunate Isles and their Union'*. Drawing by Inigo Jones, 1625. Devonshire Collection, Chatsworth. Reproduced by permission of the Trustees of the Chatsworth Settlement. Photo Courtauld Institute of Art, University of London

86 Grotto at Woburn Abbey, Bedfordshire. Photo *Country Life*

87 Grotto with Diana and Callisto. Watercolour by Isaac de Caus, *c.* 1620-30. Victoria and Albert Museum, London

88 Grotto with Mercury, and Europa and the Bull. Watercolour by Isaac de Caus. Victoria and Albert Museum, London

89 The layout of Moor Park, Hertfordshire. Drawing by Ian Mackenzie-Kerr

90 *Covent Garden Piazza*, detail showing the garden of Bedford House. Painting by an unknown artist, *c.* 1649. Collection G. H. Marwood, Esq.

91 *Parterre de broderie*. Engraving from Isaac de Caus, *Le Jardin de Wilton*, *c.* 1645

92 Figure by Nicholas Stone for the Venus Fountain at Wilton, near Salisbury, Wiltshire. Photo Julia Trevelyan Oman

93 Figure by Nicholas Stone for the Diana Fountain at Wilton. Photo Julia Trevelyan Oman

94 Figure by Nicholas Stone of Susanna for the fountain at Wilton. Photo Julia Trevelyan Oman

95 The Susanna Fountain at Wilton. Engraving from Isaac de Caus, *Le Jardin de Wilton*, *c.* 1645

96 The Wilderness at Wilton with a statue of Bacchus. Engraving from Isaac de Caus, *Le Jardin de Wilton*, *c.* 1645

97 One of the coronet fountains at Wilton. Engraving from Isaac de Caus, *Le Jardin de Wilton*, *c.* 1645

98 The immediate façade of the grotto at Wilton today. Photo *Country Life*

99 *Topographical View of Wilton*, detail showing the grotto façade. Painting by an unknown artist, *c.* 1700. Collection the Earl of Pembroke. Photo A. C. Cooper

100 Interior of the grotto, Wilton. Engraving from Isaac de Caus, *Le Jardin de Wilton*, *c.* 1645

101 The water parterre, Wilton. Engraving from Isaac de Caus, *Le Jardin de Wilton*, *c.* 1645

102 Figure by Nicholas Stone for the water parterre, Wilton. Photo Julia Trevelyan Oman

103 The amphitheatre, Wilton. Engraving from Isaac de Caus, *Le Jardin de Wilton*, *c.* 1645

104 Aerial view of the garden at Wilton from the house. En-

graving from Isaac de Caus, *Le Jardin de Wilton*, c. 1645

105 *Topographical View of Wilton*, detail showing the Pegasus Cascade. Painting by an unknown artist, c. 1700. Collection the Earl of Pembroke. Photo A. C. Cooper

106 Dawley, former county of Middlesex. From W. Kip, *Britannia illustrata*, 1707

107 Staunton Harold, Leicestershire. From W. Kip, *Britannia illustrata*, 1707

108 Haigh, Lancashire (now Greater Manchester). From W. Kip, *Britannia illustrata*, 1707

109 Self-portrait. Drawing by Inigo Jones, c. 1620. Devonshire Collection, Chatsworth. Reproduced by permission of the Trustees of the Chatsworth Settlement. Photo Courtauld Institute of Art, University of London

110 *Anne of Denmark*, detail showing the Great Gate at Oatlands. Painting by Paul van Somer, 1617. Royal Collection, reproduced by gracious permission of Her Majesty Queen Elizabeth II

111 Inigo Jones's Italian gate for the west garden at Arundel House, London. Drawing by John Smythson, 1618. British Architectural Library – RIBA Drawings Collection

112 *Thomas Howard, Earl of Arundel*, detail showing a view of the east garden at Arundel House. Painting by an unknown artist, c. 1627. Collection the Duke of Portland, Welbeck Abbey. Photo National Portrait Gallery, London

113 *Aletheia Talbot, Countess of Arundel*, detail showing the view into the garden at Arundel House. Painting by Daniel Mytens, 1618. National Portrait Gallery, London (on loan to Arundel Castle). Photo Courtauld Institute of Art, University of London

114 View of an unfinished grotto at Albury Park, Surrey. Engraving by Wenceslas Hollar. Victoria and Albert Museum, London

115 Plan of the garden at Danvers House, Chelsea. Drawing by John Aubrey, 1691. Bodleian Library, Oxford, MS Aubrey 2, f. 59^r

116 Danvers House, Chelsea. Engraving from W. Kip, *Britannia illustrata*, 1707

117 *Arthur, 1st Baron Capel and his family*, detail showing the garden at Little Hadham. Painting by Cornelius Johnson, c. 1639. National Portrait Gallery, London

118 *View towards the east front of Hadham Hall, Hertfordshire*. Painting by an unknown artist, late seventeenth century. Collection Hadham Hall. Photo National Portrait Gallery, London

119 *Garden Scene in 'The Shepherd's Paradise'*. Drawing by Inigo Jones, 1633. Devonshire Collection, Chatsworth. Reproduced by permission of the Trustees of the Chatsworth Settlement. Photo Courtauld Institute of Art, University of London

120 Rycote, Oxfordshire. Detail from W. Kip, *Britannia illustrata*, 1707

121 *Durdans House, Surrey*, detail showing house and garden. Painting by L. Knyff, 1673. Trustees of Berkeley Castle. Photo Courtauld Institute of Art, University of London

122 Design for a *parterre de broderie*. Engraving from André Mollet, *Le Jardin de plaisir*, 1651

123 Design for a *compartiment de gazon*. Engraving from André Mollet, *Le Jardin de plaisir*, 1651

124 Arethusa Fountain by Francesco Fanelli, now at Bushy Park, Richmond. Photo National Monuments Record

125 Reconstruction of André Mollet's reform of the gardens at Wimbledon. Drawing by Ian Mackenzie-Kerr

126 Design for a wilderness of the type planted at Wimbledon. Engraving from André Mollet, *Le Jardin de plaisir*, 1651

127 Design for a maze of the type planted at Wimbledon. Engraving from André Mollet, *Le Jardin de plaisir*, 1651

128 The garden front at Wimbledon, 1671. Engraving by Henry Winstanley, 1678. British Museum, London

129 Plan of a house and garden. Engraving from André Mollet, *Le Jardin de plaisir*, 1651

130 The Venus Fountain at Bolsover Castle, Derbyshire, c. 1630–33. Photo *Country Life*

131 *Henrietta Maria as Chloris in 'Chloridia'*. Drawing by Inigo Jones, 1631. Devonshire Collection, Chatsworth. Reproduced by permission of the Chatsworth Settlement. Photo Courtauld Institute of Art, University of London

132 *Portrait of an Unknown Lady*. Painting by Anthony Van Dyck, c. 1635. Royal Collection, reproduced by gracious permission of Her Majesty Queen Elizabeth II

133 *Mrs Watte*. Painting by an unknown artist, formerly collection of Lord Clinton. Photo National Portrait Gallery, London

134 *Jane Shurley, Baroness Holles of Ilfield*. Painting by an unknown artist, 1630. Collection the Marquess of Bath, Longleat. Photo Courtauld Institute of Art, University of London

135 The garden as an emblem of patience. From George Wither, *Emblemes*, 1635

136 The bowling green as a setting for the drama of the faithful soul. From Francis Quarles, *Emblemes*, 1635

137 Garden emblem. Engraving from Henry Hawkins, *Partheneia Sacra*, 1633

138 The *hortus conclusus* of the Virgin. Engraving from Henry Hawkins, *Partheneia Sacra*, 1633

139 The 'Sermon on the Mount' at Packwood House, Warwickshire. Photo National Trust

140 *Edward Herbert, 1st Baron Herbert of Cherbury*. Miniature by Isaac Oliver, c. 1610–15. Collection the Earl of Powis

141 *William Style of Langley*. Painting by an unknown artist, 1636. Tate Gallery, London. Photo A. C. Cooper

142 Democritus of Abdera. Engraving by Christian le Blon, from the title-page of R. Burton, *Anatomy of Melancholy*, 1628

143 The garden at Wotton, Surrey, designed by John Evelyn, 1652. Drawing by John Evelyn, 1653. Evelyn MSS, Evelyn Trustees, Christ Church, Oxford

144 Plan of the garden of Sayes Court, Deptford. Drawing by John Evelyn, 1653. Evelyn MSS, Evelyn Trustees, Christ Church, Oxford

Index

Numbers in italics
refer to illustrations

Abel 178
Abingdon, *s.v.* Norris
Achilles 21
Agrippa, Cornelius 103, 124
Albert, Archduke 74
Alberti, Leone Battista, and the
  Renaissance garden 15
Albury Park, Surrey, garden
  174–5, *114*
Aleotti, G. B. 76, *36, 37*
Amboise, Château d' 51
Amboise, Georges, Cardinal d'
  29, 35
amphitheatre 156, *103*
Ancy-le-Franc 57
Andromeda 158
Anet, Château d' 57, 187, *27*
Anne of Denmark, Queen of
  Great Britain 9, 10, 45, 74,
  112, 138, 179, *43*; gardens
  of: Somerset House 87 93,
  43, 44, 45, Greenwich 93–7,
  49, Oatlands 121
Antaeus, Hercules and 178
Anteros 199
Apollo 91, 92, 93, 98, 102, *48*
Appleton House, Yorkshire,
  garden 123–4, 214–15
arbours: at Hampton Court 28,
  Nonsuch 39, Hatfield House
  106, Massey's Court 110, in
  a masque 113, 200, Enstone
  132, Wilton 153
Arcadia 178
Archimedes 75
architecture 202
Arethusa 189, *124*
Arion 126
Arundel House 19; garden
  169–74, *111, 112, 113*
Arundel, Aletheia Talbot,
  Countess of 171, 174
Arundel, Henry FitzAlan, 12th
  Earl of 39, 63
Arundel, Thomas Howard,
  Earl of 19, 43; Italian
  journey 168; gardens:
  Arundel House 169–74, *112,
  113*, Albury and Tart Hall
  174–5, *114*
Astraea 46–7
Aubrey, John 117, 127, 148,
  176–9, 224, *115*
Augustyn, Brise 28
Aurora 9
Austen, Ralph 211
automata 75–8, *42*
aviaries 102, 134, *57*;
  Kenilworth Castle 51;
  Greenwich 96–7;
  Wimbledon House 191
Aymery, Leonard d' 74

Babington, John 134
Babington, Ury 189
Bacchus 76, 152, 158, *96*
Bacon, Francis (Lorf Verulam
  and 1st Viscount St Albans)
  12, 40, 120, 130, 132,
  170–71, 177, 224; garden
  127; essay 'Of Gardens' 135
Baldi, Bernardino 76
Baldinucci, Filippo 82
banqueting house (*s.v.* also
  summer house): Nonsuch
  39, 68, Wimbledon House
  62, 194, Cobham Hall 70,
  Danvers House, Chelsea 178
Basil, Simon 104, 168
Bate, John 133–4, *83, 84*
Bedford, Edward Russell, 3rd
  Earl of 120, 139
Bedford, Lucy Harington,
  Countess of 11, 12, 18, 87;
  gardens of: Twickenham
  Park 120–22, *72*, Woburn
  139–41, *86*, Moor Park
  141–6, *89*, Bedford House
  146–7, *90*
Bedford House, garden 146–7,
  90
Bell, Robert 104
Belvedere, Villa, garden and
  influence of 17 18, 169, *6*
Bembo, Cardinal Pietro 169
Besson, Jacob 111
Blois, Château de 29, *9*
Blomfield, Reginald 13, 211
Boboli, gardens 21, 79, 156,
  160, 167
Boccaccio 82
Böckler, Georg Andreas 165
Bol, Cornelius 171, 174
Boleyn, Queen Anne 34
Bolsover Castle, Derbyshire,
  garden 199–200
Bomarzo, garden 21, 82
Bourbon, Charles de 126
Bracciolini, Poggio 169
Bramante, Donato, and the
  garden 17–18, 169, *6*
Broderie, Madame de la 106
Brown, 'Capability' 11, 146
Browne, Sir Thomas 223
Brunelleschi, Filippo 75
Brunswick, Duke of 56, *24*
Buckett, Rowland 105, 106
Buckingham, Edward Stafford,
  3rd Duke of 24
Buckingham, George Villiers,
  Duke of 138, 139, 147, 179
Buontalenti, Bernardo 79, 82,
  92, 141
Burghley, William Cecil, Lord
  12, 45; garden 51–6

Burton, Robert 215–17, *142*
Bury 51
Bushell, Thomas 130–33, 211,
  82

Caccini 92
Cain 178
Callisto 141
Callot, Jacques 181, *119*
Cambridge, Sidney Sussex
  College, garden 115
Campbell, Colin 148
Campion, Thomas 98
canal, *s.v.* moat
Capel, Arthur, 1st Baron,
  garden 181–5, *117*
Capel, Henry 181
Caprarola, garden 167
Carew, Thomas, masque
  Coelum Britannicum 161–4
Caron, Antoine 92
cascade, at Wilton 158, *105*
Castello, Villa 20
Catherine de Medici, Queen of
  France 92, *48*
Cato 217
Caus, Isaac de 10, 178; life and
  writings 138, 164–5;
  Whitehall grotto 138–9;
  Woburn grotto 139–41, *86*;
  Moor Park 141–6, Wilton
  147–61; Lavington 180
Caus, Salomon de 10, 19, 21,
  85, 156, 165, 170, *35, 45, 47,
  50, 51, 53, 55, 57*; life 73–4,
  188; work for Anne of
  Denmark 87–97; for Henry,
  Prince of Wales 97–103; for
  Robert Cecil 103–10; for
  Frederick, Elector Palatine
  110, *64*; writings 111–12,
  118
Cavendish, Thomas 24
Cecil, Robert, *s.v.* Salisbury,
  Earl of
Cellini, Benvenuto 38
Ceres 82
Chamberlain, John 123, 124
Chambers, Sir William 158
Charles the Bold, Duke of
  Burgundy 32, 33, *12*
Charles V, Holy Roman
  Emperor 62
Charles I, King of England 11,
  12, 19, 38, 120, 132, 138, 139,
  158, 159, 161, 164, 167, 181,
  185, 199; introduces classical
  sculpture into gardens 170;
  garden at St James's Palace
  188–9

Charles II, King of England 223
Charleval 57
Chastleton, Oxfordshire, garden 12, 122, *74*
Chaundler, Thomas 104, 105, 106
Chloris 200
Cicero 217
Cincinnatus 217
Cleopatra 149
Cleyn, Francis 138
Clifford, Lady Anne, *s.v.* Pembroke
Cobergher, Wencel 74
Cobham, William Brooke, 7th Lord 69–70
Cobham Hall, Kent, garden 69–70
Colonna, Francesco, influence of his *Hypnerotomachia Poliphili* 14, 16–17, 22, 40, *2, 3, 4*
Concord 164
Condé, Prince de 74
Cork, Richard Boyle, 1st Earl of 164
Cornwallis, Sir Charles 97, 101
Cornwallis, Sir William 9
Coussin, Laurence 191
Ctesibius 75
Cumberland, George Clifford, 3rd Earl of 159
Cupid 102, 149, 156, 208, *92*
Cyllene 9

Dallington, Robert 16
Danby, Henry Danvers, Earl of 176
Danckerts, Hendrik 28
Daniel, Samuel 91, 120, 123, 159, 179
Danvers, Charles 176
Danvers, Elizabeth Dauntsey, Lady 180
Danvers, Magdalen Herbert, Lady 177
Danvers, Sir John 10, 177, 148; gardens: Chelsea 176–80, *115, 116*, Lavington 180–81
Dauntsey, Elizabeth, *s.v.* Danvers
Davenant, Sir William 200
Davies, John 47–8
Dawley, Middlesex, garden 161, *106*
Dee, John 112, 133, 134
Democritus of Abdera 219, *142*
Diana 21, 56, 65, 125, 141, 149, 194, *31, 33, 93*; of Ephesus 21; and Actaeon 66–8
Diocletian, Emperor 217
Donne, John 120, 159, 177
Dorset, Richard Sackville, Earl of 159
Dowsby Hall, Lincolnshire 117–18, *70*
Dragon 84
Drayton, Michael 120
Drebbel, Cornelius 112
Du Cerceau, Jacques Androuet 29, 31, 53, 57
Dugdale, Sir William 50

Durdans House, Epsom, Surrey, garden 186, *121*
Dürer, Albrecht 111
Dutton, Ralph 13

Eglantine 46–7, *19*
Elizabeth, Queen of Bohemia and Electress Palatine 74, 92, 98, 100, 103, 110, 111, 168
Elizabeth I, Queen of England 10, 12, 63, 65, 98, *19*; and the garden 45–9; as Venus at Theobalds 56; as the Pillar at Wimbledon House 62; as Diana at Nonsuch 66ff; portrait with garden at Welbeck 70; entertained at Elvetham 125–6
Elvetham, entertainment 125–6
engineering, role of in relation to garden 75, 111
Enstone, Oxfordshire, 'Marvels' 130–33, *81, 82*
Eros, 199
Este, Ippolito d', Cardinal of Ferrara 20, 82
Este, Villa d', gardens and influence of 20–21, 82, 85, 110, 112, 134, 168, 181, *7*
Europa 141
Evelyn, Captain George 222, *143*
Evelyn, John 14, 21, 104, 175, 216; and gardens 222–3, *143, 144*
Exeter, Thomas Cecil, 1st Earl of 57, 105

Fairfax, Sir Thomas, garden 123
Fairy Queen 48
Faithorne, William 175, 188
Fame 105
Fanelli, Francesco 189, *124*
Fanshawe, Sir Henry 123; garden 123–4
Ferdinand, Grand Duke of Florence 92
Ficino, Marsilio 82, 215
Fiennes, Celia 148, 156
Flora 9, 152, 158, 200
Florence, nymph of 20
Fludd, Robert 112
Fontainebleau 126, *77*; gardens 29, 38, 83, 160, *11, 40*
fountains 14; Belvedere 18; Villa d'Este 20–21; Henry VIII's 32, 35, 36; Fontainebleau 38, 83, *40, 52*; Kenilworth 51; Theobalds 53; Wollaton 57; Wimbledon House 62, 191, 194; Nonsuch 65–6; Pratolino 78–9; Somerset House 90–91, 189; in masques 92, 113; Greenwich 96; Hatfield House 104–5, *61*; Massey's Court 124; Ware Park 124; Enstone 130; Bacon commends 135; Moor Park 144, 145, 146; Wilton 148–9, 152, *92, 93, 94, 95, 97*;

Hadham Hall 181; Bolsover 199, *130*; in portraits 203–6; Wotton 222
Francesco de Medici, Grand Duke of Tuscany 21, 79
Francini, Tommaso and Alessandro 83, 84, 85, 97, *40, 42, 52*
Francis I, King of France 23, 25, 38
Frederick, King of Bohemia and Elector Palatine 103, 111, 168; garden 110
Frederick Henry of Orange, Prince 161, 188

Gaillon, garden 29–31, 35–8, 39, 40, 126, *10*
garden, as an image of monarchy 9–10, 20, 33, 43, 46ff, 92, 113, 200; nineteenth-century re-creations of 11–12; research on history of 13; the Humanist garden 14–17, *2*; the medieval garden 14, 24, 49, *2*; the high Renaissance garden 17–19, *6*; the Mannerist garden 19–22, 135–8; idea of in sixteenth century 20; French Renaissance gardens 29–31, *9, 10, 11*; Burgundian 32, *12*; and Renaissance engineering 75ff, 112; in the masques 200–03; the *hortus conclusus* in the Stuart period 206, *138*; melancholy and the garden 215–19, *140, 141, 142*
Gardiner, Stephen, Bishop of Winchester 38
gates, garden 171, 174, 185
Gerard, John 52, 69
Germolles, castle 32
Gheeraerts the Younger, Marcus 87, 90
Giambologna 179, *54*
giants: at Pratolino 78, 82, *54*, at Richmond 98
Giovio, Paolo 63
Golden Age 20
Goodrowse, William 87
Gorhambury, Hertfordshire, garden 127
Government 164
Graces 46, 48
Greenwich Palace, garden 93–7, *49*; gardens of Queen's House 189
grottos 18, 78, 165; Alberti's advocacy of 15; the Mannerist 75–8; Pratolino 78–9, *38, 39*; St Germain-en-Laye 84–5, *41, 42*; Somerset House 87, 90–91; on Daniel's 'Tethys' Festival' 91, 92; Greenwich 96–7; of Pan and Apollo 98; of Orpheus 98; Hortus Palatinus 110; Enstone 130–32, *81*; Whitehall 138–9; Woburn Abbey

139–41, *86*; designs for by Isaac de Caus 140–41; Moor Park 144, 145, 146; Bedford House 147; Wilton 156, 165, *98, 99, 100*; Albury 174–5, *114*; Danvers House, Chelsea 178–9; Lavington 180; possible at Hadham Hall 181; possible at Temple Newsam 185; Rycote 185; Wotton 222
Gryffyn, Edward 38
Gunter, Edward 38

Hadham Hall, Hertfordshire, garden 181–5, *117, 118*
Hagar 132
Haigh, Lancashire, garden 161, *108*
Hall, Edward 25
Ham House, Petersham, Surrey, garden 117, 118, *69*
Hammond, Lieutenant 148, 156
Hampton Court Palace, garden 25–34, *8*
Hardwick Hall, Derbyshire 69
Harington of Exton, Sir John 120
Hatfield House, Hertfordshire 12, 18, 113; garden 103–10, *59, 60, 62*
Hawes, Stephen 43
Hawkins Henry 209–10, *137, 138*
Henrietta Maria, Queen 11, 63, 130, 160, 161, 179, 181, 191, *131*; interest in gardens 186–7; gardens: Somerset House, Greenwich and Oatlands 189–91, *124*, Wimbledon House, 191–7, *125, 128*; gardens in her masques 200–03
Henry, Prince of Wales 10, 12, 74, 86, 90, 111, 147, 170, 188, *56*; gardens 97–103, 123
Henry VII, King of England 23, 97
Henry VIII, King of England 10, 23, 25; gardens: Hampton Court 25–34, Whitehall 34–8, Nonsuch 38–9; rivalry with Francis I 31, 38
Henry II, King of France 83
Henry III, King of France 126
Henry IV, King of France 92, 144, 161; gardens 83–6, *40, 41*
Hentzner, Paul 53
Heraldry, use of in gardens: Hampton Court 25ff, Nonsuch 39, 65, Kenilworth 51, Theobalds 53, Temple Newsam 185
Herbert of Cherbury, Edward Herbert, Lord 177, 216, *140*
Herbert, George 123, 177, 210
Herbert, Magdalen, *s.v.* Danvers
Hercules 21, 38, 76, 82, 164, 178, *37*

Hermes Trismegistus 203
Hero of Alexandria 75–8, 110,
 111, 133, 134, 165, 168, *36,
 37*
Hertford, Edward Seymour,
 Earl of 48; entertainment at
 Elvetham 69, 125–6
Hesdin, castle 32
Hesperides, apples of 21, 76, *37*
Hesse, garden 56, *24*
Highgate, James I entertained
 at 9
Hill, Thomas 42, 120, *17*
Hilliard, Nicholas 70
Hippolytus 21
History 202
Hoefnagel, Georg 65
Holinshed, Ralph 69
Hollar, Wenceslas 146, 174, *114*
Hondius, Jodocus 39, 64, 65
Honselaersdijk palace 161
Hours 48
Huygens, Lodewijk 148, 156
Hypnerotomachia Poliphili, s.v.
 Colonna

Ingram, Sir Arthur 185
Isabella, Archduchess, Regent
 of the Netherlands 74
Isabella of Portugal, Duchess of
 Burgundy 32
Ishmael 132
islands: at Richmond 98–9,
 56, Hatfield 105–6;
 development of 125ff, *75, 76,
 77, 78, 79, 80*
Ives, Simon 130

Jackson, Gilbert 203
James, Richard 170
James I, King of England, and
 VI of Scotland 9, 73, 93, 97,
 103, 105, 127, 138, 141, 147,
 171, 188
Jennings, Mountain 103, 104,
 105–6, *59*
Jones, Inigo 10, 19, 43, 74, 83,
 87, 92, 103, 104, 106, 118,
 138, 158, 159, 178, 191, 199,
 58, 85, 109, 119; and Wilton
 garden 148, 156, 160, 161;
 use of gardens in stage
 scenery 164, 181, 200–03;
 influence on garden design
 168ff; and Arundel House
 garden 171–4; garden gates
 by 171, *110, 111*; possible
 connection with Danvers
 House, Chelsea 180; possible
 connection with Hadham
 Hall 185, *117*; work on
 Oatlands garden 189–91, *110*
Jones, Walter 122
Jonson, Ben 87, 98, 120, 122,
 123, 139, 147; Highgate
 entertainment 9; *Oberon*
 102–3, *58*; *Pleasure
 Reconciled to Virtue* 103;
 *Neptune's Triumph for the
 Return of Albion* and *The
 Fortunate Isles and their
 Union* 139, *85*; *Love's*

Welcome to Bolsover 199–200,
 130; *Chloridia* 200–02, *131*
Jonson, Garrett 105
Julius II, Pope 17, 169
Juno 200

Kenilworth Castle,
 Warwickshire 125; garden
 50–51, 113, *20*
Kip, William 87, 127, 161, 177,
 178, 185, 223, *106, 107, 108,
 116*
knots 40–42, 70–71, 135, *16,
 17, 18*; Thornbury 24;
 Hampton Court 33; Pymms
 46; Theobalds 52, 53;
 Wimbledon House 62, 191;
 Nonsuch 65; Hatfield 106;
 Hortus Palatinus 110;
 Dowsby 118
Knyff, Leonard 178, 185, 186
Kratzer, Nicholas 38

Labyrinth 102, *17, 18*;
 Nonsuch 39, 65; Theobalds
 53; Wilton 123; Wimbledon
 194
Lady of the Lake 124
lake, *s.v.* pond
Laneham, Robert 50
Lannoy, Guillebert de 32, 34
Lante, Villa, Bagnaia 21, 83–4,
 156
Lavington, Wiltshire, garden
 180–81
Leak, John 165
Lee, Sir Henry 62
Leicester, Robert Dudley, Earl
 of 50–51
Leland, John 29
Lely, Sir Peter 203
Ligorio, Pirro 20–21, 82
Lockey, Rowland 70
Leonardo da Vinci 75
Loggan, David 115
loggia: Wimbledon House 62,
 Somerset House 93
Louis XII, King of France 29
Louis XIII, King of France 84,
 110, 111, 138, 153
Lumley, John, Lord 39, 63ff
Luxembourg, Palais du, garden
 160, 161, 197
Lyming, Robert 104

Madama, Villa 19
Maia 9
Maiano, Giovanni da 32
Mandelslo, Sieur de 90, 96
Mantegna, Andrea 169
Mantua, Duke of 169
Marcus Aurelius, Emperor 156
Marie de Medici, Queen of
 France 92, 106, 161, 188;
 garden of 83–6
Markham, Gervase 40
Mars 38, 82
Marvell, Andrew 123; and
 gardens 210–11, 214–15
Mary I, Queen of England 39,
 63

masques, gardens in 113,
 161–4, 200–03, *131*
Massey's Court, Llanerch,
 Denbighshire 107, *63*
Massinger, Philip 123
May, Thomas 120
maze *s.v.* labyrinth
Medici, Cosimo de 169
Medici, Ferdinando de,
 Cardinal of Florence, garden
 167–8
Medici, Lorenzo de 169
melancholy, and the garden
 215–19
Memnon, speaking statue 102,
 110, 165, *57*
Mercogliano, Pacello de 29
Mercury 9, 110, 141, 189
Merlin 125
Michelangelo, Buonarroti 111,
 141
Midas 98
Milton, John 216
moat: Theobalds 53,
 Kenilworth 125
Modena, Nicholas 38
Mollet, André 11, 63, 160,
 175; influence on Wilton
 161; life 187–8; work in
 England: St James's Palace
 188–9, *123*, Wimbledon
 House 191–7 *125, 126, 127*,
 Le Jardin de plaisir 194–6
 129
Mollet, Claude 83–4, 97, 117,
 153, 160, 187–8, *40*
Mollet, Claude, the Younger
 188
Mollet, Jacques 187
Mollet, Noël 188
Montacute, Somerset, garden
 12
Montaigne, Pierre 21, 168
Moor Park, Hertfordshire 18,
 160; garden 141–6, *89*
More, Sir Thomas 70
Moretti, Egidio 170
Moryson, Fynes 14, 78, 79,
 122, 169
mount: Hampton Court 28, 29,
 Theobalds 53, in a masque
 113, New College, Oxford
 115, Elvetham 126,
 Haughton 127, *79*, Bacon
 commends 135
Mountain, Didymus 42, *16*
Muses 46, 91, 92, 93, 158, *48*
Mytens, Daniel 138, 171, 174

Najera, Duke de 32
Napoli, Gerolamo da 29
Nash, Joseph 12
Nature, Mother 21
Nedeham, John 42
Neptune 85, 91, 105, 110, 125,
 126
Nero, Emperor 17
Neumayr von Ramssla, J. W.
 90–91, 96
Neville, Sir Henry 71
Newcastle, William Cavendish,
 Earl of 199

Newcourt, R. 175, 188
Nonsuch Palace, Surrey,
 garden 38–9, 63–9, *30, 31,
 32, 33, 34*
Norris, Bridget Wray, Baroness
 185
Norris, Elizabeth Norris,
 Baroness 185, *120*
Norris, James Bertie, Lord
 (later Earl of Abingdon) 185
Northampton, Henry Howard,
 Earl of 117
Northampton House, London,
 garden 117, *71*
Northumberland, Henry Percy,
 9th Earl of 70
Nôtre, André le 194, 223, *129*

Oatlands Palace: park gate 171,
 110, garden 189–91
Obel, Matthias de L' 69
Oliver, Isaac 70, 216, *140*
Orme, Philibert de L' 57, 83
Orpheus 85, 98, 102, *42*
Ourlian, Nicholas 28
Overbury, Sir Thomas 216
Ovid 15, 68
Oxford: New College, garden
 115, *67*, Wadham College,
 garden, 115, *66*

Packwood House,
 Warwickshire, garden
 211–14, *139*
Palladio, Andrea 168, 171
Pan 9, 98, 102
Parkinson, John 69, 186
Parnassus 87, 90, 158, *44, 46,
 47, 48*
parterres de broderie 196;
 Fontainebleau 83, *40*;
 Hortus Palatinus 110; Moor
 Park 145; Wilton 148–9, 160,
 91; in stage scenery 181; St
 James's Palace 188;
 Wimbledon House 195;
 water parterres: St Germain-
 en-Laye 84, Hortus Palatinus
 110, Wilton 156
pastoral, *s.v.* Golden Age,
 Arcadia
Peacham, Henry 170
Peele, George 46
Pegasus 91, 92, 158, *105*
Pembroke, Anne Clifford,
 Countess of 120; influence
 on Wilton garden 159–60
Pembroke, Henry Herbert, 2nd
 Earl of 147
Pembroke, Mary Talbot,
 Countess of 123
Pembroke, Philip Herbert, 4th
 Earl of 11; gardens: Moor
 Park 141–6, Wilton 147–61
Pembroke, Susan de Vere,
 Countess of 147
Pembroke, Thomas Herbert,
 8th Earl of 153
Pembroke, William Herbert,
 3rd Earl of, garden 122–3,
 142, 214

perspective, use of in garden planning 117, 118, 203
Perseus 84, 158
Petty, William 170
Philip the Good, Duke of Burgundy 32
Philo of Byzantium 75–6
Pighius, Stephanus Vinandus 21
pillar emblem 62
Pitti Palace, s.v. Boboli gardens
Platter, Thomas 33, 39, 65, 66
Pliny the Elder, and the garden 14–15, 79
Plot, Robert 132
Poesy 202
ponds 125ff, 77, 78, 79, 80; Hampton Court 28; Elvetham 125–6, 75; Gorhambury 127; Theobalds 127; Bacon's dislike 135; Wilton 152
Portland, Richard Weston, Earl of 158, 203
Pratolino, garden 21, 78–83, 84, 134, 167, 38, 39, 46; influence of 91, 98, 110, 140, 145, 161, 181
Primaticcio, Francesco 38
Proserpina 82
Prynne, William 206
Pydectes 158

Quarles, Francis 208–9, 211, 136

Ramelli, Agostino 111
Ramus, Petrus 111
Raphael 19, 111
Religion 164
Reputation 164
Richelieu, Cardinal 158
Richmond Palace, garden 23, 24, 97–103, 140, 56
Rigdon, Sir William 117
rivers, artificial, s.v. streams
Robinson, William 13
Roe, Sir Thomas 120, 170
Rogers, William 47
Romano, Giulio 19
Roos, William Cecil, Lord 170
Rubens, Peter Paul 138, 160, 199
Rudolf II, Holy Roman Emperor 122
Rueil, garden 158, 165

St Germain-en-Laye: garden 83–6, 112; influence 110, 117, 144–5, 160, 41
St James's Palace, garden 19, 161, 188–9
Salisbury, Robert Cecil, Earl of 18; gardens: Pymms 46, 103, Hatfield 103–10
Sandrart, Joachim 171
Sandys, George 167
San Gallo, Antonio 19

satyrs 9, 102
Saxony, Duke of 35, 90
Sayes Court, Deptford, Kent, garden 222, 144
Scamozzi, Vincenzo 148, 168, 171
Schott, François 21
sculpture, use of antique in gardens 18, 19, 152, 167, 170, 174, 188–9; use of contemporary 15, 20, 51, 53, 65, 144, 149, 152, 153, 178–9, 180
Selden, John 170
Serlio, Sebastiano 57, 156
Serre, Sieur de la 188
Servi, Constantino dei 74, 98
Shakespeare, William 49, 103
shepherds, statues of 178–9
Siberechts, Jan 56–7, 26
Silenus 102
Skipton Moyne, Yorkshire, garden 186
Smythson, John 118, 171, 174
Smythson, Robert 56–7, 60, 62, 87, 91, 120, 145, 191, 25, 29, 44
Somer, Paul van 171
Somerset, Edward Seymour, Duke of 45, 87
Somerset, Frances Howard, Countess of 113
Somerset House, London 45; garden 87–93, 189, 43, 44, 45
Sorbière, Monsieur de 107
Spenser, Edmund 47
sphinxes, statues of 178–9
spring 113
Stalbridge Park, Dorset, garden 164
Staunton Harold, Leicestershire, garden 161, 107
Stone, Nicholas: Whitehall sun-dial 38; Wilton 149, 92, 93, 94, 95, 102; Danvers House 178–9
streams, artificial: Hatfield 104–5, Ware Park 124, Gorhambury 127, Theobalds 127, Lavington 180
Strode, William 203
Stukeley, William 130, 158, 164
Sturtevant, Simon 105
Style, William 217, 141
Sueur, Hubert le, 19, 138, 169, 203; at Wilton 153; at St James's Palace 189
summer house (s.v. also banqueting house): Theobalds 53, Hatfield 105–6, Massey's Court 107, Gorhambury 127, Moor Park 144, Wollaton 164, Temple Newsam 185, Wimbledon House 191
sun-dials 112, 115, 122, 67; Hampton Court 25, 28; Whitehall 38; symbolism of 211, Packwood House 211
Susanna 132, 149, 94, 95

Switzer, Stephen 165
symbolism: in topiary 15, in Mannerist garden 19ff, at Hampton Court 33, Pymms 46, Pratolino 82, Jacobean symbolic gardens 112–25, pond 125–6, of Wilton 158–60, of Danvers House, Chelsea 179–80, the Stuart symbolic garden 203ff

Tart Hall, garden 175
Tè, Palazzo del 19
Temple Newsam, Yorkshire, garden 185
Temple, Sir William 141
terrace 115; Kenilworth 51; Somerset House 87; Hatfield 104; Massey's Court 107, Hortus Palatinus 110, Northampton House 117, Ham House 117, Wollaton 118, Wotton describes 134, Moor Park 144, 146, Bedford House 146, Wilton 156, 158, Arundel House 174, Hadham Hall 181, Temple Newsam 185, Rycote 185, Wimbledon House 191
Tethys 91
Thames, River 91, 92
Theobalds 45, 98; garden 51–7, 103, 127, 23
Thomas, F. Inigo 13
Thornbury Castle, Gloucestershire, garden 24, 29, 62
Thorpe, John 52, 56–7, 71, 117
Thynne, Francis 69
Tiber, River 83, 96
Tipping, Avray 12
Titian 141
Tmollus, Mount 98
Toledo, Duke of, garden 167
topiary: development of 14–15, Hampton Court 33, Nonsuch 39, Wimbledon House 62, Chastleton 122, Bacon's dislike 135
Tradescant, John 105, 106, 189
Tresham, Lady 106
Tresham, Sir Thomas 210
Trevelyon, Thomas 42, 46, 70, 106, 18
Tribolo, Niccolò 20
Triggs, Inigo J. 12
Trinity 123
Truth 164

Urfé, Honoré, d' 147, 189

Valla, Lorenzo 76
Van Dyck, Sir Anthony 138, 181, 203, 132
Varchi, Benedetto 20
Vasari, Giorgio 20
Vaughan, Henry 206

Vavasour, Sir Thomas, garden 117
Venus 21, 65, 149, 156, 199, 92, 130; labyrinth of 53
Verdier, Saulnier du 147
Vergil 20, 47, 189
Verneuil 57
Vieri, Francesco de 82, 91
Virgin Mary, hortus conclusus of 49, 209–10, 138
Virtues 46
Vitruvius 51, 111, 112
Vries, Vredeman de 52, 53, 70, 21, 22

Walpole, Sir Robert 153
Ware Park, Hertfordshire, garden 123–4
water, s.v. fountains, ponds
Watson, Anthony 39, 64
Webb, John 185
Wedel, Lupold von 34
Weston, s.v. Portland
Whitehall Palace: garden 34–8, 13, 14, grotto 138–9
Wilderness: Bacon's 135, Moor Park 144, Bedford House 146, Wilton 149–52, 96, Wimbledon House 194
Willoughby, Sir Francis 57
Willoughby, Sir Percival 118
Wilson, Thomas 105
Wilton, Wiltshire: garden 122–3, 147–61, 214, 91–105, influence of 161, 185, 106, 107, 108
Wimbledon House, garden 57–63, 191–7, 28, 29, 125, 128
Winstanley, Henry 62, 185, 191
Wisdom 164
Wither, George 206–7, 135
Woburn Abbey, grotto 139–41, 86
Wollaton Hall, Nottinghamshire: garden 56–7, 25, 26, orchard 118, summer house 164
Wolsey, Cardinal Thomas, gardens 23–4, 34
Woolridge, John 165
Worcester, Edward Somerset, 4th Earl of, garden 115
Worcester Lodge, Nonsuch, garden 15–16, 68
Works, Office of 42
Wotton, Surrey, garden 216, 222–3, 143
Wotton, Sir Henry 124, 134, 178, 214
Wray, Edward 185
Wyn, Sir Richard 191
Wyngaerde, Anthonis van 27, 28, 32, 35, 96

Zarlino, Giorgio 112
Zephyrus 9, 200
Zouche, Edward la Zouche, 11th Baron 69